Employee Rights and Employer Wrongs

How To Identify Employee Abuse

And How To Stand Up For Yourself

Suzanne Kleinberg and
Michael Kreimeh

Other Books by Suzanne Kleinberg

From Playstation® to Workstation: A Career Guide for Generation Text Surviving in a Baby Boomer World.

It's All About the Elizabeths: A Financial Management Guide for Canadian Teens

Employee Rights and Employer Wrongs:

How To Identify Employee Abuse

And How To Stand Up For Yourself

Suzanne Kleinberg and Michael Kreimeh

Potential To Soar Publishing

Toronto, Canada

Canadian Cataloguing in Publication Data

Library and Archives Canada Cataloguing in Publication

Kleinberg, Suzanne, 1963-
      Employee Rights and Employer Wrongs: How to Identify Employee Abuse and How to Stand Up For Yourself / Suzanne Kleinberg; Michael Kreimeh, illustrator.

Includes index.
ISBN 978-0-9866684-2-5

1. Employee rights--Canada. 2. Labor laws and legislation--Canada.
3. Bullying in the workplace--Law and legislation--Canada. 4. Work environment--Canada. I. Kreimeh, Michael, 1970- II. Title.

HF5549.5.E428K54 2011   331.01'10971   C2011-901281-2

Potential To Soar Publishing
Thornhill, Ontario

Dedication

This book is dedicated to all the hard working Canadians trying to earn an honest living in such diverse, complex and always changing work environments.

Table of Contents

Introduction

Have you ever wondered if your boss is treating you within your legal rights? Many employees put up with unwarranted stress, excessive workloads, and violation of rights because they are either in fear of losing their jobs, unsure of their legal rights or a combination of both.

During times of economic uncertainty, many employers knowingly (and sometimes unknowingly) take advantage of this fear by pushing employees to the limit. Just because an employer does not overtly threaten your job does not mean that you haven't been bullied. Unethical actions can be equally interpreted as menacing and exploitative. And unless you have a few hundred dollars handy, you cannot even get a consultation with an employment lawyer to understand your rights.

For many, the workplace has become a stressful, self-esteem crushing and frightening place that impacts health, relationships and emotional balance. As employees, we all need a little guidance and hope to cope with the daily grind. This book will cover what the basic employee rights are in Canada for full-time permanent, non-union employees.

This book is in no way a substitute for the advice of an experienced labour lawyer. It is more of a guide to help you decide if it is worth pursuing legal or government assistance. It is **NOT** to be taken as legal advice for individual cases, as each case always has unique circumstances.

Preface

Nearly half (49%) of North American employees have been affected by workplace bullying, either being a target themselves or having witnessed abusive behavior against a co-worker. 41% of people in Canada say they have experienced discrimination of some type when applying for a job in the last five years. A large majority of those who feel they have been discriminated against did nothing about it and most were unhappy with the outcome. Less than 5% of the wrongful dismissal cases actually go to court due to quick settlements. This small percentage reflects only the cases that have actually been pursued which are a small fraction of potential cases of unfair termination.

Canadians who suffer from workplace hostility experience stress-related health problems, including anxiety, panic attacks, sleep disorders and depression, just to name a few. Prolonged exposure to stress in the workplace can lead to other serious health concerns, such as problems related to cardiovascular, neurological and immune system health. Also, victims often decide to quit their jobs and end up trading the stress of bullying for the stress of being unemployed.

Too many people tolerate unfair, and in some cases abusive, workplace environments because they do not feel that they have any options. This book was developed with those people in mind. When you are unsure of your rights but unsure whether you need a lawyer, this book is designed to fill that gap and help you understand what your rights are and what your first steps may be. We have also included some sample letters that you may want to use to address your employer.

Hopefully, this book will guide you to a better work environment and happier, more balanced, life.

Employee Rights

What is an Employee?

Before we get into the rights afforded to employees in Canada, let's start off by looking at the legal definition of what an employee is. There are a lot of words that are used to describe a person who provides services to an employer: employee, contractor, consultant, worker, staff, and so on.

When we refer to an "employee", we are limiting the discussion to a person who is employed for an indeterminate period to regularly work the standard number of hours fixed by the employer and is not held by a collective bargaining agreement (union) or temporary contract. In other words, an employee, for the purposes of this book, is someone who works directly for a company in return for financial compensation without the benefit of union membership or contract limiting length of employment.

You can go to your provincial government's website and see a variation of this definition in "legalese". Each province's definition of an employee differs slightly so it is easy to get confused. However, to be consistent, we will use the above consistent definition as it is easy to understand.

Employee's Responsibilities

In order to determine whether you are being treated unfairly, you need to ensure that you are living up to your end of the employment contract. It is essential that you fulfill your responsibilities as an employee. Aside from the job description, an employee's responsibilities generally include (but not limited to):

• Showing up on time for work.
• Putting in the required hours.
• Behaving honestly.
• Following the employer's instructions (unless safety or the law would be breached).
• Keeping trade secrets.
• Doing the job to the best of one's ability.
• Contributing to a positive work environment.

Employer's Responsibilities

What's more challenging, however, are the employers' responsibilities. In the absence of a detailed written employment contract, both employers and employees often find that there are grey areas that may cause confusion or problems in the employment relationship further in the future.

Once individuals are in an employment relationship, they are protected by federal and provincial laws. Each province, for example, legislates basic working conditions, such as minimum wages, hours of work, rest periods, eating periods, overtime pay, paid public holidays, vacation with pay, pregnancy or parental leave, and termination or severance notice and pay. Many of these are minimums and an employee may be entitled to additional protection.

Other laws affecting the workplace govern health and safety, human rights, retirement, benefits, workers' compensation, and unemployment insurance, just to name a few. With variations in the laws across Canada, it is strongly recommended that specific employment situations should be referred to an experienced labour lawyer for clarification.

What is The Difference Between a Federal Employee and Provincial Employee?

The majority of people are under the jurisdiction of the Employment Standards of their province. However, about 10% are federally regulated. In general, employees that fall within federal jurisdiction include:

Interprovincial and international services such as railways; highway transport; telephone; pipelines; canals; ferries, tunnels, bridges; shipping and shipping services; radio and television broadcasting; air transport and aircraft operations; banks; the protection and preservation of fisheries; endeavours declared by Parliament to be for the general advantage of Canada such as grain elevators; flour and seed mills, feed warehouses and grain-seed cleaning plants; uranium mining and processing; certain individual endeavours such as Hudson Bay Mining and Smelting Company; most Federal Crown corporations, such as the Canada Mortgage and Housing Corporation and Canada Post Corporation. Federal public service employees are also covered by federal Labour Code.

This distinction is important when you need to refer to applicable laws for your situation. As well, if you need to file a complaint, your provincial/federal status will determine which governmental body you need to file it with. If you are unsure, one indicator may be if your business is shut down on Remembrance Day (November 11th). If it is, then you are probably regulated by the Federal Labour Code.

Human Resources – Whose Side Are They On?

It is easy to think that your company's Human Resources ("HR") department is in place to protect the employee and stand up for the "little guy". This assumption could not be more wrong. One of the key reasons why HR is in place is to protect the company. Sure, they have policies and procedures that appear to address the employee's needs for fairness and respect and sure, HR must act on them, however, their true goal is to warn the company's executive team of impending lawsuits or potential bad publicity.

HR reps are highly trained in how to get you to weaken your own potential case and help the employer build its defenses against your complaint. HR departments might actually try to help you fix your problem, but at the same time they are going to be helping their employer prepare its defense. Everything you do or say will be used against you later, if the need arises.

However, you still have to go through the HR process. If you have a harassment or discrimination claim, you <u>must</u> follow HR procedures, otherwise it will appear that your claim lacks validity and will negatively impact you in any future lawsuit or complaint.

If you do file a harassment claim with HR, please be sure that you have all the information to provide for them at your initial meeting to show that this is a serious offense. As well, be sure that this is something that you want to do and follow through with completely. Ask yourself the following:

- Is this a first or repeated offense?
- Were there any witnesses to corroborate your side?
- Is there any other way to verify the occurrence (documents, emails, etc.)?
- What was the impact of the offense (to you, your team, etc.)?
- What would happen if you did not report the offense? You need to consider this before you go to HR along with what you feel is the seriousness of the offense.
- Does the manager have a past record of similar offenses?
- How difficult is the situation to cope with? In other words, how close are you to going to a third party (government labour board or lawyer) in order to resolve the problem?
- How well do you trust your HR department and/or representative to conduct the investigation fairly, objectively and thoroughly? If the HR department is weak, then retaliation is a possibility from your manager. If this is the case, you will need to record any perceived retaliation.
- How important is confidentiality? While it is promised, it is rare as the HR rep will need to discuss the situation with various management personnel in order to provide a status or investigate.

This list is not to deter you. It is to ensure that when you file a complaint, you are fully prepared so that you will be taken seriously and that you understand what is expected of you.

Keeping this in mind and your continuing willingness still wish to move forward, make an appointment with HR to discuss your situation. Make sure that the HR personnel take copious notes and give you a copy to review before the investigation proceeds. As well, make certain that s/he explains the process thoroughly.

For example, in many corporations, when HR receives a complaint, they complete a standard grievance form and give it to you to sign. Part of their investigation usually includes notifying the person that your complaint is about. Then they put the complaint in a file until another similar complaint is filed. If your boss harasses you and, for whatever reason, does not harass anyone else, then your complaint may sit in that file and s/he would not be reprimanded. And if there is no other manager to transfer you to (e.g. there is only on accounting department in the company), then it may lead to an awkward situation for you.

As well, if you file a legitimate complaint against a manager that is perceived as a "good guy", then you may get a cold shoulder from co-workers if word gets out. Remember, if you experience retaliation or the conduct continuing, you must report it.

However, there are also certain protections afforded you when you report a complaint. Some of these positives include:

- You may establish a form of protection from further harassment or wrongful dismissal.
- You may inspire other people to come forward that could reinforce your claim.
- Your complaint establishes a basis for future complaints/lawsuits.
- Your complaint will put your "victimizer" on notice and will be added to his/her personnel file.

This is not to discourage you but to enlighten you of the possible situations you may find yourself in and to prepare for them. Harassment or discrimination should not be tolerated whether there is only one victim or 100 victims. But sometimes, you need to stand up for yourself by yourself.

Basic Employee Rights

While many specifications in regard to pay, vacation time, overtime and other entitlements vary from province to province, many of the concepts are the same. Please be sure to check your provincial or federal specific website for details.

Hours of Work, Overtime, Meal and Other Breaks

Source: www.labour.gc.ca

Legislation across the country varies from province to province. While some jurisdictions are thoroughly legislated in regard to work hours, breaks, overtime or days worked, others leave some of the details up to the discretion of the employee/employer relationship.

It is important to understand what your rights are in this area because many employees don't realize that they are entitled to breaks and overtime pay.

The table below outlines the basics in each area for each jurisdiction. Please check the applicable government website or call your provincial/territorial Employment Standards Board for details or any updates.

Jurisdiction	Standard Hours	Maximum Hours	Averaging Agreements[1]	Overtime (OT) Rate[2]	Right to Refuse OT	Time Off in Lieu of OT Wages[3]	Minimum Rest Periods	Meal and Other Breaks
Federal	8 in a day; 40 in a week	48 in a week	Yes	1 ½ times reg. rate	No	No	1 day per week[4]	*Not specified*
Alberta	8 in a day; 44 in a week	12 consecutive hours in a day	Yes	1 ½ times reg. rate	No	Yes	8 hours between shifts; 1 day per week (average)[5]	½ hour during each shift in excess of 5 consecutive hours of work
British Columbia	8 in a day; 40 in a week	*N/A*[6]	Yes	1 ½ or 2 times[7] reg. rate	No	Yes	8 consecutive hours between shifts; 32 consecutive hours in a week[8]	½ hour after each 5 consecutive hours of work[9]
Manitoba	8 in a day; 40 in a week[10]	*N/A*	Yes~ 19	1 ½ times reg. rate[11]	Yes[12]	Yes	24 consecutive hours in a week[22]	½ hour after each 5 consecutive hours of work

New Brunswick	44 in a week	N/A	No	1 ½ times min. wage	No	No	24 consecutive hours in a week[13]	½ hour after each 5 consecutive hours of work
Newfound-land and Labrador	40 in a week	14 in a day	No	1 ½ times min. wage[14]	No	Yes	8 consecutive hours in a 24-hour period; 24 consecutive hours in a week[15]	1 hour immediately after each 5 consecutive hours of work
Northwest Territories and Nunavut	8 in a day; 40 in a week	10 in a day; 60 in a week[16]	Yes~[17]	1 ½ times reg. rate	No	No	1 day per week[18]	½ hour after each 5 consecutive hours of work[19]
Nova Scotia	48 in a week	N/A	Yes[20]	1 ½ times reg. rate	No	No	24 consecutive hours in a 7-day period[21]	*Not specified*
Ontario	44 in a week	8 in a day (or employee's regular work day if more); 48 in a week[22]	Yes	1 ½ times reg. rate	No	Yes	8 hours between shifts[22]; 11 consecutive hours in a day; 24 consecutive hours in a week or 48 consecutive hours in a 2-week period[38]	½ hour after each 5 consecutive hours of work; an employer and an employee may agree to split the break into two periods totaling at least 30 minutes during that period. If an employer provides another type of break, such as a coffee break, and the employee must remain at his/her workplace during that break, the employee is deemed to be performing work during that time.
Prince Edward Island	48 in a week[23]	N/A	No	1 ½ times reg. rate	No	No	24 consecutive hours in a 7-day period[24]	½ hour after each 5 consecutive hours of work

Québec	40 in a week	N/A	~[25]	1 ½ times reg. rate	Yes (limited)[26]	Yes	32 consecutive hours in a week[27]	½ hour after each 5 consecutive hours of work[28]. If an employer provides another type of break, such as a coffee break, the employee is deemed to be at work during that time.
Saskatchewan	8 in a day; 40 in a week	44/week[28]	Yes with gov't approval	1 ½ times reg. rate	Yes (limited)[29]	No	8 consecutive hours in a 24-hour period[30]; 24 or 48 consecutive hours[31] in a 7-day period (for employees who usually work 20 hours or more in a week)	½ hour within every 5 consecutive hours of work for employees working 6 hours or more[32]. Where necessary for medical reasons, an individual employee is entitled to take a meal break at another time. If an employer provides another type of break, such as a coffee break, it is deemed to be time worked.
Yukon	8 in a day; 40 in a week[33]	N/A	Yes with gov't approval	1 ½ times reg. rate	Yes[34]	Yes	8 consecutive hours between shifts[35]; 2 days per week[36]	½ hour after 5 consecutive hours of work for employees who work 10 hours or less on that day; ½ hour after 6 consecutive hours for employees who work more than 10 hours on that day. [37]

Notes :

[1]   Refers to whether the government allows employers and employees to negotiate to average hours of work over a specified period, for example, 12 hour shifts 4 days per week. This may impact the way overtime is calculated.

[2]   The overtime rate is payable for each hour or part of an hour that an employee works over the standard hours of work.

[3]   Indicates whether government specifically allows employees to trade overtime earned for time off instead of overtime wages. For example, if you have worked 8 hours of overtime, some employers will allow you to take a day off instead of 8 hours of overtime pay.

[4]   Where possible, the rest period must be on Sunday.

[5]   An employee is entitled to at least one day of rest in each work week, or to either two consecutive days of rest in each period of two consecutive work weeks, three consecutive days of rest in each period of three consecutive work weeks, or four consecutive days of rest in each period of four consecutive work weeks. An employer must provide an employee at least four consecutive days of rest after 24 consecutive work days.

[6]   No maximum hours are specified, however, an employer must not demand or allow an employee to work excessive hours that would be detrimental to the employee's health or safety.

[7]   Employees are entitled to two times their regular wage rate for any time worked in excess of 12 hours in a day.

[8]   If the employer does not provide the employee with the required rest period, it must pay the employee 1 ½ times the regular wage for time worked by the employee during the 32 hour period s/he would otherwise be entitled to have free from work.

[9]   A meal break must be counted as time worked if the employee is required to work or to be available for work during that period.

[10]   If it is provided for under a union agreement or approved by Manitoba Labour Board, an employer may increase the daily standard hours of work without paying the overtime wage rate.

[11]   Overtime does not include time that an employer provides an employee as a break if the employee is not required to stay on the business premises or be on duty during the break.

[12]   The rights of an employer do not include an implied right to require an employee to work overtime", except in defined emergency situations.

[13]   Unless the employee is not usually employed for more than three hours in any one day, the employee is required to cope with an emergency.

Where possible, the rest period is to be taken on a Sunday or to be accumulated and taken later, either a part at a time or all together. However, this does not authorize any work to be performed on Sunday that is prohibited by law (i.e. most retail businesses).

[14]   The overtime rate does not apply where an employer grants an employee's request to change his/her work schedule with one or more other employees, if the change in work schedule results in the employee working hours in excess of the standard hours of work.

[15] Where possible, the rest period must be taken on a Sunday.

[16] The maximum hours of work may be exceeded in the following cases: an accident to machinery, equipment, plant or persons; urgent and essential work to be done to machinery, equipment or plant; or other unforeseen or unpreventable circumstances; but only to the extent necessary to prevent serious interference with the ordinary working of the industrial establishment.

[17] The standard and maximum hours of work in a day and in a week may be averaged for a period of one or more weeks.

[18] Where possible, the rest period must be on Sunday.

[19] An employee taking a meal break must not work during that period.

[20] Employers and employees may agree to average hours of work where there is a pre-determined, fixed cycle of work that repeats over a specific period of time. For this agreement to be valid, it must meet certain conditions approved by the provincial government. For example, there must be a greater benefit to the employee, in the form of an extended period of time off; otherwise the employer has violated the employer's rights.

[21] An employer in an industrial undertaking must, where possible, grant the period of rest simultaneously to all employees in the establishment and grant the day of rest on Sunday.

An employer can require more than six consecutive days of work: if the Director of Labour Standards permits it; or in the case of an occurrence beyond human control, but only so far as is necessary to avoid serious interference with the ordinary operation of the employer's undertaking.

[22] Unless the total time worked on successive shifts does not exceed 13 hours or unless the employer and the employee agree otherwise.

[23] Some exemptions may apply for specific employers or industries as designated by Employment Standards Board.

[24] Where possible, the rest period must include Sunday.

[25] With the authorization of the Labour Standards Commission, hours of work may be staggered on a non-weekly basis.

[26] Employees may refuse to work more than four hours in excess of their regular daily working hours or more than 14 hours per 24-hour period — whichever is the shortest period. Employees whose hours of work are flexible or non-continuous may refuse to work more than 12 hours per 24-hour period. Employees may refuse to work more than 50 hours per week or, for employees working in an isolated area or in the James Bay territory, more than 60 hours per week unless there is an authorization by the Commission to stagger hours of work on a basis other than a weekly basis.

However, this right of refusal does not apply where there is a danger to the life, health or safety of employees or the population; where there is a risk of destruction or serious deterioration of movable or immovable property or in any other case of superior force; or if the refusal is inconsistent with the employee's professional code of ethics.

It should also be noted that an employer may not dismiss or take reprisals against an employee who refuses to work beyond his/her regular hours in order to fulfill specified parental and family obligations; but this only applies where the employee has taken reasonable steps within his/her power to deal with these obligations otherwise.

[27] A meal break must be paid if the employee is not authorized to leave his/her work station.

[28] Except in emergency circumstances or if the employee agrees to work extra hours. However, an employee's hours of work in a day must be confined to a 12-hour period. An employee is not be required to report to work more than twice in this period.

[29] An employee may refuse to work more than 44 hours in a week, except in emergency circumstances, and is protected against punishment arising from this refusal.

[30] In addition, no employer may punish an employee who refuses to work according to a schedule that does not allow for 8 hours of rest where no emergency circumstances exist.

[31] Employees in an establishment with more than ten employees are entitled to the longer (48 hour) rest period in every seven days and where possible, the rest period must include Sunday.

[32] Employers are not required to provide a meal break where: an accident occurs, urgent work is necessary or other unforeseeable or unpreventable circumstances occur; where the Director of Labour Standards is satisfied that the employer and the majority of employees agree.

Where an employer is not required to grant a meal break, employees must be allowed to eat while working once they have worked for 5 hours. A meal break must be paid if the employee is required or to be at the disposal of the employer during that period.

[33] Unless the employer is exempt by the Director of Employment Standards, the standard hours of work of an employee working a split shift must be confined to the 12-hour period immediately following the start of the employee's shift.

[34] An employee may refuse to work overtime for just cause provided that the refusal and cause for refusing are given to the employer in writing.

[35] Unless an emergency situation arises. Under certain circumstances, the Director of Employment Standards may order that the rest period be shortened to 6 consecutive hours.

[36] Where possible, the rest period must include Sunday. However, if an employer requires an employee to work regularly in excess of the daily standard hours of work, the employer may require the employee to work up to 28 continuous days without a day of rest in addition to seven more continuous days when the additional work is necessary in order to complete a project on which the employee was employed during those 28 days. An employee who has such a work schedule is entitled to at least one day of rest for each continuous seven days of work and to take the accrued days of rest continuously with each other.

[37] A meal break must be paid if the employee is required to work during that period.

[38] In exceptional circumstances (e.g., emergencies, urgent repair work), an employee may be required to work during a rest period, but only so far as is necessary to avoid serious interference with the ordinary working of the employer's operations.

Current Provincial Minimum Wage

Source: www.labour.gc.ca

Each province and territory has its own minimum wage. Any increases in the minimum wage are regulated by the province or territory. Therefore, one provincial government's increase to the minimum wage is no guarantee that other provinces will follow accordingly.

Province	Minimum Wage (2011)
Alberta	$8.80
BC	$8.00 $6.00 "First Job" Rate (less than 500 hours of work experience and no paid experience before November 2001)
Saskatchewan	$9.25
Manitoba	$9.50
Ontario	$10.25 General Workers $8.90 Liquor Servers $9.60 Student Under 18 (less than 28 hrs/wk)
Québec	Before May 2011: $9.50 General Workers $8.25 If Gratuities Apply As of May 2011: $9.65 General Workers $8.35 If Gratuities Apply

New Brunswick	$9.00
Nova Scotia	$9.65 Less than 3 months experience $9.15
PEI	$9.00
Newfoundland & Labrador	$10.00
Yukon	$8.93
NWT	$9.00
Nunavut	$11.00
Federal Rate	Going rate of province in which you work (e.g. if you work full-time for the Federal government and work in Ontario, then the minimum wage would be $10.25.)

There are certain employment arrangements that are unique. Some industries (farming or fisheries), job roles (domestic worker or commissioned salesperson) or specific circumstances (room and board or apprenticeship) may be exempt from the application of the minimum wage.

Room and Board

When room and/or board are provided by an employer and the arrangement is accepted by the employee, the employee's wages may be reduced below the minimum wage, but not by more than 50 cents per meal and 60 cents per day for lodging. Room and board will only be deemed to have been paid as wages if the employee has received the meals and occupied the room.

Example: What employers can deduct for room and board (Ontario)

Source: www.labour.gov.on.ca

The allowable amounts that an employer can count as having paid to the employee as wages for room or board or both is set out below:

- Room (weekly)
    - private $31.70
    - non-private $15.85
- Meals
    - each meal $2.55
    - weekly maximum $53.55
- Rooms and meals (weekly)
    - with private room $85.25
    - with non-private $69.40
- Harvest workers (only) weekly housing
    - serviced housing $99.35
    - unserviced housing $73.30

Check your provincial labour board for the amounts allowable in your jurisdiction.

Apprenticeship

An employer is exempt from the paying minimum wage for employees who are being trained on the job if the employees are registered under and paid according to a provincial apprenticeship Act. Many of these programs are better known as internships or co-ops. Check your provincial labour board for specific guidelines.

Other Possible Jobs Exempt from the Minimum Wage

There are other jobs that may be exempt from being guaranteed the local minimum wage. They may include (but are not limited to) the list below. Please note: as the standards are different between provinces/territories, please check your local labour board for verification of which situations will apply to you.

- Real Estate Salesperson (Commission)

- Non-Profit Playground Or Summer Camp Employee

- Commissioned Salespeople Who Work Outside The Employer's Office

- Insurance Agents

- Liquor Servers
- Extras In Films/Television
- Securities Salesperson

Minimum Hours When Called

When an employer calls an employee into work, s/he is obligated by law to pay the employee wages for no less than three hours of work, whether or not the employee is asked to do any work after so reporting. So if your employer calls you into the office whether you are expected to be in the office or not, you have a right to be pay for at least 3 hours of wages even if your employer sends you home after a few minutes.

Equal Pay Legislation in Canada by Jurisdiction

Equal pay means that an employer can't pay you less based solely on your gender. In general, if you are doing the same work with the same responsibility, skill level, effort and working conditions, then you should be paid the same as anyone else doing this job regardless of whether the other person is a man or a woman. While there may be some exemptions, such as seniority or night shift work, all areas of Canada have instituted some form of equal pay legislation.

Below are the overviews from each province/territory.

Source: www.labour.gc.ca

Federal Jurisdiction

Application	Federal public service and federally-regulated industries
Type of Prohibition[2]	Male-female pay differential
Basis for Measuring Equal Pay	Wages[4]
Basis for the Comparison of Work	Based on work of equal value performed in the same establishment, same working conditions, assessed by the combination of the skill level, effort and responsibility required. [5]
Factors that Justify a Difference in Pay	Different performance ratings; seniority; a re-evaluation resulting in demotion of an employee's position or wages; a rehabilitation assignment; a temporary training position; the existence of an internal labour shortage in a particular job classification; a reclassification of a position to a lower level; or regional rates of wages. Gender is not a reasonable justification for a difference in pay. [6]
Time Limit to File Complaint	1 year (an extension of time is possible)
Restrictions on Recovery[3]	No

Alberta

Application	Private and public sectors
Type of Prohibition[2]	Male-female pay differential
Basis for Measuring Equal Pay	Rate of pay
Basis for the Comparison of Work	The same or substantially the same work for an employer in an establishment.
Factors that Justify a Difference in Pay	The breach of the Act was reasonable and justifiable in the circumstances.
Time Limit to File Complaint	1 year[7]
Restrictions on Recovery[3]	Recovery is limited to wages, income lost and/or expenses incurred during the 2 years preceding the complaint. A limit also applies for civil proceedings.[8]

British Columbia

Application	Private and public sectors
Type of Prohibition[2]	Male-female pay differential
Basis for Measuring Equal Pay	Rate of pay
Basis for the Comparison of Work	Similar work. This must be assessed by the concepts of skill, effort and responsibility, subject to factors in respect of pay rates, such as seniority systems, merit systems and systems that measure earnings by the quantity or quality of production.
Factors that Justify a Difference in Pay	A factor that would reasonably justify the difference, other than gender.
Time Limit to File Complaint	6 months[2] (an extension of time is possible).
Restrictions on Recovery[3]	No (A limit does apply for civil proceedings). [8]

Manitoba

Application	Private and public sectors
Type of Prohibition[2]	Male-female pay differential
Basis for Measuring Equal Pay	Wages[4]
Basis for the Comparison of Work	The kind or quality of work and the amount of work required of, and done by, the employees, is the same or substantially the same.
Factors that Justify a Difference in Pay	No provisions
Time Limit to File Complaint	6 months
Restrictions on Recovery[3]	Recovery is limited to wages due and payable in the 6 months before the date the complaint was filed or, if employment was terminated, in the last 6 months of employment. [10]

New Brunswick

Application	Private and public sectors
Type of Prohibition[2]	Male-female pay differential
Basis for Measuring Equal Pay	Rate of pay[11]
Basis for the Comparison of Work	Work that is substantially the same in nature, performed under similar working conditions in the same establishment and requiring substantially the same skill, effort and responsibility.
Factors that Justify a Difference in Pay	A seniority system; a merit system; a system that measures earnings by quantity or quality of production; or any other system or practice that is not unlawful.
Time Limit to File Complaint	12 months
Restrictions on Recovery[3]	No

Newfoundland and Labrador

Application	Private and public sectors
Type of Prohibition[2]	Male-female pay differential
Basis for Measuring Equal Pay	Wages, pension rights, insurance benefits and opportunities for training and advancement.
Basis for the Comparison of Work	The same or similar work on jobs requiring the same or similar skill, effort and responsibility, performed under the same or similar working conditions in the same establishment.
Factors that Justify a Difference in Pay	A seniority system or a merit system. These factors apply only in respect of wages (i.e. not for insurance benefits or opportunities for training and advancement).
Time Limit to File Complaint	6 months
Restrictions on Recovery [3]	No

Northwest Territories

Application	Private and public sectors
Type of Prohibition[2]	General anti-discrimination
Basis for Measuring Equal Pay	Wages.[12]
Basis for the Comparison of Work	The same or substantially similar work performed by employees in the same establishment. Work is deemed to be similar or substantially similar if it involves the same or substantially similar skill, effort and responsibility and is performed under the same or substantially similar working conditions.
Factors that Justify a Difference in Pay	A seniority system; a merit system; a system that measures earnings by quantity or quality of production or performance the existence of a labour shortage in respect of the field of work or of regional differences in the cost of living; a demotion process or system; a temporary rehabilitation or training program; or any other system or factor. These cannot be based on a prohibited ground of discrimination.

Time Limit to File Complaint	2 years (an extension of time is possible)
Restrictions on Recovery [3]	No

Nova Scotia

Application	Private and public sectors
Type of Prohibition[2]	Male-female pay differential
Basis for Measuring Equal Pay	Wages[13]
Basis for the Comparison of Work	Substantially the same work performed in the same establishment, the performance of which requires substantially equal skill, effort and responsibility and that is performed under similar working conditions.
Factors that Justify a Difference in Pay	A seniority system; a merit system; a system that measures wages by quantity or quality of production; or another differential based on a factor other than sex.
Time Limit to File Complaint	6 months[14]
Restrictions on Recovery [3]	No

Ontario

Application	Private and public sectors
Type of Prohibition[2]	Male-female pay differential
Basis for Measuring Equal Pay	Rate of pay[15]
Basis for the Comparison of Work	Same kind of work performed in the same establishment under similar working conditions requiring the same skill, effort and responsibility.
Factors that Justify a Difference in Pay	A seniority system; a merit system; a system that measures earnings by quantity or quality of production; or any factor other than sex.
Time Limit to File Complaint	2 years
Restrictions on Recovery [3]	An order to pay unpaid wages made by an employment standards officer cannot exceed $10,000 per employee. An officer cannot make an order to pay unpaid wages if wages became due more than 6 months before the complaint was filed.

Prince Edward Island

Application	Private and public sectors
Type of Prohibition[2]	General anti-discrimination
Basis for Measuring Equal Pay	Rate of pay
Basis for the Comparison of Work	Substantially the same work, requiring equal education, skill, experience, effort and responsibility performed under similar working conditions.
Factors that Justify a Difference in Pay	A seniority system; a merit system; or a system that measures earnings by quantity or quality of production.
Time Limit to File Complaint	1 year
Restrictions on Recovery [3]	No. (A limit does apply for civil proceedings) [16]

Québec

Application	Private and public sectors
Type of Prohibition[2]	General anti-discrimination
Basis for Measuring Equal Pay	Salary or wages
Basis for the Comparison of Work	Equivalent work performed at the same place.
Factors that Justify a Difference in Pay	Experience; seniority; years of service; merit; productivity; or overtime. These criteria must be common to all members of the personnel in order to justify a difference in pay.
Time Limit to File Complaint	Not specified[17]
Restrictions on Recovery [3]	No

Saskatchewan

Application	Private and public sectors
Type of Prohibition[2]	Male-female pay differential
Basis for Measuring Equal Pay	Rate of pay[18]
Basis for the Comparison of Work	Similar work performed in the same establishment under similar working conditions, requiring similar skill, effort and responsibility.
Factors that Justify a Difference in Pay	A seniority system or a merit system.
Time Limit to File Complaint	Not specified
Restrictions on Recovery [3]	No

Yukon Territory (private sector)

Application	Private sector
Type of Prohibition[2]	Male-female pay differential
Basis for Measuring Equal Pay	Rate of pay
Basis for the Comparison of Work	Similar work performed in the same establishment under similar working conditions, requiring similar skill, effort and responsibility.
Factors that Justify a Difference in Pay	A seniority system; a merit system; a system that measures earnings by quantity or quality of production; or a differential based on any factor other than sex.
Time Limit to File Complaint	6 months[19]
Restrictions on Recovery [3]	No

Yukon Territory (public sector)

Application	Public sector, including municipalities and their corporations, boards and commissions
Type of Prohibition[2]	Male-female pay differential
Basis for Measuring Equal Pay	Wages[20]
Basis for the Comparison of Work	Work of equal value, assessed by the criterion of the composite of skill, effort, and responsibility required and the working conditions.
Factors that Justify a Difference in Pay	No provisions
Time Limit to File Complaint	6 months
Restrictions on Recovery [3]	No

Notes:

[1] Nunavut does not have equal pay legislation. However, the *Human Rights Act* in that territory does prohibit discrimination against an individual or class of individuals with respect to "employment or a term or condition of employment" on the ground of gender (among other grounds), regardless of whether that term or condition exists prior or subsequent to employment.

[2] In general, equal pay provisions prohibit a *pay differential* between *male and female* employees of the same employer who are performing the same or substantially similar work. However, the legislation of the Northwest Territories, Prince Edward Island and Québec prohibits *general discrimination* with respect to pay where employees perform work that is the same or substantially the same. The *Human Rights Act* of the Northwest Territories prohibits an employer from paying an employee, *on the basis of a prohibited ground of discrimination*, at a rate of pay less than that paid to other employees employed in the same establishment who are performing the same or substantially similar work. Prohibited grounds of discrimination include race, colour, ancestry, nationality, ethnic origin, place of origin, creed, religion, age, disability, sex, sexual orientation, gender identity, marital or family status, family affiliation, political belief or association, social condition and a conviction for which a pardon has been granted. The *Human Rights Act* of Prince Edward Island similarly prohibits discrimination in pay. "Discrimination" is defined as discrimination in relation to age, colour, creed, ethnic or national origin, family status, marital status, physical or mental handicap, political belief, race, religion, sex, sexual orientation or source of income of any individual or class of individuals. In Québec, the *Charter Of Human Rights And Freedoms* requires an employer to grant, without discrimination, equal salary or wages to the members of his/her personnel who are performing equivalent work at the same place. Under the *Charter*, discrimination exists where a distinction, exclusion or preference (based on race, colour, sex, pregnancy, sexual orientation, civil status, age except as provided by law, religion, political convictions, language, ethnic or national origin, social condition, or a handicap) has the effect of nullifying or impairing a person's right to full and equal recognition and exercise of his/her rights or freedoms.

[3] This refers to the most amount of money that an employee can recover from an employer in a complaint under equal pay legislation, excluding the following: punitive damages (including compensation or damages awarded on the grounds that the wrongdoer acted willfully or recklessly); compensation in respect of pain and suffering or injury to dignity, feelings and self-respect; costs; and administrative costs.

[4] "Wages" is defined as any form of compensation payable to an individual for the performance of work, including: salaries, commissions, vacation pay, dismissal wages and bonuses; reasonable value for board, rent, housing and lodging; payments in kind; employer contributions to pension funds, pension plans, long-term disability plans and all forms of health insurance plans; and any other advantage received directly or indirectly from the employer.

[5] The *Equal Wages Guidelines* provide that intellectual and physical qualifications acquired by experience, training, education or natural ability must be considered in assessing the skill required in the performance of work; however, how the employees acquired these qualifications cannot be considered in assessing the skill of different employees. The requirement to work overtime or to work shifts cannot be considered in assessing working conditions.

[6] To justify a difference in wages on the basis of one of these factors, the employer is required to establish that the factor in question is applied consistently and equitably in calculating and paying the wages of all male and female employees employed in the same establishment who are performing work of equal value.

[7] The deadline to start a civil action under the equal pay provisions is also one year. Note that the Act prevents a person from proceeding with both a civil action and a complaint regarding the equal pay provisions.

[8] A civil action applies only to the wages of an employee during the 12-month period immediately preceding the earlier of the termination of the employee's services or the beginning of the action.

[9] A civil action under the equal pay provisions must be started within 12 months of the date of the termination of the employee's services.

[10] However, if the complaint relates to a vacation allowance or wages for a general holiday, the maximum amount recoverable is limited to wages due and payable in the 22 months before the date the complaint was filed or, where the employee's employment was terminated, in the last 22 months of employment.

[11] "Pay" includes wages, public holiday pay and pay in lieu of public holidays, vacation pay and pay in lieu of vacation, benefits, initiation fees and dues checked off by an employer. It does not include deductions from wages that can be lawfully made by an employer. " Wages" includes salary, commissions and compensation in any form for work or services. It does not include public holiday pay, pay in lieu of public holidays, vacation pay, pay in lieu of vacation gratuities or honoraria.

[12] "Pay" includes any form of payment made by an employer for work performed by an employee including salary, commission, vacation pay, severance pay, pay in lieu of notice of termination, bonuses, the value of any board, rent or housing provided, contributions to a disability plan, health insurance plan or pension plan and any other advantage received directly or indirectly by the employee.

[13] "Wages" includes salaries, commissions, compensation in any form for work or services, general holidays pay and pay in lieu of minimum notice of termination. It does not include vacation pay, pay in lieu of vacation or gratuities.

[14] There is no time limit to file a complaint; however, an order cannot be made with respect to a complaint unless the failure to comply with the Act occurred within the six months preceding the receipt of the complaint or the initiation of an inquiry.

[15] The *Employment Standards Act* provides that employment standards officer can determine the amount owing to an employee and that amount will be deemed to be "unpaid wages" owing to the employee. "Wages" includes monetary remuneration payable by an employer to an employee under an employment contract, any payment an employer is required to make to an employee, and any allowances for room and board under an employment contract or prescribed allowances. It does not include the following things: tips or other gratuities; sums paid as gifts or bonuses on the discretion of the employer and not related to hours, production or efficiency; expenses and travelling allowances; or employer contributions to a benefit plan and payments to which an employee is entitled under a benefit plan.

[16] The *Human Rights Act* provides that civil proceedings under the equal pay provisions apply only to the employee's wages during the 12-month period immediately preceding the earlier of the termination of his/her services or the start of proceedings. Civil proceedings must be started within 12 months of the date that the cause of action arose. The Act bars an employee from proceeding with both a complaint under the Act and civil proceedings.

[17] However, the *Commission des droits de la personne et des droits de la jeunesse* can refuse to act on a complaint two years before the date the complaint was filed.

[18] "Pay" is defined as remuneration in any form.

[19] The complaint must be made within six months after the last date on which payment was to be made after the date on which the complaint arose.

[20] "Wages" refers to any payment for work performed by an individual, including the following: salaries; commissions; vacation pay; dismissal wages; bonuses; value for board, rent, housing or lodging; payments in kind; employer contributions to pension plans or funds, long-term disability plans or any form of health insurance plans; and any other advantage received directly or indirectly from the employer.

Statutory Holidays

Source: www.labour.gc.ca

Statutory holidays are days designated by government to celebrate a significant occasion or event such as Canada Day or New Year's Day. Employees who work on a statutory holiday normally receive a premium wage for the time worked.

Jurisdiction	Holidays [1] (days per year)	Eligibility Requirements: No Entitlement to Holiday Pay If...				Pay for Holidays Worked [2]
		length of service less than (in days):	failure to work on working day preceding or following the holiday	no wages earned for 15 of the 30 days preceding the holiday	work arrangement where employee can decide whether or not to report to work	
Federal	9	30		X[3]		regular rate of wages + 1½ times regular rate for time worked
Alberta[4]	9	30	X			a) average daily wage + 1½ times regular rate for hours worked; or b) regular rate for hours worked + paid day off
British Columbia	9	30				1½ times regular wage for first 11 hours + 2 times regular wage for each additional hour + paid day off
Manitoba	7[5]	n/a	X	X		regular wages + 1½ times regular rate for hours worked
New Brunswick	6	90	X		X	regular wages + 1½ times regular rate for time worked
Newfoundland	5	30	X	X[6]		a) regular wages + normal wages b) paid day off within 30 days; or c) one additional day of vacation
Nova Scotia	5[5]	n/a	X	X		regular pay + 1½ times regular rate for time worked

Ontario	8	n/a	X[7]		X	a) total amount of regular wages in 4 work weeks preceding week of holiday ? 20 + 1½ times regular rate for hours worked; or (b) regular rate for hours worked + paid day off
Prince Edward Island	5	30	X	X	X	a) one day's pay + 1½ times regular rate for time worked; or b) regular rate for time worked + paid day off
Québec	8	60	X	(June 24)[8]	X	wages for work done, plus a) average daily wages; or b) paid day off
Saskatchewan	9	n/a				regular wages (or pro-rated amount) + 1½ times regular rate for time worked
Northwest Territories/ Nunavut[2]	10 / 9	30	X			regular rate of wages for normal hours (or average daily wages), plus a) 1½ times regular rate for time worked; or b) paid day off
Yukon	9	30	X	X[10]		regular wages, plus (a) 1½ times regular rate for hours worked; or (b) regular rate for hours worked + another day off

Notes:

The information above applies in most cases. However, some statutes and regulations may include a number of exceptions. Some types of work and industries are specifically excluded from statutory holiday provisions in many jurisdictions.

1   The following statutory holidays are recognized by the labour boards of the various Canadian jurisdictions:

Jurisdiction	Holiday
All	New Year's Day, Good Friday (or Easter Monday in Québec), Canada Day (Memorial Day in Nfld.), Labour Day, Christmas Day
All except New Brunswick, Newfoundland, Nova Scotia, and Prince Edward Island	Victoria Day (Dollard Day in Québec), Thanksgiving Day
B.C. (British Columbia Day), New Brunswick (New Brunswick Day), Saskatchewan. (Saskatchewan Day), Northwest Territories, Nunavut, Ontario (Simcoe Day)	1st Monday in August
Federal, Alberta, British Columbia, Saskatchewan, Northwest Territories, Nunavut,, Yukon (also see note 7)	Remembrance Day (November 11)
Federal, Ontario	Boxing Day
Alberta, Ontario, Saskatchewan	Family Day (3rd Monday in February)
Northwest Territories	National Aboriginal Day (June 21)
Prince Edward Island	Islander Day (3rd Monday in February)
Québec	St. John the Baptist's Day (June 24)
Yukon	Discovery Day (3rd Monday in August)

2   This information pertains to employees who are eligible for holiday pay. It should be noted that employees do not usually have a legislated right to refuse to work on a holiday, except in Newfoundland and, for employees in most retail business establishments, in Ontario. In Manitoba, employees in retail business establishments have the right to refuse to work on Remembrance Day.

3   Holiday pay may be pro-rated for employees who are unable to establish 15 days of wages in the 30 day period because of their terms and conditions of employment.

4   In Alberta, employees are not entitled to holiday pay or a compensatory day off if a holiday falls on a non-working day.

[5] Remembrance Day is not recognized as a general holiday in the labour/employment standards legislation of Manitoba and Nova Scotia. However, employees who meet qualifying requirements are entitled, if required to work on that day, to holiday pay and wages for no less than ½ the normal working hours in Manitoba and to another day off with pay in Nova Scotia.

[6] In the case of Newfoundland, an employee must not have been absent for 15 or more of the 30 days preceding the holiday, unless for an annual vacation, a pregnancy, or a parental, adoption, bereavement or sick leave.

[7] It is not necessary to pay public holiday pay to an employee who fails to perform all of the work agreed to on a holiday and who also fails, without reasonable cause, to work all of the scheduled days of work immediately before and after the holiday.

[8] An employer in Québec is not required to grant a holiday with pay for St. John the Baptist's Day to an employee who has not been entitled to wages for 10 days in the period from June 1 - June 23.

[9] Employees in the Northwest Territories and Nunavut are not entitled to holiday pay if they are on pregnancy or parental leave.

[10] Employees in the Yukon who have been absent without pay for 14 consecutive days immediately preceding the holiday, on a leave of absence at their request, are not entitled to holiday.

Vacation Time/Pay

Most employees are eligible vacation time or vacation pay. Full-time, part-time, temporary, seasonal, term contract employees and student employees are eligible.

Vacation time is allotted time away from work while still receiving your salary. Vacation pay is money paid to you above your regular pay in the amount of no less than 4% of wages earned. Wages include regular wages, commissions, public holiday pay, overtime, merit bonuses and allowances for room and board. Wages, in this case, do not include tips and gratuities, Christmas bonus, contributions to a benefit plan, expenses or travelling allowances.

While your employer may offer more, the tables below list the minimum requirements for annual vacations with pay in employment standards legislation.

(Please check your provincial website for details and clarifications.)

Source: www.labour.gc.ca

Jurisdiction	Vacation
Alberta	2 weeks/year 3 wks/yr after 5 yrs
British Columbia	2 weeks/year 3 weeks/year after 5 years
Federal	2 weeks/year 3 weeks/year after 6 years

Manitoba	2 weeks/year 3 weeks/year after 5 years
New Brunswick	2 weeks/year 3 weeks/year after 8 years
Newfoundland	2 weeks/year 3 weeks/year after 15 years
Nova Scotia	2 weeks/year
Nunavut	2 weeks/year 3 weeks/year after 5 years
Northwest Territories	2 weeks/year 3 weeks/year after 5 years

Ontario	2 weeks/year
Prince Edward Island	2 weeks/year
Québec	2 weeks/year 3 weeks/year after 5 years
Saskatchewan	3 weeks/year 4 weeks/year after 10 years
Yukon	2 weeks/year

Federal

Length of Vacation	2 weeks; 3 weeks after 6 consecutive years of employment.
Scheduling of Vacation	Within 10 months of entitlement.
Division of Vacation Time	Not specified.
Notice Required	2 weeks.
Waiver of Vacation[1]	Yes. Pay in lieu must be given within 10 months.
Amount of Vacation Pay	4% of annual wages; 6% after 6 years
Payment of Vacation Pay (Timing)[2]	Within 14 days before vacation begins.

Alberta

Length of Vacation	2 weeks; 3 weeks after 5 consecutive years of employment.[8]
Scheduling of Vacation	Within 12 months of entitlement.
Division of Vacation Time[2]	One unbroken period; or, at employee's written request, employer can agree to two or more periods of at least one day.
Notice Required	2 weeks.
Waiver of Vacation[1]	Not specified.
Amount of Vacation Pay	4% of annual wages; 6% for employees entitled to 3 weeks of vacation.
Payment of Vacation Pay (Timing)[2]	No later than regular pay day following start of vacation; at employee's request, vacation pay must be paid at least one day before the vacation starts.

British Columbia

Length of Vacation	2 weeks; 3 weeks after 5 consecutive years of employment.
Scheduling of Vacation	Within 12 months of entitlement.
Division of Vacation Time	Periods of one or more weeks.
Notice Required	Not specified.
Waiver of Vacation[1]	Not specified.
Amount of Vacation Pay	4% of total wages earned in the year of employment (if employee has completed at least 5 calendar days of employment); 6% after 5 consecutive years of employment.
Payment of Vacation Pay (Timing)[2]	7 days before beginning of vacation or, if agreed by the employer and the employee or provided for in a collective agreement, on the employee's scheduled pay days.

Manitoba

Length of Vacation	2 weeks; 3 weeks after 5 consecutive years of employment.
Scheduling of Vacation	Within 10 months of entitlement.
Division of Vacation Time	Periods of not less than one week; where a business customarily shuts down for an extended period each year, employees can be required to take their vacation during that period.
Notice Required	15 days.
Waiver of Vacation[1]	Not specified.
Amount of Vacation Pay	2% of wages earned in the year of employment for each week of vacation. Employer must also add 2% of cash value of board and lodging to vacation pay entitlement.
Payment of Vacation Pay (Timing)[2]	Last working day before the vacation unless the employer and the employee agree otherwise.

New Brunswick

Length of Vacation	2 weeks or 1 day per month worked during vacation pay year (whichever is less); 3 weeks or 1¼ days per month worked during vacation pay year (whichever is less) after 8 consecutive years of service.
Scheduling of Vacation	Within 4 months after end of vacation pay year.
Division of Vacation Time	Not specified.
Notice Required	1 week.
Waiver of Vacation[1]	Not specified.
Amount of Vacation Pay	4% of wages earned in the vacation pay year; 6% after 8 consecutive years of employment.
Payment of Vacation Pay (Timing)[2]	At least 1 day before the vacation begins.

Newfoundland and Labrador

Length of Vacation	2 weeks; 3 weeks after 15 years of continuous employment.
Scheduling of Vacation	Within 10 months of entitlement.
Division of Vacation Time	One unbroken period, or combination of unbroken periods of 1 or 2 weeks, at employee's option; employer and employee may agree to shorter periods; employee must give notice of intention before vacation entitlement date.
Notice Required	2 weeks. If employer cancels/changes dates of employee's booked vacation, employer reimburses employee for reasonable expenses incurred with respect to cancelled/changed vacation plans.
Waiver of Vacation[1]	Not specified.
Amount of Vacation Pay	4% of total wages earned during 12-month period; 6% after 15 years of continuous employment.
Payment of Vacation Pay (Timing)[2]	At least 1 day before annual vacation, or a part of it.

Northwest Territories / Nunavut

Length of Vacation	2 weeks; 3 weeks after 6 years of employment (whether continuous or accumulated over the past 10 years).
Scheduling of Vacation	Within 10 months of entitlement.
Division of Vacation Time	Not specified.
Notice Required	Not specified.
Waiver of Vacation[1]	Yes. If employee agrees to waive right to or agrees to postpone vacation for a given year, employer must still pay vacation pay to employee.
Amount of Vacation Pay	4% of wages; 6% for an employee entitled to 3 weeks of vacation.
Payment of Vacation Pay (Timing)[2]	1 day before beginning of vacation.

Nova Scotia

Length of Vacation	2 weeks; 3 weeks after 8 continuous years of employment.
Scheduling of Vacation	Within 10 months of entitlement.
Division of Vacation Time	One unbroken period; employer and employee may agree to divide annual vacation in two or more periods, including at least one unbroken period of one week or more.
Notice Required	1 week.
Waiver of Vacation[1]	Yes (restricted).[2]
Amount of Vacation Pay	4% of wages; 6% after 8 continuous years of employment.
Payment of Vacation Pay (Timing)[2]	1 day before vacation begins; if vacation is broken, 1 day before an unbroken vacation period of at least one week.

Ontario

Length of Vacation	2 weeks.
Scheduling of Vacation	Vacation must normally be completed no later than 10 months after entitlement.[4]
Division of Vacation Time	One two-week period or two periods of one week each, unless employee requests in writing to take the vacation in shorter periods and employer agrees.
Notice Required	Not specified.
Waiver of Vacation[1]	Yes.
Amount of Vacation Pay	4% of wages earned in the applicable period (normally a 12-month period).
Payment of Vacation Pay (Timing)[2]	Normally, before vacation begins, if an employer pays an employee's wages by direct deposit or the employee does not take his/her vacation in complete weeks, the payment should be on or before pay day for the period in which the vacation falls. If the employee agrees and a wage statement sets out vacation pay, payment should be on pay day of each pay period where it accrues, or payment at a time mutually agreed upon by both parties.[5]

Prince Edward Island

Length of Vacation	2 weeks.
Scheduling of Vacation	Within 4 months of entitlement.
Division of Vacation Time	One unbroken period.
Notice Required	1 week.
Waiver of Vacation[1]	Not specified.
Amount of Vacation Pay	4% of wages.
Payment of Vacation Pay (Timing)[2]	1 day before beginning of vacation.

Québec

Length of Vacation	2 weeks; 3 weeks after five years of uninterrupted service. 1 additional week of unpaid annual leave may be taken in certain cases.[6] Employees with less than one year of uninterrupted service: one day per month of uninterrupted service during reference year (2 weeks maximum).
Scheduling of Vacation	Within 12 months following the end of the reference year.[7]
Division of Vacation Time	One unbroken period, or two periods if employee requests; with consent of employer, may be divided in more than two periods; some exceptions may apply.
Notice Required	4 weeks.
Waiver of Vacation[1]	No.[8]
Amount of Vacation Pay	4% of gross wages during the reference year; 6% of gross wages for employees entitled to three weeks of annual leave; special provisions apply to employees who are absent because of sickness, accident or maternity leave.[2]
Payment of Vacation Pay (Timing)[2]	Before beginning of vacation.

Saskatchewan

Length of Vacation	3 weeks; 4 weeks after 10 years of employment.
Scheduling of Vacation	Within 12 months of entitlement.
Division of Vacation Time	One unbroken period; or, at employee's option, two or more periods of at least one week each; employer may arrange to close his/her business and require employees to take their vacation at that time.
Notice Required	4 weeks. Where an employer does not permit an employee to take an annual holiday as scheduled by agreement, the employer must reimburse the employee for any monetary/loss s/he suffered as a result of the cancellation/postponement.
Waiver of Vacation[1]	Yes. Because of a shortage of labour, an employee can agree in writing to forego an annual vacation. The employee must be paid the annual holiday.
Amount of Vacation Pay	3 / 52 of total wages earned in year of employment; 4 / 52 of total wages for employees entitled to 4 weeks of annual holidays.

Payment of Vacation Pay (Timing)[2]	Within 14 days before each period of vacation (vacation pay may be divided). If employee foregoes annual holiday to which s/he is entitled, then employee must pay vacation pay no later than 11 months from date of entitlement.

Yukon

Length of Vacation	2 weeks.
Scheduling of Vacation	Within 10 months of entitlement.
Division of Vacation Time	Not specified.
Notice Required	Not specified.
Waiver of Vacation[1]	Yes. Employer must pay to the employee, within 10 months of the date it is due, the vacation pay to which the employee is entitled.
Amount of Vacation Pay	4% of wages earned in year of employment (if employee has been continuously employed for a period of at least 14 days).
Payment of Vacation Pay (Timing)[2]	1 day before beginning of vacation.

Notes:

[1] Refers to the possibility, for an employee, to waive an annual vacation to which he or she is entitled. This may be subject to a number of specific conditions, and therefore does not necessarily apply to all employees. Even if an employee does not take an annual vacation, his/her employer must still pay any vacation pay earned.

[2] Any earned vacation pay not yet received by the employee must be paid when his/her employment is terminated.

[3] An employee who works for an employer for less than 90% of the regular hours during a continuous 12-month period may waive his/her entitlement to a vacation by notifying the employer in writing. In this case, vacation pay must be paid by the employer no more than one month after the end of the twelve-month period in which it was earned.

[4] An employee who is taking a pregnancy, parental, family medical or emergency leave on the day on which the annual vacation must be completed, may complete the uncompleted part of the vacation immediately after the leave expires or, with the agreement of his/her employer, at a later date. Alternately, the employee may forego the remaining vacation time and receive vacation pay instead.

5　If an employee goes on strike or is locked out during a time for which his/her vacation had been scheduled by the employer, the latter must pay the employee the vacation pay that would have been paid with respect to that vacation, even if it is considered to have been cancelled.

6　Employees entitled to two weeks of annual leave and who have at least one year of uninterrupted service are also entitled, if they apply for it, to an additional week of annual leave without pay, to be taken in an unbroken period. This does not apply to employees already entitled to three weeks of annual leave with pay. An additional unpaid annual leave need not follow immediately a paid annual leave.

7　However, a collective agreement may allow the parties to defer an annual leave until the following year. In addition, an employer may allow an employee to take part or all of the annual leave during, rather than after, the reference year. An employer may also agree to defer an employee's annual leave to the following year, if the employee is absent at the end of the 12 months by reason of sickness or accident, or for family or parental matters.

8　Employers are prohibited from replacing an annual leave by a compensatory indemnity, unless a special provision is contained in a collective agreement. However, at the request of the employee, the third week of leave may be replaced by a compensatory indemnity if the establishment closes for two weeks on the occasion of the annual leave.

9　Should an employee's absence due to sickness or accident or a maternity leave during the reference year result in the reduction of his/her annual leave indemnity, then the employee is entitled to an amount equal to twice or three times (depending on whether the employee is entitled to two or three weeks of annual leave) the weekly average of wages earned during the period of work. An employee with less than one year of uninterrupted service and whose annual leave is less than two weeks is entitled to an amount proportional to the days of leave credited to his/her account. An annual leave indemnity is not to exceed the amount to which an employee would have been entitled had s/he not been on leave or absent.

Additional Notes:

A.　Normally, an employee must have completed one year of service with his/her employer in order to be eligible for two weeks of annual vacation. However, in New Brunswick and Québec, an employee with less than one year, but at least one month of service is entitled to pro-rated vacation time and pay. Furthermore, in Alberta, Manitoba, Ontario, Saskatchewan and the federal jurisdiction, employers can establish a common anniversary date for employees for the purpose of calculating vacation entitlements, but must provide prorated vacation and pay to employees with less than one year of service on that date.

B.　In Newfoundland and Labrador, an employee must have worked for at least 90% of normal working hours over a continuous 12-month period in order to be entitled to an annual vacation. Newfoundland and Labrador is the only jurisdiction with a minimum working hours requirement regarding annual leave.

C. Although the formula used to calculate vacation pay—annual wages times 4% or 6%—is common to most jurisdictions, there is relatively little consistency across Canada as regards the types of earnings (e.g., salary, tips, holiday pay) that are to be considered as "wages". The definition of wages varies in each jurisdiction. For example, definitions used in provinces such as Alberta and Ontario explicitly list the types of payments (e.g., tips, expenses, discretionary bonuses) that are not deemed to be wages for vacation pay (and other) purposes.

Right to Refuse Work

There are occasions where it may be unreasonable for an employer to insist that an employee perform his/her duties. While you don't have the right to refuse work for minor changes in the workplace, you do have the right in situations where your health or human rights are at risk.

Here are the most common issues.

Sundays or Religious Holidays

Until the 1990's, very few jurisdictions allowed any retail establishments to operate on Sundays. However, in some provinces, that has since changed due to deregulation. In the context of the deregulation of Sunday commercial activity, three provinces—Ontario, Manitoba and New Brunswick—enacted new provisions to provide retail sector employees the right to refuse Sunday work in certain circumstances, while prohibiting retaliation from employers. The purpose of such legislation was to grant a degree of protection to employees unwilling, for religious, family or other reasons, to work on Sundays.

In Ontario, except for religious reasons, employees in retail business establishments hired on or after September 4, 2001, no longer have the right to refuse to work on Sundays if they had agreed to work on that day at the moment of hiring. Provisions pertaining to Sunday work were adopted more recently in Manitoba and in New Brunswick. In both provinces, employees of specified retail business establishments can refuse to work on a Sunday by giving their employer at least 14 days' notice.

Illness

Generally, the Canada Labour Code provides protection against dismissal, lay-off, suspension, demotion or discipline because of absence due to illness or injury. An employee is protected for any absence not exceeding 12 weeks provided the employee has completed three consecutive months of employment. The employee is required to provide a doctor's certificate in a timely manner if requested by the employer. For long term disability, the employee must produce a medical certificate that states that the employee is not fit to perform the job.

For more information, go to the section in this book on "Sick Leave".

Overtime

Labour standards legislation in most Canadian jurisdictions does not provide employees with an explicit right to refuse to work overtime. However, there are some exceptions.

Manitoba's Employment Standards Code stipulates that an employer's rights do not include an implied right to require an employee to work overtime, except in cases of emergency. Employees may refuse to work overtime beyond a set limit in Ontario - after 8 hours in a day or 48 hours in a week - and Saskatchewan (44 hours in a week). This provision does not apply in an emergency, defined as any sudden or unusual occurrence or condition that could not, by the exercise of reasonable judgment, have been foreseen by the employer. In the Yukon, an employee may refuse to work overtime for "just cause." The cause for refusing must be provided to the employer in writing.

In Québec, both types of "right to refuse" provisions exist. Employees are provided with the right to refuse excess daily and weekly working hours. They are also protected against reprisal by the employer if they cannot work more than their regularly scheduled working hours due to family responsibilities. However, there are some exceptions to these provisions.

Unsafe Workplace

Workers are entitled to refuse work, or to refuse work with certain machinery or equipment, if they believe it is dangerous to either their own health and safety, or the health and safety of another worker, without retaliation from their employer. If a worker refuses work, the worker must immediately inform the worker's supervisor or employer.

The Labour Code indicates that the danger perceived by the employee "…must relate to a machine, thing or to the physical condition of the work place". The Code, therefore, protects the employee from dangers that exist in the work place. The Code does not appear to go so far as to protect the employee in cases where the danger is caused by his/her own medical condition.

In the case where a worker is injured on the job site, medical certificates should be taken into consideration, along with all the other relevant facts, in order to determine whether the danger was caused by a machine or condition at the work place or by the employee's own medical condition.

For more information, please check your provincial/territorial labour board for more detailed information.

Civic Duty

Jury Duty

Employers must give employees time off to attend jury selection and to serve as jurors. A juror is considered to be on unpaid leave for the period of jury duty. Although the employers are not legally obligated to pay employees for lost wages while on jury duty, the employee is considered to be in continuous employment for the purposes of calculating annual vacation, termination entitlements, as well as for pension, medical or other employee benefit plans. The employee is also entitled to all increases in wages and benefits which he or she would have received if not on jury duty.

An employer cannot dismiss, suspend or reassign an employee who has been summoned or who has served as a juror, take discriminatory measures or reprisals against the employee or impose any other penalty. It is an offence for an employer to directly or indirectly threaten to cause or causes an employee loss of position or employment or threaten to impose or impose on an employee any monetary or other penalty because of the employee being summoned for jury service.

As soon as jury duty ends, an employee must be returned to his or her former position or comparable position.

An employee who is penalized solely for performing jury duty may file a complaint with their provincial labour board.

Reservist Leave

Recently, military reservists working as civilians did not have a guaranteed right to return to their position upon completion of their deployments, unless such protection had been negotiated contractually. Now, employers must provide statutory job protection to civilians serving as military reservists in the Canadian Forces.

Recent changes to the provisions permit reservist employees to take leaves of absence, without pay, when deployed to a Canadian Forces operation outside Canada or to pre-deployment or post-deployment duties in connection with such an operation. Such leaves also extend to reservist employees deployed to a Canadian Forces operation inside Canada for the purpose of providing assistance in dealing with an emergency or its aftermath.

The new provisions require employers to provide a leave of absence for the prescribed period, or, if no period is prescribed, for the period which is necessary to accommodate the Canadian Forces operation. Employers are not required to contribute to any benefit or pension plans during the leave period unless otherwise agreed to in an employment contract.

Similar to other leave provisions, employees wishing to take reservist leave would be required to provide written notice four-weeks in advance of the period of leave. If the employee receives notice of deployment less than four weeks before it will begin, written notice must be provided to the employer as soon as is reasonable and realistic. In addition, the written notification must include the date on which the unpaid leave is to begin and the expected date of return to work. If an employee intends to return to work prior to the date previously specified in the written notification, he or she must give the employer notification at least one week before the date proposed to return to work.

The reservist leave provisions are intended to apply to all employers, regardless of size in British Columbia, Ontario, Saskatchewan, Manitoba, New Brunswick, Nova Scotia, Prince Edward Island and the federal government in providing job protecting for reservist employees.

Voting

Every employee who is an elector is entitled, during voting hours on polling day, to have three consecutive hours for the purpose of casting his or her vote. If your hours of work do not allow for three consecutive voting hours, your employer must allow you the time off necessary to meet that requirement.

Here is an example: Assuming voting times do not change, a Toronto employee scheduled to start work no earlier than 12:30 p.m. or to finish work by 6:30 p.m. will not need extra time off to vote. If an employee is scheduled to work such that they do not have three consecutive voting hours before or after their shift, the employee must be permitted to start late or finish early. The time off may be scheduled when "convenient" for the employer, so it is up to the employer to determine whether an employee is permitted a late start or an early finish. Employers may not make a deduction from the wages of an employee or impose a penalty on an employee for the time he or she is allowed for voting. You should be paid as if you had worked a full shift.

Maternity, Parental and Adoption Leave

With the growing demand for a greater work-life balance, provincial governments are recognizing the need for new parents to have the opportunity to bond with the newest member of their family while not risking their role in the workplace. Even in the case of adoption, the Labour Code allows parents time to create a strong family foundation.

It is not only mothers that are allowed a leave of absence. Legally, fathers are just as entitled to time off on the arrival of a new child and more fathers are enjoying this opportunity.

This table shows the standard amount allowed in each jurisdiction.

Jurisdiction	Pregnancy & Parental Leave
Alberta	15 weeks maternity leave 37 wks parental leave
British Columbia	17 weeks pregnancy leave 35 weeks parental leave for birth mother 37 weeks parental leave for father
Federal	17 weeks maternity leave 37 weeks parental leave combined duration not to exceed 52 weeks
Manitoba	17 weeks maternity leave 37 weeks parental leave
New Brunswick	17 weeks maternity leave 37 weeks parental leave combined duration not to exceed 52 weeks

Newfoundland	17 weeks maternity leave 35 weeks parental leave
Nova Scotia	17 weeks maternity leave 52 weeks parental leave
Nunavut	17 weeks maternity leave 37 weeks parental leave combined duration not to exceed 52 weeks
Northwest Territories	17 weeks maternity leave 37 weeks parental leave combined duration not to exceed 52 weeks
Ontario	17 weeks pregnancy leave 35 weeks parental leave (or 37 weeks if pregnancy leave not taken)
Prince Edward Island	17 weeks maternity leave 35 weeks parental leave
Québec	18 weeks maternity leave; 5 weeks paternity leave 52 weeks parental leave
Saskatchewan	18 weeks maternity leave 34 weeks parental leave for primary caregiver 37 weeks for other parent

Yukon	17 weeks maternity leave 37 weeks parental leave

Maternity Leave

The purpose of this type of leave is to allow mothers to take time off work following the birth of a child.

An employee who gives birth is, under certain conditions, entitled to 17 weeks' unpaid leave (15 weeks in Alberta, 18 weeks in Québec and Saskatchewan). Employees must give their employer notice in writing a few weeks prior to the start of such leave. In some jurisdictions, the leave can also start up to 16 or 17 weeks prior to the expected due date, terminating 17 or 18 weeks after the actual date of delivery, depending on the jurisdiction. Extensions are also possible in some jurisdictions. When she comes back to work, the employee usually returns to her former position or be assigned equivalent duties, with the same salary and benefits.

Generally, the employee must have worked for the same employer for a certain period, except in British Columbia, New Brunswick and Québec, which do not have such a requirement.

In the federal and Québec jurisdictions, a pregnant woman or nursing mother may ask her employer to temporarily modify her duties or to assign her to another position if continuation of her present duties puts her health or that of her unborn child or nursing infant at risk. This request must, however, be accompanied by a certificate from a qualified physician. If it is impossible to reassign the employee or to modify her duties, she may take leave immediately.

In several jurisdictions, labour standards legislation stipulates that benefits may continue throughout the leave period provided the employee makes all the contributions she would normally have made within a reasonable period of time. In some jurisdictions she may also be required to pay the employer's share of these benefits.

Under federal jurisdiction, an employer may not dismiss, lay off or demote an employee because of her pregnancy or intention to take maternity leave. The employer also may not use an employee's pregnancy as grounds for denial of promotion or training.

During maternity leave, eligible employees may receive Employment Insurance maternity benefits for 15 weeks, after serving a 2-week waiting period.

Some employers provide a supplemental unemployment benefit plan that partially or wholly makes up the difference between Employment Insurance maternity benefits and the worker's salary.

Parental Leave

Parental leave is designed to provide either or both parents with time to spend with their newborns. For the mother, parental leave provisions commonly stipulate that the leave be taken immediately after maternity leave, thereby extending the total leave period. For the father, parental leave provisions allow time off to help with the care of the newborn; sometimes language used that is gender-specific to the father is referred to as paternity leave.

In all Canadian jurisdictions, employees who meet eligibility requirements are entitled to unpaid parental leave ranging from 12 to 52 weeks. Employees must give notice in writing to the employer a few weeks prior to the start of such leave. When they come back to work, employees must normally return to their former position or be assigned equivalent duties with the same salary and benefits.

In ten jurisdictions, the full parental leave is available to both parents if they are eligible. However, in Alberta, New Brunswick, the Yukon and the federal jurisdiction, parental leave may be shared between both parents as long as the total period of leave does not exceed the legislated maximum.

Some jurisdictions allow employees to continue their participation to the benefit plans during the leave provided they make all contributions they would normally have made within a reasonable period of time. In some jurisdictions the employee may be required to pay the employer's share of these benefits.

During their parental leave, eligible employees may receive 35 weeks of Employment Insurance parental benefits. A limited number of employers have a supplemental unemployment benefit plan that partially makes up the difference between Employment Insurance parental benefits and the worker's salary.

Adoption Leave

Adoption leave, by definition, is a period of leave granted to adoptive parents to care for a newly adopted child. In most jurisdictions, adoption leave is included under parental leave. Adoptive parents are entitled to a parental leave that is equivalent, in terms of duration and eligibility requirements, to what is offered to natural parents (excluding maternity leave). Three provinces nevertheless have distinct provisions regarding adoption leave.

Prince Edward Island's Employment Standards Act provides for 52 weeks of leave for adoptive parents (compared to 35 weeks of parental leave for natural parents). Eligible adoptive parents in Newfoundland and Saskatchewan are entitled, respectively, to 17 and 18 weeks of adoption leave to which can be added a further 35 (Newfoundland) or 34 (Saskatchewan) weeks of parental leave for a combined total of 52 weeks of leave in both cases.

The full period of adoption leave is available to each eligible parent in Prince Edward Island and Newfoundland. In Saskatchewan, on the other hand, the 18 weeks of adoption leave are only provided to the parent who is to be the primary caregiver. Nevertheless, both the primary caregiver of an adopted child and his/her spouse are entitled to the full period of parental leave (34 and 37 weeks respectively). Adoption leave, just as parental leave, must be taken within a set period of time following the adoption or arrival of the child in the employee's care.

Jurisdiction	Maternity Leave[1] (in weeks)	Parental Leave[1] (in weeks)	Adoption Leave[1] (in weeks)
Federal	17	37[4]	37[4]
Alberta	15	37[4]	37[4]
British Columbia	17	37[3],[5]	37[5]
Manitoba	17[2]	37[2],[5]	37[5]
New Brunswick	17	37[4]	37[4]
Newfoundland and Labrador	17	35[5]	52[5],[8]
Northwest Territories	17	37[5]	37[5]
Nova Scotia	17	52[3],[5]	52[5]
Nunavut	17	37[5]	37[5]
Ontario	17	37[3],[5]	37[5]
Prince Edward Island	17	35[4]	52[4]
Québec	18[2],[6]	52[2],[5],[6]	52[5]
Saskatchewan	18	37[5],[7]	52[8]
Yukon	17[2]	37[2],[4]	37[4]

Eligibility requirements: To qualify for maternity or parental leave, an employee must normally have completed a specific period of continuous employment. However, some provinces—British Columbia, New Brunswick and Québec—do not require a specific length of service. Ontario requires 13 weeks of service; Newfoundland and Labrador as well as Prince Edward Island require 20 continuous weeks; and Saskatchewan requires 20 weeks in the 52 weeks preceding the requested leave. The federal jurisdiction permits an employee to take the leave after six months of continuous service, and Manitoba after seven months. Alberta, Nova Scotia and the three territories require 12 months of service. In addition, in all jurisdictions, a medical certificate must be provided or may be requested by the employer, and an employee must notify the employer, usually two to four weeks in advance (six weeks in Alberta), of his/her intent to take maternity or parental leave.

Notes:

1   A number of jurisdictions allow maternity and/or parental leave (for natural or adoptive parents) to be extended under certain circumstances, such as late births or health problems of the mother or child.

2   In all Canadian jurisdictions except Manitoba, Québec and the Yukon, the combined duration of maternity and parental leave cannot exceed 52 weeks.

3   In the case of an employee who has taken maternity leave, the maximum parental leave is 35 weeks.

4   The Alberta legislation stipulates that there is no requirement to grant parental leave to more than one parent at a time if both parents of a child work for the same employer. In the Yukon, parents who share a parental leave cannot normally take their leave at the same time, whether or not they work for the same employer. In the Federal jurisdiction, Alberta, New Brunswick and Yukon, parental leave may be taken by one parent or shared between two parents but the total combined parental or adoption leave cannot exceed 37 weeks. In Prince Edward Island, parental or adoption leave may be taken by one parent or shared between two parents but in either case the combined leave cannot exceed 35 weeks of parental leave or 52 weeks of adoption leave.

5   A majority of jurisdictions, namely British Columbia, Manitoba, Newfoundland and Labrador, Northwest Territories, Nova Scotia, Nunavut, Ontario, Québec and Saskatchewan (with respect to parental leave) permit both parents to take the full parental or adoption leave. In the other jurisdictions, parental leave can normally be shared between parents.

6   An employee is entitled to a paternity leave of not more than 5 uninterrupted weeks without pay at the time of the birth of his child. This leave must be taken at the earliest in the week in which the child is born and end no later than 52 weeks after the birth.

7   In Saskatchewan, an employee who is entitled to maternity or adoption leave may not take more than 34 weeks of parental leave.

8   In Newfoundland and Labrador, an eligible employee is entitled to 17 weeks of adoption leave, to which can be added 35 weeks of parental leave. In Saskatchewan, the primary caregiver of an adopted child is entitled to 18 weeks of adoption leave and 34 weeks of parental leave. The other parent may take up to 37 weeks of parental leave. In both provinces, an eligible adoptive parent may therefore take up to 52 weeks of cumulative leave.

Leave for Parental Reasons

Jurisdiction	Maximum Leave Duration—Unpaid (in weeks)[1]				Eligibility Requirements		Seniority During Leave[2]	Maintenance of Benefit Plans During Leave
	Maternity	Parental (with / without mat. leave)[3]	Max. Total (mat. + par.)	Adoption[4]	Length of Service[5]	Min. Notice[6]		
Federal	17	37 / 37	52	37	6 consec. months	4 weeks	Accrual	Yes
Alberta	15	37 / 37	52	37	52 consec. weeks	6 weeks[7]	Maintained	Not specified
British Columbia	17	35 / 37	52	37	N/A	4 weeks	Maintained	Yes
Manitoba	17	37 / 37	54	37	7 consec. months	4 weeks[8]	Not specified	Yes
New Brunswick	17	37 / 37	52	37	N/A	2 weeks (maternity leave); 4 weeks (parental leave)[9]	Accrual	Not specified
Newfoundland and Labrador	17	35 / 35	52	52[10]	20 consec. weeks	2 weeks	Maintained	No
Northwest Territories / Nunavut	17	37 / 37	52	37	12 consec. months	4 weeks	Maintained	Not specified
Nova Scotia	17	35 / 52	52	52	12 consec. months	4 weeks	Maintained	Yes (at employee's cost)
Ontario	17	35 / 37	52	37	13 weeks	2 weeks	Accrual[11]	Yes
Prince Edward Island	17	35 / 35	52	52	20 continuous weeks	4 weeks	Maintained	No[12]
Québec[13]	18	52 / 52[14]	70	52	N/A	3 weeks	Maintained	Yes[15]
Saskatchewan	18	34 / 37	52	37 / 52[16]	20 weeks in 52 weeks preceding leave	4 weeks[17]	Accrual	Yes
Yukon	17	37 / 37	54	37	12 continuous months	4 weeks	Maintained	Not specified

Notes:

1 All jurisdictions specify the period during which maternity and parental leave may be taken. For example, employees covered by the Canada Labour Code may take their maternity leave from 11 weeks before to 17 weeks after the date of confinement. As for parental leave, it must be completed within the 52-week period following the birth of the child, or following the day on which the child comes into the employee's care.

Legislation in some jurisdictions allows employees to extend their maternity leave for medical or other reasons. Seven jurisdictions (Alberta, British Columbia, Newfoundland and Labrador, Ontario , Prince Edward Island , Saskatchewan, and Yukon) guarantee at least six weeks of post-natal leave. This minimum post-natal leave is unconditional in British Columbia. It applies to employees who are not taking parental leave in Newfoundland and Labrador and Ontario, and to those who gave birth later than the expected date in Prince Edward Island and Saskatchewan. In Alberta, the minimum post-natal leave is to be charged against any remaining maternity leave first, then against parental leave, reducing the latter accordingly. Finally, employees in Yukon (see below) are entitled to this minimum period only if they have pregnancy-related health problems. It is worth mentioning that legislation in Nova Scotia provides that maternity leave may not end sooner than one week after the date of delivery.

Manitoba, Québec, Nunavut and the Northwest Territories provide a maternity leave extension if the actual date of delivery occurs later than the estimated date of birth; such an extension is equal to the period of time between the two dates. In the Northwest Territories and Nunavut, this is limited to six additional weeks of leave. Only employees who have less than two weeks of regular maternity leave remaining after delivery are entitled to this extension in Québec.

In British Columbia, pregnancy leave may be extended for six consecutive weeks if the employee is unable to return to work for reasons related to the birth or the termination of the pregnancy. Parental leave may be extended by up to five additional weeks when a child suffers from a physical, psychological or emotional condition requiring additional parental care. Similarly, in Québec, an employee's maternity leave may be extended if required due to her state of health or that of her child, for a duration indicated in a medical certificate. In Saskatchewan, maternity leave can be extended for up to six weeks if an employee is unable to return to work for medical reasons. And, in Yukon, an employee who requires leave because of health problems associated with her pregnancy cannot be required to return to work during the six weeks that follow the date of birth or termination of the pregnancy.

Finally, statutes in both Québec and the federal jurisdiction contain special leave provisions for pregnant (or nursing) employees if the employee's current job functions could pose a risk to the employee's health or to that of the fetus or child.

2 The column 'Seniority During Leave' deals with whether or not an employee's seniority for length of service continues to build while they are on leave for parental reasons or whether their seniority is maintained at the level held by the employee prior to the start of their leave.

3   A majority of jurisdictions, namely British Columbia, Manitoba, Newfoundland and Labrador, the Northwest Territories, Nova Scotia, Nunavut, Ontario, Québec and Saskatchewan (with respect to parental leave) permit both parents to take the full period of parental or adoption leave. In the other jurisdictions, parental leave can normally be shared between parents. However, legislation in Alberta stipulates that there is no requirement to grant parental leave to more than one parent at a time if both parents of a child are employed with the same employer. In Yukon, parents who share a parental leave cannot normally take their leave at the same time, whether or not they work for the same employer.

4   Indicates the maximum duration of leave for adoptive parents. In most jurisdictions, adoptive parents are entitled to the same parental leave as birth parents. In Newfoundland and Labrador and Saskatchewan a distinct adoption leave is available to eligible adoptive parents in addition to parental leave.

5   This requirement refers to the length of continuous service (with the exception of Saskatchewan) with the same employer.

6   Refers to the minimum period of written notice an employee must give his or her employer prior to taking a maternity, adoption or parental leave. However, in most jurisdictions, an employee may be exempted from notice requirements in certain situations (e.g., early birth, pregnancy-related health problems, unforeseeable placement date for adopted child, etc.).

7   If an employee who intends to take maternity leave fails to give the necessary notice, she is still entitled to maternity leave if within 2 weeks after she ceases to work, she provides her employer with a medical certificate indicating that she is not able to work because of a medical condition arising from her pregnancy, and giving the estimated or actual date of delivery.

8   [12] In Manitoba, an employee who fails to give sufficient notice is entitled to a shorter parental leave. The length of the parental leave is reduced by a period equal to the number of days by which the notice given is less than four weeks.

9   In New Brunswick, an employee must also, four months before the projected date of delivery or as soon as her pregnancy is confirmed, whichever is later, advise her employer of her intent to take a leave and the anticipated commencement date in the absence of an emergency. Where an employee becomes an adoptive parent, he or she must give four months' written notice (or provide written notice as soon as possible in the event of an emergency) of his/her intent to take leave, as well as providing proof of actual or expected placement and notification of the start date and duration of the leave.

10   This amount represents the aggregate of 17 weeks of adoption leave and 35 weeks of parental leave.

11   Although employees in Ontario continue to accrue seniority during any maternity or parental leave for the purposes of calculating an employee's length of service, the period of an employee's leave is not included when determining whether an employee has completed a probationary period under an employment contract.

12   An employer is not required to pay employee pension benefits in respect of any period of maternity leave granted to an employee.

13   An employee in Québec is entitled to five days of leave (including two days with pay if s/he has at least 60 days of uninterrupted service) following the birth or adoption of a child. This leave may not be taken once 15 days have passed since the child's arrival in the home of his mother or father. An employee who adopts the child of his/her consort is entitled to two days without pay. In addition, a female employee may be absent from work without pay for an examination by a physician or midwife related to her pregnancy.

14   In addition to other leaves, an employee is entitled to a paternity leave of not more than 5 uninterrupted weeks without pay at the time of the birth of his child. This leave must be taken at the earliest, in the week in which the child is born, and no later than 52 weeks after the birth.

15   An employee's pension and benefit plans are maintained through the course of their leave if employees who make contributions to their benefit plans continue to make these contributions for the duration of the leave.

16   In Saskatchewan, the primary caregiver of an adopted child is entitled to 18 weeks of adoption leave and 34 weeks of parental leave. The other parent may take up to 37 weeks of parental leave.

17   An employee in Saskatchewan who fails to give her employer a written application for a maternity leave and who does not provide a medical certificate attesting that there were verified medical reasons to cease work immediately is entitled to 14 weeks of unpaid leave (compared to 18 weeks otherwise).

Leave for Personal Reasons

Leave for personal reasons can provide employees with periods of time off, with or without pay, to deal with family obligations or other personal commitments. This measure improves employee morale and helps recruit and retain staff. It may also help reduce conflict between employees who have access to leave for family responsibilities and those who do not because they have no dependants. An benefit of personal leave is that it allows employees to avoid the necessity of having to use vacation time for personal needs.

In general, this type of leave does not exist in labour standards legislation. However, labour standards legislation may include a variety of other leaves intended to help employees meet their personal obligations. Among these other leaves available in some jurisdictions are;

- annual vacation leave,
- bereavement leave (9 jurisdictions),
- leave for family responsibility (3 jurisdictions),
- court/jury leave (at least 10 jurisdictions have legislation pertaining to court/jury duty leave),
- marriage leave (Québec).

The total number of days of personal leave available in one year is limited, as is the number of days employees may take consecutively.

Compassionate Care Leave

Jurisdiction	Max. Leave Duration [1]	Eligibility Requirements			Sharing of Leave Between Care-givers[2]	Fraction-ing of Leave[3]	Family Members for Whom Employees May Take Compassionate Care Leave	Seniority / Benefits Protected
		Service[4]	Notice [5]	Medical Cert.				
Federal	8 weeks	*N/A*	*N/A*	If requested in writing by employer within 15 days of return to work	Yes	Periods of at least one week each	See Annex A	Seniority: Yes[6] Benefits: Yes[7]
British Columbia	8 weeks; A further period of leave is possible[8]	*N/A*	*N/A*	Required – must be provided as soon as possible	No	Periods of at least one week each	See Annex A	Seniority: *Not specified[9]* Benefits: Yes[10]
Manitoba	8 weeks	30 days	One pay period before starting leave (or less in some cases)[11]; 48 hours before ending leave[12]	Required – must be provided as soon as possible[13]	No	One or two periods of at least one week each	See Annex A	Seniority: *Not specified* Benefits: Yes[14]
New Brunswick	8 weeks[15]	*N/A*	Employer must be advised "as soon as possible"	If requested in writing by employer within 15 days of return to work	Yes	Periods of at least one week each	See Annex A	Seniority: Yes[16] Benefits: *Not specified*
Newfoundland and Labrador	8 weeks[17]	30 days	Employer must be notified 2 weeks before leave[18]	If requested in writing by employer within 15 days of return to work	Yes	Periods of at least one week each	See Annex A	Seniority: *Not specified* Benefits: No (unless otherwise agreed)[19]

Nova Scotia	8 weeks[20]	3 months	Employer must be notified as soon as possible	If requested in writing by employer	No	Periods of at least one week each	See Annex A	Seniority: *Not specified* Benefits: Yes (at employee's cost)[21]
Nunavut	8 weeks	*N/A*	N/A	If requested in writing by employer within 15 days of return to work	Yes	Periods of at least one week each	See Annex A	*Not specified*
Ontario	8 weeks; A further period of leave is possible[22]	*N/A*	Employer must be advised in writing	If requested by employer – must be provided as soon as possible	Yes	Periods of at least one week each	See Annex A	Seniority: Yes Benefits: Yes[23]
Prince Edward Island	8 weeks[24]	*N/A*	N/A	If requested in writing by the employer within 15 days of return to work	Yes	Periods of at least one week each	See Annex A	*Not specified*
Québec	12 weeks (per 12 months) (104 weeks in certain cases)[25]	3 months	Employer must be advised "as soon as possible"	If requested by employer, a document justifying the absence must be provided	No	*Not specified*	See Annex A	Seniority: *Not specified* Benefits: Yes[26]
Saskatchewan	12 weeks per 52 week period[27] (extension to 16 weeks in some cases[28])	13 weeks	*N/A*	If requested in writing by employer	No	*Not specified*	See Annex A	*Not specified*

| Yukon | 8 weeks | N/A | N/A | If requested in writing by employer before leave starts or within 15 days of return to work | Yes | Periods of at least one week each | See Annex A | *Not specified* |

Notes:

1   In the federal jurisdiction, British Columbia, Manitoba, New Brunswick, Newfoundland and Labrador, Nova Scotia, Nunavut, Ontario, Prince Edward Island and Yukon, leave must be taken within a specified 26-week period, generally starting on the first day of the week in which a medical certificate attesting to the family member's medical condition is issued. However, leave in these jurisdictions (except Manitoba) automatically ends on the last day of the week in which the family member's death occurs. In Newfoundland and Labrador, under exceptional circumstances, an additional period of three days- to be taken immediately after the end of the week during which the death occurred - can be provided.

2   Refers to whether or not the leave must be shared between employees who provide care or support to the same person.

3   Refers to the number and minimum duration of periods in which compassionate care leave may be taken.

4   Refers to the minimum length of service that an employee must have completed with his/her current employer to qualify for leave.

5   Refers to the minimum period of notice that an employee must give to his/her employer before starting the leave. In New Brunswick, the notice will also have to indicate the anticipated duration of the leave.

6   The Canada Labour Code provides that seniority continues to accrue during a period of compassionate care leave. An employee also has the right to be informed in writing of every employment, promotion and training opportunity that arises during the period in which s/he is on leave and for which s/he is qualified.

7   Seniority and pension, health and disability benefits continue to accumulate during the leave period, provided the employee makes his/her contributions (if any) within a reasonable time. When calculating other benefits, employment before and after the leave is deemed to be continuous.

8   If the family member survives past the 26-week period specified in the medical certificate, the employee is entitled to take another period of compassionate care leave provided s/he furnishes his/her employer with another medical certificate. Moreover, the right to compassionate care leave is in addition to the five unpaid days per year of family responsibility leave that is provided for under British Columbia's Employment Standards Act. Family responsibility leave can be used to meet responsibilities related to the care, health or education of a child in the employee's care or the care or health of any other member of the employee's immediate family.

9   However, it should be noted that the periods of employment before and after the leave are deemed to be continuous for the purposes of calculating appropriate notice of termination and entitlement to annual vacation.

10   The employee is entitled to all increases in wages and benefits to which s/he would have been entitled had s/he not taken leave. Moreover, the employer is required to continue to make payments to a pension, medical or other plan when the latter is taking compassionate care leave, provided that the employee pays his/her share of the cost (where applicable).

11   A shorter notice period may be given where circumstances so require.

12   If the employee decides to end his/her leave before it has expired.

13   In addition to stating that the family member has a serious medical condition with a significant risk of death within 26 weeks, the required medical certificate must also indicate that the family member requires the care or support of one or more family members.

14   In Manitoba, employment before and after the leave is deemed to be continuous for the purpose of pension and other benefits.

15   Furthermore, under the Employment Standards Act of New Brunswick, an employee is entitled to three unpaid days per year of family responsibility leave, which can be used to meet responsibilities related to the health, care or education of a person in a close family relationship with him/her.

16   Seniority continues to accrue during the leave (unless the employee would have been dismissed, suspended or laid off had s/he not been granted leave). Moreover, the employee is deemed to have been continuously employed during the leave.

17   Under Newfoundland and Labrador's Labour Standards Act, an employee with at least 30 continuous' days of service with his/her employer is entitled to take up to seven unpaid days of family responsibility and/or sick leave per year.

18   The notice must also indicate the intended length of the leave. However, a valid reason for not providing the notice exempts the employee from this requirement.

19   Unless the employer and employee agree otherwise, the period of leave does not count towards the application of the rights, benefits and privileges provided under the Labour Standards Act. However, the period worked upon resumption is considered to be continuous with the period worked prior to the leave.

20   Furthermore, under Nova Scotia's Labour Standards Code, an employee is entitled to three unpaid days' leave per year due to the sickness of a child, parent or family member or for medical, dental or other similar appointments during working hours.

21   In Nova Scotia, an employee has the option of maintaining, during the period of leave, a benefit plan in which s/he participated prior to the leave. However, s/he is required to pay the employer's share of the benefit plan cost, unless the employer agrees to continue his/her contribution. The employer is required to notify the employee in writing of the option to maintain a benefit plan and of the deadline for deciding whether or not to exercise that option.

22   Where the employee takes an 8-week period of family medical leave and the family member survives beyond the 26-week period specified in the medical certificate, the employee is entitled to take another period of family medical leave provided s/he furnishes his/her employer with another medical certificate. Furthermore, in addition to family medical leave, an employee whose employer regularly employs 50 employees or more can take up to 10 days per year of unpaid emergency leave which may be used, among other things, in case a family member or other prescribed individual (including a spouse, child, child of the spouse, parent, grandparent, grandchild, sibling or a relative who is dependent on the employee for care or assistance) has an illness, injury or medical emergency.

23   Time spent on leave is to be included in the calculation of the employee's seniority and length of service. During the leave, the employee continues to participate in specified employment benefits—pension, life insurance, accidental death, extended health, and dental plans—unless he or she elects in writing not to do so. The employer must continue paying its share of premiums unless the employee gives written notice that s/he does not intend to pay his or her contributions, if any.

24   Furthermore, under the Employment Standards Act of Prince Edward Island, an employee who has completed at least six months of continuous service with his/her employer is entitled to take up to three days of unpaid leave per year to meet responsibilities related to the care or health of a person who is a member of his/her immediate or extended family.

25   An employee's absence may be extended to 104 weeks if a child of the employee under the age of 18 has a serious and potentially fatal illness. Moreover, under Québec's *Act respecting labour standards*, an employee can take up to ten unpaid days per year of family responsibility leave to fulfill obligations relating to the care, health or education of his/her child or the child of his/her spouse, or because of the state of health of his/her spouse, father, mother, brother, sister or grandparent.

26 In Québec, an employee who continues to pay regular contributions is entitled to maintain his/her participation in any group insurance and pension plans recognized in his/her place of employment. The employer must also continue to pay its share of the cost.

27 An employee can also take this leave due to his/her own serious illness or injury. In addition, it should be noted that an employee with at least 13 weeks' service is entitled to up to 12 unpaid days' leave per year for non-serious illness or injury (of the employee and/or a member of his/her immediate family), unless it can be demonstrated that the employee has a record of chronic absenteeism and there is no reasonable expectation of improved attendance.

28 An employer is prohibited from dismissing, suspending, laying off, demoting or disciplining an employee because of absence (except for just cause) if, during the period of absence, the employee is receiving compassionate care benefits (or is serving the waiting period for benefits) under the Employment Insurance Program and his/her absence, in combination with absences due to his/her serious or non-serious illness or injury and/or that of a family member, does not exceed 16 weeks in total in a 52-week period.

Personal Emergency Leave

Some employees have the right to take up to 10 days of unpaid job-protected leave each calendar year due to illness, injury and certain other emergencies and urgent matters. This is known as personal emergency leave.

Only employees who work for employers that regularly employ at least 50 employees are eligible for personal emergency leave. When determining whether the 50-employee threshold has been met, all employees (not just full-time salaried employees) of the employer are counted. Part-timers and casual employees are all included as one employee each in the count.

When a single employer has multiple locations, all employees employed at each location are to be counted.

For example:

An employer owns 5 sandwich shops with 12 employees employed in each shop. This employer regularly employs 60 employees. All employees at all 5 locations are entitled to personal emergency leave.

Reasons for Which an Unpaid Personal Emergency Leave May Be Taken

Any of the following may be considered reason for personal emergency leave:

- Personal illness, injury or medical emergency, **or**
- Death, illness, injury, medical emergency or urgent matter relating to the following family members:
    - A spouse (married or common-law, opposite sex or same sex);
    - A parent, step-parent, foster parent, child, step-child, foster child, grandparent, step-grandparent, grandchild or step- grandchild of the employee or the employee's spouse;
    - The spouse of an employee's child;
    - A brother or sister of the employee;
    - A relative of the employee who is dependent on the employee for care or assistance.

Illness, Injury or Medical Emergency

All illnesses, injuries and medical emergencies of the employee or of a specified family member, as listed above, will qualify an employee for personal emergency leave. It does not matter whether the illness, injury or medical emergency was caused by the employee's own actions or by external factors. For example, an employee who sprained his knee while showing off to his friends when waterskiing would still be entitled to personal emergency leave, even though the injury was a result of his own carelessness.

Generally, employees are entitled to take personal emergency leave for pre-planned (elective) surgery. Although such surgery is scheduled ahead of time (and therefore not a medical "emergency"), surgeries performed because of an illness or injury will entitle an employee to personal emergency leave.

Employees are not entitled to personal emergency leave for medically unnecessary cosmetic surgery unrelated to an illness or injury.

Urgent Matter

An employee is eligible for personal emergency leave because of the death, illness, injury or medical emergency of, or an "urgent matter" concerning, a specified family member, as listed above. An urgent matter is an event that is unplanned or out of the employee's control, <u>and</u> raises the possibility of serious negative consequences, including emotional harm, if not responded to.

Examples of an "Urgent Matter":

- The employee's babysitter calls in sick.

- The house of the employee's elderly parent is broken into, and the parent is very upset and needs the employee's help to deal with the situation.

- The employee has an appointment to meet with his or her child's counselor to discuss behavioural problems at school. The appointment could not be scheduled outside the employee's working hours.

Examples of Events That Do Not Qualify As an Urgent Matter:

- An employee wants to leave work early to watch his daughter's track meet.

- An employee wants the day off in order to attend at her sister's wedding.

Sick Leave

Sick leave enables employees to take time off work when ill. It is not really leave for family obligations although it may sometimes be used as such.

Employees may not be dismissed, suspended, laid off or demoted when on sick leave in 8 jurisdictions (federal jurisdiction, Québec, Yukon, Newfoundland, New Brunswick, Nova Scotia, PEI and Saskatchewan) and is unpaid.

Manitoba employers will be required to provide unpaid family leave to deal with personal illness or the needs of their families. In all of these jurisdictions, the leave period is unpaid. In addition, employees may not be dismissed, suspended, laid off or demoted when using sick leave entitlements.

Alberta, British Columbia, the Northwest Territories and Nunavut don't have any statutes in their employment/labour standards for sick leave.

In Ontario employers are not required to provide unpaid or paid sick leave, or paid benefit plans for sickness to employees. However, employees who work for employers that regularly employ at least 50 employees or more are entitled to unpaid emergency leave in certain situations including employee illness.

In provinces or territories where unpaid leave for illness is not required, it is left at the employer's discretion within its workplace policies. In addition, some employers provide paid sick leave, personal days, and paid time off on top of legislated leave for illness.

Generally, some of these days may be taken each year without a medical certificate. If the employee needs to take a longer sick leave because of health reasons, he may be entitled to take longer unpaid sick leave and/or obtain a doctor's certificate. S/he may then be eligible for

Employment Insurance sickness benefits or benefits from other compensation plans for work-related illness or injury.

Sick leave may also be combined with maternity leave if there are complications related to the birth of a child.

Family Medical Leave

Family medical leave is unpaid, job-protected leave of up to eight weeks in a 26-week period.

Family medical leave may be taken to provide care or support to certain family members of whom a qualified health practitioner has issued a certificate indicating that s/he has a serious medical condition with a significant risk of death occurring within a period of 26 weeks.

There is no requirement that an employee be employed for a particular length of time, or that the employer employ a specified number of employees in order for the employee to qualify for family medical leave.

Care or support includes, but is not limited to: providing psychological or emotional support; arranging for care by a third party provider; or directly providing or participating in the care of the family member.

The specified family members for whom a family medical leave may be taken are:

- the employee's spouse (including same-sex spouse)
- a parent, step-parent or foster parent of the employee or the employee's spouse
- a child, step-child or foster child of the employee or the employee's spouse
- a brother, step-brother, sister, or step-sister of the employee
- a grandparent or step-grandparent of the employee or of the employee's spouse
- a grandchild or step-grandchild of the employee or of the employee's spouse
- a brother-in-law, step-brother-in-law, sister-in-law or step-sister-in-law of the employee
- a son-in-law or daughter-in-law of the employee or of the employee's spouse
- an uncle or aunt of the employee or of the employee's spouse
- a nephew or niece of the employee or of the employee's spouse
- the spouse of the employee's grandchild, uncle, aunt, nephew or niece

Family medical leave may also be taken for a person who considers the employee to be like a family member. Employees wishing to take a family medical leave for a person in this category must provide their employer, if requested, with a completed copy of the Compassionate Care Benefits Attestation form, available from Human Resources and Skills Development Canada (www.hrsdc.gc.ca) whether or not they are making an application for EI Compassionate Care Benefits or are required to complete the form to obtain such benefits.

The specified family members do not have to live in the same province in order for the employee to be eligible for family medical leave.

Under the Federal Employment Insurance Act, six weeks of employment insurance benefits (called "compassionate care benefits") may be paid to EI eligible employees who have to be away from work temporarily to provide care to a family member who has a serious medical condition with a significant risk of death within 26 weeks and who requires care or support from one or more family members.

The right to take time off work under the family medical leave provisions is not the same as the right to the payment of compassionate care benefits under the federal Employment Insurance Act. An employee may be entitled to family medical leave whether or not he or she has applied for or is qualified for the compassionate care benefits.

The employee does not have to have the medical certificate before he or she can take the leave. If the employee could not subsequently produce a copy of the certificate and/or purported to take leave beyond the 26-week period, the employee would not be entitled to any of the protections afforded to employees on such a family medical leave.

An employer is entitled to ask an employee for a copy of the certificate of the qualified health practitioner to provide proof that he or she is eligible for a family medical leave. The employee is required to provide the copy as soon as possible after the employer requests it. The certificate must state that the family member has a serious medical condition with a significant risk of death occurring within a specified 26-week period. The employee is responsible for obtaining and paying the costs (if any) of obtaining the certificate.

Difference between Family Medical Leave and Personal Emergency Leave

Family medical leave and personal emergency leave are two different types of leave. Personal emergency leave is unpaid, job-protected leave of up to 10 days each calendar year. It may be taken in the case of personal illness, injury or medical emergency and the death, illness, injury, medical emergency of, or urgent matter relating to, certain family members, including dependent relatives.

Family medical leave, on the other hand, is unpaid, job-protected leave of up to eight (8) weeks in a 26 week period. It is taken to provide care or support to certain family members who have a serious illness with a significant risk of death.

Further, while only employees who work for employers that regularly employ at least 50 employees are entitled to personal emergency leave, this is not a requirement for family medical leave.

The list of persons for whom a family medical leave may be taken is not identical to the list of persons specified for personal emergency leave.

An employee may be entitled to both leaves. They are separate leaves and the right to each leave is independent of any right an employee may have to the other leave. An employee who qualifies for both leaves would have full entitlement to each leave.

Length of Family Medical Leave

A family medical leave can last up to eight weeks within a specified 26-week period.

The eight weeks of a family medical leave do not have to be taken consecutively. An employee may take a single week of leave at a time. However, if an employee only takes part of a week off work as family medical leave, it is still counted as a full week of leave.

That is because "week" is defined for family medical leave purposes as a period of seven consecutive days beginning on a Sunday and ending on a Saturday. Week is defined in this way to correspond with the beginning and end of the week set for EI entitlement purposes.

Example 1

Felicia begins a family medical leave on Wednesday, May 21. First week of leave is defined as beginning on the preceding Sunday, May 18 and will end on Saturday, May 24. Felicia will be considered to have used one full week of the 8 weeks of family medical leave as of Saturday, May 24.

Example 2

Connie takes two days off work for family medical leave on Monday, July 19 and Tuesday, July 20. The week of family medical leave is defined as beginning on the preceding Sunday (July 18) and will end on Saturday, July 24. Although Connie chose to return to work on Wednesday, July 21 (and be paid her regular wages for that work) she will be deemed to have used one full week of the 8 weeks of family medical leave as of Saturday, July 24.

Rights During Family Medical Leave

Employers do not have to pay wages when an employee is on family medical leave.

Employees who take family medical leave are entitled to the same rights as employees who take pregnancy or parental leave. For example, an employer cannot threaten, fire or penalize in any other way an employee for taking, planning on taking, being eligible or being in a position to become eligible to take a family medical leave.

The table below is a comparison of your allowance for each type of leave.

Jurisdiction	Emergency Leave	Compassionate Care Leave	Pregnancy & Parental Leave
Alberta	Nil	6 weeks	15 weeks maternity leave 37 wks parental leave
British Columbia	5 days family responsibility 3 days bereavement	6 weeks	17 weeks pregnancy leave 35 weeks parental leave for birth mother 37 weeks parental leave for father
Federal	3 days bereavement (paid) 12 weeks sick leave	6 weeks	17 weeks maternity leave 37 weeks parental leave combined duration not to exceed 52 weeks
Manitoba	Nil	6 weeks	17 weeks maternity leave 37 weeks parental leave
New Brunswick	5 days bereavement 3 days family responsibility 5 days sick leave	6 weeks	17 weeks maternity leave 37 weeks parental leave combined duration not to exceed 52 weeks
Newfoundland	3 days bereavement (1 day paid) 5 days sick leave	6 weeks	17 weeks maternity leave 35 weeks parental leave

Nova Scotia	3 days bereavement	6 weeks	17 weeks maternity leave 52 weeks parental leave
Nunavut	Nil	6 weeks	17 weeks maternity leave 37 weeks parental leave combined duration not to exceed 52 weeks
Northwest Territories	Nil	6 weeks	17 weeks maternity leave 37 weeks parental leave combined duration not to exceed 52 weeks
Ontario	10 days unpaid/year (only in organizations with 50 or more employees)	6 weeks	17 weeks pregnancy leave 35 weeks parental leave (or 37 weeks if pregnancy leave not taken)
Prince Edward Island	3 days bereavement	6 weeks	17 weeks maternity leave 35 weeks parental leave
Québec	4 days bereavement (1 with pay) 1 day for marriage 10 days parental or family obligations 5 days for birth (2 paid)	6 weeks	18 weeks maternity leave; 5 weeks paternity leave 52 weeks parental leave
Saskatchewan	5 days bereavement	6 weeks	18 weeks maternity leave 34 weeks parental leave for primary caregiver 37 weeks for other parent

Yukon	1 week bereavement 1 sick day per month	6 weeks	17 weeks maternity leave 37 weeks parental leave

Family Responsibility Leave

Family responsibility leave entitles employees to five days of unpaid leave during each employment year to meet responsibilities related to the care, health or education of a child in the employee's care or the care or health of any other member of the employee's immediate family.

It is defined as immediate family as the spouse, child, parent, guardian, sibling, grandchild or grandparent of an employee, and any person who lives with an employee as a member of the employee's family.

An employer cannot refuse to grant family responsibility leave. While there is no request process set out, employees are expected to give the employer reasonable notice of family responsibility leave and sufficient information for the employer to ascertain that the employee is entitled to the leave.

The entitlement to five days' unpaid leave each year does not carry over from year to year if unused. In addition, a portion of a day taken off work may be counted as one full day of family responsibility leave for the purposes of calculating an employee's remaining entitlement.

The request does not need to be made because of a crisis or emergency. It must be related to the care or health, and in the case of a child, education, of a member of the employee's immediate family.

Examples

- Thomas is notified by school authorities that his child has been injured in a school yard accident and taken to hospital. Family responsibility leave should be allowed.

- Yuki has an appointment to meet with a school counselor to discuss behaviour issues. The appointment is during her scheduled working hours. Family responsibility leave should be allowed.

- Bassam has to accompany his elderly, disabled parent to attend a medical appointment. Family responsibility leave should be allowed.

- Raj wants to accompany his child on a school recreational activity excursion. Since this activity is not related to the care, health or education of the child, it does not justify family responsibility leave.

- Bob wants two days family responsibility leave to go to Edmonton to help his son pack up his belongings after his second year at university and drive him home to Terrace, where he will live with his parents and work for the summer before going back to Edmonton to continue his studies. Since Bob's son is over the age of nineteen, this activity is not related to the education of a child in the employee's care and does not justify family responsibility leave.

Vacation Entitlement After Leave Of Absence

Example

Kate commences work on June 1, 2009. Due to family responsibilities, in December, 2010, she requests a two-month unpaid leave of absence to attend to a sick parent. The employer approves the unpaid leave. Kate returns to work in February 2011.

Kate is entitled to 2 weeks' paid vacation effective June 1, 2010 regardless of the fact that she has taken a 2-month leave of absence approved by the employer.

Jurisdiction	Maximum Leave Duration (leave unpaid unless indicated otherwise)				Length of Service Requirements
	Family Responsibility	Sick Leave (for employee's illness/injury)	Bereavement[i]	Compassionate Care / Serious Family Illness[ii]	
Federal	N/A	12 weeks	3 days immediately following date of death (with pay)[iii]	8 weeks	*Bereavement leave with pay:* 3 consecutive months of service; *Sick leave:* 3 consecutive months of service
Alberta	N/A	N/A	N/A	N/A	N/A
British Columbia	5 days/year	N/A	3 days	N/A	N/A
Manitoba	N/A	N/A	N/A	8 weeks	**Compassionate care leave: *30 days***
New Brunswick	3 days/year	5 days/year	5 days	8 weeks	N/A
Nfld. and Labrador	7 days/year (combined)		1 paid day + 2 unpaid days[iv]	N/A	*Bereavement leave with pay:* 1 month of continuous service; *Family responsibility and sick leave:* 30 days of continuous service
Nova Scotia	3 days/year[v]		3 consecutive working days; or 1 day[vi]	8 weeks	**Compassionate care leave: *3 months***
Ontario	*Emergency leave:* 10 days/year[vii] (combined)			N/A[viii]	No length of service requirement. However, emergency leave only applies to employees of an employer that regularly employs 50 employees or more.
P. E. I.	3 days/12-month period	3 days/12-month period	3 days; or 1 day	8 weeks	**Family leave and sick leave: *6 months of continuous service***
Québec[ix]	10 days/year	26 weeks/12 months	1 paid day + 4 unpaid days; or 1 unpaid day	12 weeks/12 months; (104 weeks if child under 18 years of age has potentially fatal illness)	*Sick leave:* 3 months of uninterrupted service; *Serious family illness:* 3 months of uninterrupted service; *Bereavement leave; family responsibility leave:* N/A
Saskatchewan	12 days/year (non-serious illness/injury)	12 days/year (non-serious illness/injury); 12 weeks/52-week period (serious illness/injury)	5 days	12 weeks/52-week period (serious illness/injury); extended to 16 weeks in some cases[x]	*Bereavement leave:* 3 months of continuous service; *Leave for illness/injury of employee or family member:* 13 consecutive weeks of service[xi]
N.W.T. / Nunavut	N/A	N/A	N/A	8 weeks (Nunavut)	N/A
Yukon	N/A	1 day/month of service[xii]	1 week	8 weeks	N/A

Notes:

[i] In every case, bereavement leave applies with regard to the funeral or death of an employee's spouse, father, mother, child or sibling. It also applies, in a lesser number of jurisdictions, to grandparents, grandchildren, in-laws, and other specified persons, such as guardians or wards.

[ii] In the federal jurisdiction, Manitoba, New Brunswick, Nova Scotia, Nunavut, Prince Edward Island and Yukon, leave may be taken where a specified family member of an employee (normally a child, spouse or parent, although provisions in some jurisdictions cover additional relatives) has a serious medical condition with a significant risk of death within 26 weeks, as attested by a medical certificate.

[iii] In the federal jurisdiction, bereavement leave may be taken during the normal working days that occur in the three days immediately following the date of death. Employees who do not meet length of service requirements are entitled to leave *without* pay.

[iv] Employees who do not meet length of service requirements are nevertheless entitled to two days of bereavement leave *without* pay.

[v] Three days per year of unpaid leave may be taken due to family illness (i.e., the sickness of a child, parent or other unspecified family members) or for medical, dental or other similar appointments during the employee's working hours.

[vi] The shorter bereavement leave periods in Nova Scotia, Prince Edward Island and Québec apply with respect to the death of more distant relatives (e.g., specified in-laws).

[vii] In Ontario, eligible employees can take an emergency leave because of personal medical reasons, the death, illness or injury of a child, spouse, same-sex partner, parent, grandparent, grandchild, or sibling. An emergency leave may also be taken by reason of an "urgent matter" involving any of these relatives.

[viii] Bill 56 amends the Ontario Employment Standards Act, 2000 to provide for up to eight weeks of "family medical leave".

[ix] In addition, Québec's legislation provides employees the right to be absent from work for one day, without reduction in wages, on their wedding day or on the day of their civil union. One day without pay is provided on the wedding day, or on the day of the civil union, of the child, father, mother, brother or sister of an employee or of a child of his or her consort. The employee must advise his/her employer of such an absence not less than one week in advance.

[x] An employee is entitled to leave without pay while receiving compassionate care benefits (or serving the waiting period for benefits) under the Employment Insurance program, up to a maximum of 16 weeks per 52-week period.

[xi] Moreover, an employee is not entitled to leave for a non-serious illness or injury if it can be demonstrated that s/he has a record of chronic absenteeism and there is no reasonable expectation of improved attendance.

[xii] A maximum of 12 days of sick leave may be accumulated in Yukon.

Bereavement Leave

Bereavement Leave provides that employees are entitled to up to three days of unpaid leave on the death of a member of the employee's immediate family.

It defines immediate family as the spouse, child, parent, guardian, sibling, grandchild or grandparent of an employee, and any person who lives with an employee as a member of the employee's family. This definition does not include a parent-in-law unless that person lives with the employee as part of the employee's family.

There is no requirement for an employee to give notice to the employer if s/he intends to take bereavement leave. The leave should be taken within a reasonable time period. Further, the employee is not required to take all three days, nor does the leave have to be taken on consecutive days.

The entitlement to bereavement leave is not an annual entitlement. If an employee suffers more than one death in the family in one year, he or she would be entitled to bereavement leave for each of those deaths.

Marriage Leave (Québec only)

Québec provides a leave of one day without reduction in wages for the employee's wedding/civil union, and one day without pay on the wedding day of the employee's child, father, mother, brother, sister, or step-child.

Organ Donor Leave

Organ donor leave is unpaid (except in Saskatchewan), job-protected leave of up to 13 weeks, for the purpose of undergoing surgery to donate all or part of certain organs to a person. In some cases, organ donor leave can be extended for an additional period of up to 13 weeks.

An employee is entitled to organ donor leave whether he or she is a full-time, part-time, permanent, or contract employee.

The employee must meet the following criteria to qualify for organ donor leave:

- Have been employed by his or her employer for at least 13 weeks;
- Undergoes surgery to donate all or part of one of the following organs to another person:
  - Kidney
  - Liver

- Lung
- Pancreas
- Small bowel

Employees who take organ donor leave are entitled to the same rights as employees who take pregnancy or parental leave. For example, employers cannot threaten, fire or penalize in any way an employee who takes or plans on taking an organ donor leave.

The employee's entitlement to organ donor leave is in addition to the personal emergency leave entitlement.

Whistleblower Protection

Some jurisdictions have instated protection for "whistleblowers" or employees that report wrongdoings within a company. In general, the whistleblower protection applies to the disclosure of the following wrongdoings in or relating to:

- An act or omission constituting an offence under a provincial or federal Act or regulation;
- An act or omission that creates a substantial and specific danger to the life, health or safety of persons, or to the environment, other than a danger that is inherent in the performance of the duties or functions of an employee;
- Gross mismanagement, including public funds or public assets; and
- Knowingly directing or counseling a person to commit any of the above-mentioned wrongdoings.

Below is a list of whistleblower legislation. Where a province is not listed, no explicit legislation protection currently exists.

Jurisdictions	Employees Affected	Protection
New Brunswick	All employees covered by the Employment Standards Act.	An employer is prohibited from dismissing, suspending, laying off or otherwise penalizing, or discriminating against, an employee if the reason for this action is related in any way to the giving of information or evidence by the employee against the employer with respect to the alleged violation of a New Brunswick or Federal Act or regulation in the conduct of its business.
Nova Scotia	Provincial Public Servants	Public servants are covered by whistleblower protection legislation where the Civil Service Disclosure of Wrongdoing Regulations under the Civil Service Act provide a procedure for the disclosure of wrongdoings in the civil service and protect employees against reprisals.
Ontario	Provincial Government Employees	Ontario Public Service Act deals with whistleblower protection for provincial government employees; however, these provisions, which were inserted into that Act in 1993, have not been enacted into law.
Saskatchewan	All employees covered by the Labour Standards Act. The law specifies that the provisions on the protection of whistleblowers do not apply to an employee whose actions are vengeful.	An employer is prohibited from discharging or threatening to discharge, taking any retaliation against or discriminating against an employee who reported, or proposed to report, an alleged illegal activity to a lawful authority (police or law enforcement agency or any person responsible for supervising the employee), or who testified or could testify in an investigation or proceeding conducted under a Saskatchewan or Federal Act.

| Manitoba | Public Servants & Private Employees | Employees who reasonably believe that they have information that could show that a wrongdoing has been committed or are about to be committed can make a disclosure to their supervisor or designated officer or to the Ombudsman in writing.

A person is prohibited from giving any punishment against an employee, or directing that one be given, because the employee has, in good faith, sought advice about making a disclosure, made a protected disclosure, or cooperated in an investigation. "Reprisal" is defined as any of the following measures taken against an employee: a disciplinary measure; a demotion; termination of employment; or any measure that adversely affects the employment or working conditions of the employee. A threat to take any of these measures also constitutes a reprisal.

An employee or former employee who alleges that a reprisal has been taken against him/her can file a complaint with the Labour Board of Manitoba. If a reprisal has been taken against the complainant, it can make an order requiring a person to take all necessary measures to:

- Permit the complainant to return to his/her duties.
- Pay compensation to the complainant equivalent to what s/he will have received if the reprisal had not occurred.
- Pay an amount to the complainant equal to any expenses and any other financial losses that s/he has incurred as direct result of the reprisal.

Protection for private-sector employees who provide information:

Individuals other than employees of the public service are allowed to make a disclosure if they reasonably believe that they have information that could show that a wrongdoing has been or is about to be committed in the public service – provided that the information is in writing.

Private-sector employers cannot take any reprisals against an employee for the sole reason that the employee has, in good faith, provided information about an alleged wrongdoing. Employers are also prohibited from taking such measures for the sole reason that they believe that an employee will provide information. The following are considered to be "prohibited measures": any disciplinary measure; a demotion; termination of employment; any measure that adversely affects the employment or working conditions of an employee; or a threat to take any of these measures. |

Employer Wrongs

Employer's Rights

It goes without saying that when two parties enter into a binding agreement, both parties have rights so that each can be protected. This, too, is the case in the employer/employee agreement/relationship. So, naturally, an employer has rights as well but, just what are they? Sadly, an astounding number of employees throughout Canada have an insufficient understanding of their own rights let alone the right of their employers. It is imperative that we understand just what are within an employer's rights with regards to its business practices towards its employees. Can an employer use secret surveillance devices to monitor employees? Can it access your credit report?

The following are some of the most common issues that are often confused in the Canadian workplace today.

Pay Cheque Deductions

What is an employer allowed to deduct from your pay cheque other than taxes (federal, provincial, CPP/QPP, EI/QPIP)? Employees may deduct your RRSP deductions that you designate, any legal deductions such as garnishments and family support deductions, company compulsory deductions such as union dues and your portion of benefit plan premiums, recovery of pay advances, corrections of payroll errors and voluntary deductions such as Canada Savings Bonds and charitable donations.

Some employees may want to buy products from their employers. These items may even be a condition of employment, which employees need to perform their job. Common examples are mechanics and construction workers. Employers can make the tools a condition of employment and can deduct the cost from employees' wages only if the tool:

1. remains the property of the employee.
2. is not unique to this particular employer.
3. is available for purchase from different suppliers.
4. can reasonably be expected to be used at different employers in the same occupation.
5. is voluntarily bought from the employer instead of another supplier.

What deductions are your employer prohibited from withholding from your pay? An employer <u>cannot</u> deduct:

- The cost of any losses, breakage, shortages or thefts caused or committed by customers or other employees.
- Offset any faulty work you may allegedly have completed.
- Lost, stolen or shoplifted items (including dine-and-dash incidents).

- The difference between the daily till balance and the register's daily tally or any other cash shortage if other employers or individuals had access or could have gained access to the till.

- Being late if you worked those hours. However, please note that if you showed up 8:08am for an 8am shift, your employer has the right to insist you go away until 8:30am so you lose ½ hour's wages (for hourly employees) or request you stay until 5:08am.

- Inventory shortages.

- Uniforms and special clothing required by employers.

- Business supplies.

- Interest charges or other fees for cash advances or cashing cheques.

- Education expenses that only benefit the employer.

- Workplace safety and health legislation states any equipment, device or clothing required to be worn to help with rescue or to provide protection from health and safety hazards at a workplace must be provided and paid for by employers. There are exceptions for safety headwear and some safety footwear.

- Damages to their property. This includes: the cost of car accidents and parking tickets involving company vehicles; dishes broken by employees, etc.

- Any other deductions that are of no direct benefit to the employees.

Make sure you verify with your Provincial Labour Board for specifics on the above.

Reimbursements

Many employees expect that the employer is obligated to reimburse them for expenses incurred by the employee. That is not the case unless the employer has a company policy stating otherwise. Therefore, you should not assume that your employer is required to reimburse you for mileage for business use of your car, providing your own equipment, or laundering your uniform.

Drug and Alcohol Testing

Although at present there is no Canadian law requiring mandatory drug testing of employees, some private sector companies have put drug testing policies in place. The Federal government has also implemented policies for prisoners and military personnel.

Appellate courts in different provinces have issued conflicting decisions about an employer's ability to conduct pre-employment drug testing. Random drug and alcohol testing has been found to violate human rights legislation, unless the employer can demonstrate that testing is required for safety reasons. If there is a legitimate need for a sober employee such as operating heavy machinery or driving a delivery truck, employers are allowed to random monitoring.

Urinalysis is the main technology used to test for the presence of certain drugs. False positives may be obtained from the urine sample of an employee who has, for example, consumed innocuous substances such as poppy seeds, over-the-counter cold medications, or herbal teas. Another concern relates to the highly personal information that can be gleaned from these tests. A urine specimen can be analyzed to reveal whether an employee is pregnant, is using prescription or other legitimate medications, or is being treated for conditions such as heart disease, bipolar disorder, epilepsy, diabetes or schizophrenia. It has been suggested that employers could potentially use these tests for genetic screening to exclude individuals with any condition deemed likely to diminish work performance.

Perhaps the greatest limitation to the use of urinalysis as a means of drug testing is its inability to confirm whether or not an employee is actually impaired. Urinalysis indicates only whether a person has consumed a drug in the recent past (in the case of marijuana, for example, trace amounts can be detected in urine up to four weeks after use). It cannot demonstrate present drug use or present or past impairment. Nor can the test determine the quantity consumed of any drug that it detects.

Hair analysis, however, is being promoted in some quarters as less intrusive and more reliable than urinalysis. Traces of drugs that have been circulating in the body can be detected in hair months or even years later (depending on the length of the hair sample). At best, it can detect only that a given substance has been in someone's body. It provides no evidence if the person had actually been impaired on the job. Plus, results can be skewed when hair has been bleached or dyed. There have been suggestions that hair testing may be biased against people with coarse black hair, which contains high melanin levels, since drugs bind with melanin in the hair. Finally, because hair testing is more expensive than urinalysis, cost may be a barrier to the acceptance of this drug-testing technique.

Saliva analysis is the latest technique being promoted to test for the presence of illegal drugs. Collection of a sample is easier and less intrusive than urine collection; analysis can be conducted immediately at the scene; and the results can indicate whether drugs were taken recently – unlike urine testing. Saliva analysis tools can detect marijuana, cocaine, opiates and methamphetamines. Saliva testing is already being used widely in the United States and is gaining favour in Canada.

Not surprisingly, the influence of the American "war on drugs" has also been felt by Canadian subsidiaries of American firms. In November 1991, the Canadian Civil Liberties Association filed a complaint with the Ontario Human Rights Commission on behalf of four employees of Imperial Oil Limited. The basis of the complaint was that Imperial Oil's drug testing program, which commenced in January 1992, discriminated on the basis of "handicap" under the Ontario Human Rights Code. Imperial Oil was the first private company in Canada to institute a comprehensive drug testing policy that included random drug testing and a requirement to disclose previous substance abuse problems. Apparently, the development of this policy was the result of advice received from Imperial Oil's major shareholder, Exxon Corporation, an American company.

On June 23, 1995, the Ontario Human Rights Board of Inquiry rendered the first decision in that province in the area of substance abuse testing. On August 10, 1995, it ordered Imperial Oil Ltd. to pay damages to an employee. The company had forced the employee to reveal that he had once had an alcohol problem, had demoted him, and had retaliated when he launched a human rights complaint. Imperial Oil appealed the board's decision to the Ontario Divisional Court, where it was dismissed.

On a further appeal before the Ontario Court of Appeal, the Board's decision was reversed in part. The Court recognized that minimizing the risk of impairment resulting from substance abuse, and thus ensuring a safe workplace, was a legitimate objective rationally connected to work performance and that Imperial Oil acted honestly and in good faith. However, the Court noted that blood tests for drugs did not indicate actual impairment. On the other hand, breathalyzer tests for alcohol did indicate impairment and were thus a reasonable requirement for employees in safety-sensitive jobs. However, automatic dismissal of employees who failed the breathalyzer test was inconsistent with Imperial Oil's duty to accommodate employees. Therefore, alcohol testing was an occupational requirement, provided that sanctions were tailored to the employee's circumstances. Finally, the mandatory disclosure, reassignment and reinstatement provisions of the policy were discriminatory and were not occupational requirements because they were not reasonably necessary to ensure that employees in safety-sensitive jobs were unimpaired.

Imperial Oil resumed random drug testing for employees in safety-sensitive positions in July 2003 by means of saliva analysis. This led to a challenge by the union. In a December 2006 award, the Board of Arbitration held that random drug testing was not permissible even though saliva testing, unlike the previous urine testing program, could detect current cannabis impairment. Imperial Oil argued that random drug testing with a method that could determine actual impairment should be permitted in the same way that breathalyzer tests are permitted. The Arbitrator noted that saliva testing could not be compared to a breathalyzer test. Since the sample must be sent to a lab for analysis, the test would not prevent an intoxicated employee from proceeding to work.

Consensual Relationships between Managers and Subordinates

In Cavaliere v. Corvex Manufacturing, an employee was dismissed for cause without notice for engaging in sexual relationships with two subordinates spanning a decade. The employee argued that the relationships were consensual, and therefore the employer did not have cause. It's a complicated situation, because both the dismissed employee and both women were married, the husband of one of the women worked for the same employer, as did the employee's daughter, and the activities took place in the workplace, parking lots, and various other compromising situations around the small town.

The Judge found cause ruling that managerial employees have an implied obligation in their employment contracts to ensure that the workplace does not become corrupted due to sexual harassment and to protect the employer from potential legal action for such harassment. He rejects the argument that the relationships were consensual because the employees were subordinates and therefore 'vulnerable'.

In addition, after the first incident, the employer gave the employee a warning to avoid any sort of relationship with female employees, a warning which the employee ignored by entering into a new affair almost immediately.

Workplace Privacy

A number of jurisdictions, including the Federal Government, British Columbia, Alberta and Québec, have introduced privacy legislation covering the employment relationship. Previously, few rules governed how employers gathered and managed personal information respecting employees. Employers operating in jurisdictions with privacy legislation are now expected to establish policies for the collection, storage and disclosure of employee information.

New legislation also further limits the circumstances in which employers may conduct surveillance for the purpose of discovering employee wrongdoing or poor performance. Employers must also be aware that, under privacy legislation, they are accountable for any personal information transferred to suppliers; therefore, precautions should be taken to ensure the confidentiality and security of such information.

Employees should be aware that technology has given employers a powerful ability to collect information from employees in several different ways. Some example of data collection are through:

- background checks on credit and criminal records;
- resumes, cover letters and job applications;

- video surveillance of work premises and off-duty conduct;
- Global Positioning Systems for couriers, delivery and transport workers;
- telephone monitoring;
- keystroke logging;
- monitoring internet activities;
- "smart" ID cards that track attendance, access to the workplace and drug and dental plans;
- biometrics (fingerprint, handprint, voice and eye scanning to verify employee identity);
- drug and alcohol tests.

Whether any particular method of collection is permissible depends on whether:

a)   the employee is aware of the monitoring;
b)   consent was obtained;
c)   the level of intrusiveness of the collection;
d)   the appropriate balance between employer and employee interests was fair; and
e)   the facts of the situation warranted such collection.

Details are examined below.

Credit Checks

When staffing positions that require high levels of trust relating to financial matters, employers may conduct credit checks to determine the appropriateness of an applicant. In Ontario, for example, employers may conduct credit checks for these reasons. However, employers are required to notify an applicant in writing that they are conducting a credit check and identify the consumer reporting agency that will be conducting the credit check (e.g. Equifax, TransUnion).

Arguably, the Personal Information Protection and Electronic Documents Act ("PIPEDA") also requires federally regulated employers to obtain consent from applicants to collect personal information from credit reporting organizations, identify how the credit information will be used, and limit the use of that information to the hiring process. Even if PIPEDA does not directly apply to applicants and current employees, PIPEDA does provide employers with a set of best practices to handle personal information, such as ensuring that the individual's credit information is reasonably collected and appropriately safeguarded and disposed.

The Information and Privacy Commissioner of Alberta ruled on the appropriateness of credit checks. In this case, the complainant was required to consent to a credit check when applying for a job. The employer's policy was to conduct background checks on all applicants, regardless of what position they applied for. The employer organization was governed by Alberta's Personal Information Protection Act, which is similar to PIPEDA, meaning that an applicant's information must be reasonably required for the purpose for which it is being collected. In this case, information was being collected for the purpose of employment.

The Commissioner found that there was no correlation between the applicant's ability to manage her credit and the position of Receptionist/Administrative Assistant. The position involved managing nominal amounts of "petty cash" and did not necessarily require her to have a company credit card. Nor could the report be used to verify past employment, as the employer admitted that there were other, less invasive and more effective ways to probe into an applicant's employment history during the interview process.

Ultimately, the Commissioner confirmed that, in certain circumstances, an employer would certainly have legitimate business interests in collecting the kind of information contained in credit checks to prevent employee fraud. However, given the type of position that the complainant applied for, the other options to test her reliability during the interview process, and adequate supervision upon hiring, the employer could not justify the collection of credit information for the purposes of employment under Alberta's private sector privacy law.

Security Check

Under certain circumstances, it is permissible for an employer to conduct a security check on prospective employees. The Federal Privacy Commissioner has approached security and credit checks in a similar way as federal and provincial human rights commissioners. Relevant factors to determine the reasonableness of a security check include:

- The presence of expressed and meaningful consent of employee.

- The nature of the work and position (e.g. pilots, atomic energy plants workers, ports, airports or other security and safety sensitive positions).

- Legal requirements that support conducting security checks in a given sector.

- The current security environment, locally, nationally, and internationally.

The Commissioner found that security checks for spouses can be reasonable in certain circumstances and do not require spousal consent. However, the Commissioner also found that it is not reasonable to disclose information for security checks to a foreign government.

In a security-related case before the Federal Privacy Commissioner, the employer's requirement to collect fingerprints and driver's license information from drivers in order to allow them automatic access to a railway's inter-modal terminal was found to be reasonable, given the nature of the transported cargo, heightened security concerns, and safeguards taken by the employer to encrypt the data collected and restrict access to personal information within the company.

Personnel Files, Résumés and Employment References

The Federal Court of Canada has ruled that providing a poor reference (MacNeil v. Canada) and noting criminal charges on an employee's record is not a privacy breach under the federal Privacy Act.

When an employer is contacted to provide a reference for a current or former employee, both public and private sector privacy legislation requires that the employer obtain employee consent before disclosing personal information. Although not required by law, it would be considered practical for employers to follow this practice. Employer references should not contain information that is not true. This means that employers are not obliged to provide a positive reference if that reference would be untrue.

However, in references, a former employer can only provide job related information such as job title, salary, performance, start date and end date. They cannot provide non-related information such as age, disabilities, family status, race, personal lifestyle, results of drug testing, medical records, WSIB claims, or if you filed a discrimination complaint.

While PIPEDA applies to personal information of employees of federally regulated organizations, it is unclear whether the definition of "employee" includes external applicants applying for a job and their résumés, job applications and interview documentation. Some provincial privacy acts, such as Alberta's PIPA have express provisions that apply to résumés and job applications.

Medical Information

Personal health information is protected by PIPEDA, the Privacy Act and provincial health privacy legislation in four provinces: Alberta, Manitoba, Ontario, and Saskatchewan. In addition, human rights codes, common law and constitutional law principles have been relied upon to protect individual's personal health information. Given the high level of sensitivity of personal health information, consent is generally required from the employee for its collection and disclosure, unless the employer is compelled to produce records by court order, statute or contract.

Despite the substantial privacy protections afforded to personal health information, the Federal Privacy Commissioner has recognized that employers have legitimate purposes for collecting and using this type of personal information with the following guidelines:

- Sick leave policies that meet PIPEDA's consent requirements to disclose information to internal and external practitioners are valid.

- Verify that an employee's absence is for genuine medical reasons.

- Medical certification of an employee in a safety sensitive position who is coming off sick or disability leave is reasonably justified if the employer follows proper consent and access procedures prescribed by the Act.

- Occupational health and safety officers must obtain consent to contact medical staff and obtain information on an employee's medical exam.

- Occupational health and safety officers, doctors, and nurses are bound by codes of ethics such that they cannot provide management with more personal information than necessary.

Therefore, if consent is not a legal requirement, it is strongly recommended that an employer administering sick leave, medical certifications or insurance benefits obtain consent to collect and disclose medical information from the employee before or at the time of collection and avoid collecting information about an employee's diagnosis.

Provincial Health Privacy Legislation:

Alberta Health Information Act:
http://www.qp.alberta.ca/570.cfm?frm_isbn=9780779752607&search_by=link

Manitoba Personal Health Information Act:
http://web2.gov.mb.ca/laws/statutes/ccsm/p033-5e.php

Ontario Personal Health Information Protection Act:
http://www.e-laws.gov.on.ca/html/statutes/english/elaws_statutes_04p03_e.htm

Saskatchewan Health Information Protection Act:
http://www.qp.gov.sk.ca/documents/english/Statutes/Statutes/H0-021.pdf

Videotape Surveillance

In some cases, an employer may videotape employees at work, but only under specific conditions and circumstances. The Federal Privacy Commissioner approaches surveillance cases as balancing the rights of the employer's legitimate business interests and the employee's reasonable expectation of privacy. In PIPEDA, the Commissioner set out the main factors to consider when determining whether video surveillance of the workplace is appropriate.

1. Is the video camera demonstrably necessary to meet a specific need?

2. Is it likely to be effective in meeting that need?
3. Is the loss to privacy proportional to the benefit gained?
4. Is there a less privacy invasive way to achieve the same goal?

In Eastmond v. Canadian Pacific Railway before the Federal Court, CP Rail had installed six digital video recording surveillance cameras in its mechanical facility area. The court adopted the Privacy Commissioner's four- part test (listed above) but came to the opposite conclusion on additional evidence.

In Eastmond, the result was that in terms of surveillance cameras, there has to be a line drawn between the secret collection of information and the collection of information by cameras whose locations are known, as well as employees made aware that recordings are being made and the use of those recordings. However, the court also condemned the use of surveillance cameras to record the productivity of workers.

The appropriate use of video cameras will also depend on the locations of the video cameras. Cameras focused on exits and entrances may be easier to justify in instances where security can be established as an issue in the workplace. However, cameras trained on other work areas without being able to adequately capture the activity the video surveillance was meant to monitor have been found unacceptable by the Federal Privacy Commissioner. Privacy Commissioners generally do not look favourably on employers who monitor employees as a deterrent or for prevention purposes without establishing that there is an existing problem. A web cam was also considered not permissible.

Workplace monitoring guidelines issued by some provincial commissioners' offices emphasize that the employer:

- must have compelling concerns to justify monitoring.

- should use the least intrusive means possible.

- should notify employees about the surveillance.

- should explain the reasons for the surveillance, its use, possible disclosure and consequences of the information being collected.

Can My Employer Videotape Me When I Am Off-Duty?

The Federal Privacy Commissioner found that in some cases (e.g. investigating insurance fraud) off-duty video surveillance conducted by a private investigator on behalf of the employer was justified because in that instance:

1. There was evidence proving that the employer suspected that the trust relationship with the employee was broken by an alleged false workplace injury claim.

2. All other less privacy intrusive ways to obtain the required information were exhausted.

3. The employer limited its collection of personal information to the greatest extent possible.

Overall, video surveillance of employees may or may not be legal depending on its necessity, effectiveness, and the extent of its impact on employee privacy interests.

.

Global Positioning System (GPS)

The Federal Privacy Commissioner has ruled on the use of personal information collected from employees using Global Positioning Systems (GPS). In one case, the employer implemented GPS in its installation, repair, and construction vehicles in order to locate, dispatch, and route its employees to various job sites. The employer cited enhanced efficiency, improved customer service, and employee safety as justifications for installing GPS in its vehicles. Some employees were concerned, however, that GPS would also be used to monitor their work performance, and that personal information collected by the technology would be used to justify disciplinary action.

The Commissioner used the following analysis, which is similar to the analysis for video surveillance, to assess the appropriateness of using GPS in that case:

- Is the measure absolutely necessary to meet a specific need?
- Is it likely to be effective in meeting that need?
- Is the loss of privacy proportional to the benefit gained?
- Is there a less privacy-invasive way of achieving the same end?

The Commissioner accepted most of the employer's reasons for installing GPS. The Commissioner determined that when the purpose for using GPS is appropriately defined, limited, and communicated to the employees beforehand, the use of the technology may be acceptable under PIPEDA. However, the Commissioner cautioned that "systematically using GPS to check up on workers and try to determine how well they are doing their jobs would be going too far. Employers do not have carte blanche to use GPS to constantly monitor their workforce."

Monitoring of Telephone Calls, Email or Websites Visited

Criteria similar to those used for judging video surveillance have also been used to evaluate other forms of surveillance, such as telephone, email and internet monitoring, and keystroke logging.

In addition to the four factors outlined by the court in Eastmond case mentioned above for video surveillance, when faced with a case involving email, internet, telephone or keystroke monitoring, privacy commissioners will generally consider:

- The invasiveness of the monitoring.

- Evidence that there is a problem that monitoring is meant to address.

- Whether the employee is aware of the purposes for which the monitoring device is being used.

- If the activity being monitored is related to the enterprise, or within the realm of personal activity that often occurs in the workplace (e.g. online banking, purchases, accessing personal email accounts, personal phone calls).

1. Monitoring Telephone, Internet and Computer Use

The Federal Privacy Commissioner has recognized that companies monitor calls between their telephone operators and customers for "quality assurance" purposes. These types of telephone conversations would be within the normal course of employment and are clearly related to the employer's business.

As of 2010, there has been no definitive court ruling on monitoring employee telephone calls or email. Labour arbitration cases on the surveillance of employee email and internet use have tended to confirm that an employer's proprietary interest in his/her computer networking systems diminishes an employee's reasonable expectation of privacy because:

- There is a presumption that the employer owns the computing system that employees use in the course of employment;

- The employer's proprietary rights in the system extend to all information contained therein;

- Information contained in the system is likely to be business-related and thus less deserving of privacy protection; and

- The nature of the employment relationship allows the employer to maintain control over their employees' work in order to protect the employer's legitimate business interests.

Note that the normal course of employment typically includes any time spent or activities conducted on the employer's premises, including breaks and lunch hours.

An employer generally has a right to access its computer system as it would any other property it owns. One of the leading labour law cases enforcing this standard is International Association of Bridge, Local Union no. 97, and Structural and Ornamental Ironworkers and Office and Technical Employees' Union, Local 15. An arbitrator ruled that email on employer-owned systems have no reasonable expectation of privacy because the employer has a right to search their computer system as they would with any other type of company property.

In terms of searches of computer files stored on the employer's network or computer, courts have taken a similar property-rights approach. In Québec, a court ruled in Tremblay that an employer could search an employee's workplace computer for child pornography. This decision was based, in part, because the employer, a local police service, owned the computer that the files were stored on, and because the police officer employee had indicated that the files in question were work-related. Ultimately, the court determined that the employee had no reasonable expectation of privacy in work-related files stored on the employer's computer.

In terms of investigation of misuse of technology, there have been a few cases that have led to justifiable dismissal. In Di Vito v. Macdonald Dettwiler & Associates ("MDA"), Mr. Di Vito and Mr. Mathers, the plaintiffs, both worked for MDA, a high tech company. An e-mail composed by another MDA employee was sent to Mr. Di Vito. The e-mail was based on a monologue performed by a comedian and described, in a vulgar and derogatory fashion, sexual acts with an obese woman. The monologue had been altered so that it referred to a specific employee of MDA who suffered from a weight problem. Just over a year later, Mr. DiVito retrieved the "joke" from a file he had saved it on and sent it to Mr. Mathers. Mr. Mathers forwarded the "joke" to three other MDA employees and printed out a hard copy. A month later someone posted a copy of the "joke" on one of the office bulletin boards. The existence of the "joke" on the board was brought to the attention of the supervisor. The posted copy of the e-mail showed that the e-mail had been sent to Mr. Di Vito. He was called in by the supervisor for an explanation on the "joke's" distribution.

Mr. Di Vito admitted he had received the message and forwarded it to several employees, including Mr. Mathers. Mr. Mathers also acknowledged that he had received the copy but didn't say that he had printed out a copy of the joke or that he had forwarded it to other employees as well. When asked on three separate occasions if they had both disclosed everything they knew, they both said they had. Eventually the woman who was the subject matter of the joke found a copy of the email in her inbox. She was understandably upset and notified management.

Upon hearing this, Mr. Di Vito admitted that he knew that Mr. Mathers had distributed the email to a number of other employees. Mr. Mathers, again after a series of denials, finally admitted that he had forwarded the "joke". Both the employees were fired and brought a wrongful dismissal action against MDA.

The employer, in trying to establish cause, said that the plaintiffs had engaged in hurtful and malicious conduct toward a co-worker that had seriously affected the work environment. Their termination was necessary to rehabilitate the working environment. Also, the plaintiffs had been dishonest in their dealings with management during the investigation and could no longer be trusted.

The B.C. Supreme Court said there was nothing humorous about the e-mail. It was humiliating for the female employee and by posting it on the bulletin board, she was publicly embarrassed. Further, there was an aggravating factor in that the e-mail was not just sent once; it was stored for more than a year and then sent again. This defeated any argument on the plaintiffs' part of a momentary lack of judgment.

But the Court was not persuaded that the conduct of the plaintiffs, in so far as the distribution of the mail was concerned, was sufficient grounds for their dismissal. Such conduct, by itself, warranted a severe reprimand but not dismissal for cause. However, the Court held that the conduct, combined with the dishonesty during the investigation, did amount to just cause. The dishonesty was a breach of the employees' implied duties of honesty and faithfulness and constituted serious misconduct.

Similarly, in Westcoast Energy Inc v. Communications, Energy and Paperworkers' Union of Canada, a grievance was filed by Dan Bourdon, the employee, challenging the termination of his employment. Mr. Bourdon sent multiple, anonymous, sexually harassing e-mails to a female co-worker on four occasions. He had used the company's computer and network in order to send the messages.

However, he had used an Internet based e-mail system (Hotmail) and not a work e-mail system. The employee became worried and began to think someone was stalking her. Using a special program, the company was able to trace the e-mails back to Mr. Bourdon's computer at work. When confronted with this information, Mr. Bourdon lied several times to the employer and said that the e-mails were sent by his supervisor. When the dismissal went before an arbitrator, the termination was revoked and substituted with a long suspension. The arbitrator took into account the fact that the employee had worked for the company for 24 years, had no previous discipline record, and would have to deal with the shame and loss of credibility he brought upon himself. In this instance even though the employee was engaged in completely inappropriate behavior and was dishonest, the arbitrator held that there was not sufficient cause for dismissal.

An employer can also monitor an employee's Internet usage to determine where the employees have been, for how long and in what activities they engaged while online. Such information is stored either on the employee's own computer or on the company's server. While access to Internet use is often crucial to the employee's ability to do the job well, it also allows employees to "surf the Net" on company time. This is a legitimate concern for employers and in certain circumstances can provide cause for termination.

For example, Dominic Petruzzi was a technical inspector for CAE Electronics in Montreal. After a routine audit of employees' Internet activity, it was discovered that Mr. Petruzzi had spent 329 hours over a four month period of time (there were 640 working hours in that period of time) surfing the Internet at work. The majority of the time was spent visiting adult pornographic websites. His employment was terminated. A grievance was filed by Mr. Petruzzi. He tried to say that there was some error on the part of the employer because he never spent more than two hours a day on the Internet. The panel didn't believe his defense and held that the employer had cause to terminate him.

Some conclusions with respect to cause for termination that can be drawn from these cases are:

- Employees **do not** have a reasonable expectation of privacy in e-mails sent or received on work e-mail systems.

- The contents of the e-mails might allow for termination with cause of the employee.

- The sending of inappropriate, even harassing e-mails is not always sufficient to establish cause. If the employee has committed some other breach of employment obligations (such as being dishonest during the investigation), just cause will be easier to establish.

- When e-mails become physically threatening or violent, this should be sufficient just cause for dismissal.

- Monitoring of Internet use in the workplace is allowed by the employer. Just cause may be established where there is excessive use.

2. Keystroke Monitoring on Workplace Computers

The Alberta Privacy Commissioner has ruled that secret employee monitoring by way of keystroke logging violates Alberta's public sector privacy law. The case was brought by an individual who lost his job as a computer technician at a public library after he discovered and complained about a keystroke logging program that was monitoring his computer use. Under Alberta privacy law, public bodies can collect personal information without consent where the information "relates directly to and is necessary for an operating program or activity of the public body". The employer, Parkland Regional Library, argued that the keystroke logging was necessary in order to ensure that the employee was not using the computer for personal purposes and was being sufficiently productive. In his decision, the Alberta Privacy

Commissioner stated that he was not convinced by the employer's justifications, noting that there are other, much less intrusive means to monitor employee productivity and address concerns about working time. The Commissioner also noted that there was no good reason in this case not to inform the employee that he was being monitored.

3. Workplace Policies May Put Employees "On Notice"

If an employer clearly communicates their policies on appropriate workplace email, internet and computer usage, and notifies employees about monitoring practices, employees may have a diminished expectation of privacy in their online communications and computer use. In Briar v. Canada (Treasury Board) four employees of a correctional facility in British Columbia were disciplined for using the Correctional Service of Canada's email system to broadcast offensive materials in the workplace. They filed a complaint arguing that their privacy rights had been violated by the employer's email monitoring. The Public Servants Staff Relations Board held that because the situation was not a case of random surveillance and because the employer made the internet usage and monitoring policies very clear, the employees had no reasonable expectation of privacy in the circumstances.

Fingerprint Scans and Other Biometrics

Biometrics is emerging as a new tool for employers to manage attendance and security in the workplace. Biometrics raise privacy concerns because they verify a person's identity using a person's unique physical characteristics such as their fingerprint, handprint, eye scan, or voice pattern.

In Turner v. Telus, the Federal Court was faced with a complaint made by Telus Communications employees about their employer's use of voice recognition technology, which is used for logging work-related information and absence reporting. The employees also alleged that they were threatened with progressive discipline by Telus for refusing to consent to the collection of their "voice print".

One of the employees, Turner, had previously filed a complaint with the Federal Privacy Commissioner. The Commissioner found that the portion of the complaint concerning the collection of the voice print was not well-founded. However, the part of the complaint concerning the collection of personal information by the absence-reporting application was.

The employees asked the court to prevent Telus from implementing E-Speak in the workplace. The employees had refused to consent to the collection of their "voice print" in order to enroll them in the new system. Voice prints or patterns, as well as other types of biometric information, are considered personal information under the Personal Information Protection and Electronic Information Act ("PIPEDA").

The Federal Court dismissed the employees' application. The judge found in favour of Telus, ruling that:

1. An employer's use of biometric voice authentication was reasonable in the circumstances.

2. An employer could not force employees to use the system, but was free to implement it.

3. Employers can discipline those who do not consent to reasonable collections.

4. Progressive discipline does not constitute "withholding goods or services" under PIPEDA.

While upholding the decision on appeal, the Federal Court did not accept the finding that the employer was exempted from obtaining consent from the employees. An organization may collect personal information without the knowledge or consent of the individual only if the collection is clearly in the interests of the individual and consent cannot be obtained in a timely way. In the Telus case, the Court found that the employees were available to provide consent – but they chose not to.

The case law has shown that employers can justify using biometrics at arbitration or before the Privacy Commissioner if they have evidence to prove that:

1. The use of biometrics is a business advantage for the company (i.e. it is cost efficient, it improves security).

2. A security or attendance problem exists and the biometrics are implemented to remedy such problems.

3. The chosen biometric is the least intrusive means to achieve the employer's objective.

4. Adequate safeguards are in place to protect the personal information used in the biometric system.

Notably, an arbitrator recently reinstated three employees of a company who were fired after they refused to enroll in a biometric hand scanning system because of their religious belief that doing so might identify them as followers of Satan with the "Mark of the Beast." The arbitrator held that the employer must attempt to accommodate the employees. An employee's religious beliefs do not need to be objectively reasonable or generally accepted, only sincerely held. "Their refusal should have been treated as a significant human rights issue, not a disciplinary matter."

Lie Detector Tests

A polygraph (lie detector) is an instrument that measures and records several physiological responses such as blood pressure, pulse, respiration, breathing rhythms, body temperature and skin conductivity while the subject is asked and answers a series of questions, on the theory that false answers will produce distinctive measurements.

Employees have the right to refuse to take lie detectors tests requested by their employers. Even for an employer to ask or require that they take a lie detector test is a violation of their rights. These rules apply to applicants for employment as well.

No one can disclose to an employer that an employee has taken a lie detector test, and no one can disclose to an employer the results of a lie detector test taken by an employee.

Search and Seizure

Are you safe from your employer's intrusions into areas normally subject to your exclusive control (i.e. locker, desk drawer, etc.)? The answer may be a little murky.

In Ontario, it is generally agreed that there is no statutory protection of privacy for employees while on the employer's premises. There is ambiguity about whether or not the law protects privacy and if so, at what point. There is certainly an acknowledged right to protection from unreasonable search and seizure under the Charter which applies in criminal situations although an employer / employee relationship creates some different considerations.

Generally, everything that belongs to the employer could be the object of a search without the employee's consent provided it is not "unreasonable".

The case of Canada Post Corp. v. C.U.P.W.8 (Plant Security National Policy Grievance) probably offers the best guidance on this issue. It dealt with a union grievance arising from the establishment of security rules by Canada Post. These rules included the right of the company:

a. To demand inspection of any items carried in and out of the plant.

b. To impose a prohibition on bringing personal belongings such as handbags, packages or parcels into the work area without written permission of the plant manager.

c. To search lockers issued by the corporation to employees and the right to inspect vehicles entering or leaving the plant.

The union argued that the rules, although implemented with some justification, went too far and would result in an unwarranted violation of the privacy of employees. Canada Post argued that the rules were necessary due to a security problem related to the uniqueness of its operations.

The arbitrator ruled that the corporation had the right to restrict items brought into the plant. Canada Post could conduct inspection of employee belongings prior to bringing them into the plant. The arbitrator also held that since the lockers were provided by the corporation, the corporation had the right to require visual inspections of lockers. However, the arbitrator held that the right of employees to privacy extended to "those personal effects which are normally carried by individuals as they go about their day-to-day business" and concluded that employees were free from spot checks of these effects "unless there is an express general principle of law which permits it, or unless consent has expressly or impliedly been given".

Common Employer Wrongs

Dismissals

Wrongful Dismissal

You hear the phrase "wrongful dismissal", but what is it really? A wrongful dismissal simply means that an employer fails to provide reasonable notice of termination. Most people equate the term 'wrongful' to mean some form of misconduct. This is not the case. Wrongful dismissal damages are provided only to compensate for lack of notice and not for misconduct, however, courts may award additional damages in a wrongful dismissed action for 'bad faith' conduct in the manner of termination over and above damages for failure to provide adequate notice.

Many people assume that any termination/severance package received is reasonable and that their employer would never try to take advantage of them. This concept ignores the fact that the employer is running a business and it makes business sense to pay less rather than more. Using that basic principle, it is rare that the opening offer will be its best offer. (Negotiation is discussed in a later chapter.) There is, however, a minimum level that an employer cannot go below legally. These payments are referred to as "statutory termination and severance pay". Termination pay is given instead of the required notice of termination of employment. For example, if you are entitled to 2 weeks' notice, then you would get two weeks' pay and benefits.

Severance pay is paid to a qualified employee who has his/her employment "severed". It compensates for loss of seniority and job-related benefits and recognizes an employee's years of service. You qualify for severance when you have worked for an employer for at least 5 years and the company has a payroll of at least $2.5 million. For example, if you qualify for severance pay, your employer will give you a lump sum payment equal to one week's regular pay for each year you were employed up to a maximum of 26 weeks for 26 years. You also get credit for full months of employment. Severance pay is not the same as termination pay, which is given instead of the required working notice of termination of employment. For example, if you worked for 10.5 years, your employer would pay you 10.5 weeks' regular pay as your severance pay.

But what if the employer adds a few weeks to the minimum payment? To the inexperienced person, it may appear that the employer is being generous, when in fact it is not. To demonstrate, take a five-year Ontario employee who is entitled to severance and termination pay in the equivalent of 18 weeks. In this situation, the employee is entitled to 18 weeks' pay at a minimum and without signing a release. If the employer seeks a signed release of common law entitlements (i.e. promise not to sue the employer) in exchange for 20 weeks, the employee would receive only two weeks over Employment Standards minimum payments and in exchange for giving up rights to potential damages which could represent 12 months pay or more. Common law entitlements are based on several factors including the person's age, position, years of service, and the availability of alternate employment. Unlike statutory notice, common law notice is based on what a court believes is reasonable in the circumstances. In monetary terms, an employee could be leaving tens of thousands of dollars on the table.

It should be understood that Employment Standards minimum payments are payable without an employee having to sign any release whatsoever. In other words, the employer would be obligated, in the above example, to pay 18 weeks pay and the employee would retain the right to bring a civil claim.

It is therefore extremely important that an employee understand what minimum payments they are entitled to. The closer the offer is to the minimum, the worse the offer. The assessment of whether common law damages will be significantly greater than minimum payments can only be assessed by a qualified lawyer.

Just Cause

"Just cause" is a legal term that means an employer is justified in terminating an employee without providing termination notice or termination pay. There is no clear-cut method of determining what will constitute just cause. Each case is unique and must be reviewed with attention to all of the facts of the situation.

When resolving whether there is just cause for dismissal without notice in your situation, courts will look at answering the following two questions: (1) was misconduct by the employee proven?; and (2) was the level of the misconduct justifiable to dismiss the employee without any notice? If the answer to both questions is *yes*, then just cause dismissal was reasonable; however, if an answer to either question is *no*, then the employer was obligated to give reasonable termination notice or termination pay.

What is the measure of misconduct that justifies termination for just cause? There are a number of factors. Firstly, a court will look at whether the employee's misconduct caused an irreparable disruption in the employment relationship, by either violating an important condition of the employment contract, or destroying the employer's trust in the employee. If the misconduct resulted in any of these events, then there is just cause.

Secondly, a court will look at the seniority of the employee in the organization. The more senior an employee, the more serious the conduct.

Thirdly, a court will look to see whether the employer gave any warnings (written or verbal) prior to termination. Where there was no warning prior to the dismissal that the misconduct was connected to, except in the most serious of cases (e.g. stealing, violence, leaking corporate secrets, etc.), the employer will have a harder time proving just cause in court.

Lastly, courts will look at whether the employee's misconduct was tolerated prior to the dismissal. If misconduct occurred before and the employer tolerated this behaviour through inaction (i.e. not providing the employee with a formal warning that the misconduct would not be tolerated) then the employer's actions will be under scrutiny if the employee was dismissed without notice.

It is difficult enough for an individual to be suddenly told that his/her employment has come to an end. One of the top three stresses for adults in our society is losing a job. It is doubly so when the employer informs the employee that s/he has been terminated for "cause". The standard statement regarding "cause" is provided by the Ontario Court as follows:

"If an employee has been guilty of serious misconduct, habitual neglect of duty, incompetence, or conduct incompatible with his duties or prejudicial to the employer's business, or if he has been guilty of willful disobedience to the employer's orders in a matter of substance, the law recognizes the employer's right to summarily dismiss the delinquent employee."

Not every act of misconduct should lead to termination. The conduct by the employee must be serious enough to end the employment relationship. The types of conduct which the law recognizes as justifying termination have included: incompetence, insubordination or disobedience, abusive language or behaviour, violence, chronic absenteeism, persistent lateness, intoxication, dishonesty, theft, destruction of property and sexual harassment.

When there is a cause for termination, the employer has no obligation to provide the employee with notice or termination pay. It is therefore not unusual for an employer to allege cause, even though it will be difficult to prove in order to discourage an employee from bringing an action for wrongful dismissal. Some employers try to take advantage of a terminated employee's shock and vulnerability.

In addition, an employee's entitlement to termination/severance payments and eligibility for EI benefits may be affected by allegations of cause for termination. Given all that is at stake, employees, in such circumstances, are urged to consult with a lawyer to determine their rights going forward and the strength of any case for wrongful dismissal they may have against the employer.

Dishonesty

Not every employee who faces termination will have a legitimate lawsuit for wrongful dismissal. A termination is "wrongful" when an employee is terminated without cause and is not provided with reasonable notice of his/her termination.

In a recent case (Misty Rae v. Attrell Hyundai Subaru), the employer, an auto dealership, alleged cause for termination based upon dishonesty. The employer alleged that the plaintiff had created fictitious work orders to cover up the fact that she was having work done on family members' vehicles and not paying for the work done. The terminated employee conceded that she had brought her sister's car to the dealership for inspection by a technician. Parts were required but were not available at the dealership. The former employee took the car away with the intention of bringing the car back at a later time to have the parts installed. The employee did not make payment for the inspection undertaken by the technician.

The employee acknowledged that she owed the defendant for the work done on her sister's car. The facts of this case, even with the admission by the employee, did not establish that the plaintiff had acted dishonestly or established cause for termination. The judge noted: "when just cause consists of allegations of dishonesty there must be clear and cogent proof". The evidence in this case did not provide the level of proof required.

"Dishonesty" includes not only theft or fraud but any form of untrustworthy behaviour. Just cause based on dishonesty may happen whether the conduct in question occurs before the start of employment (e.g. lying on your résumé), during the course of employment or in relation to matters unconnected with employment. In determining when just cause for dishonesty exists, the courts are primarily concerned with whether the conduct of the employee is such that s/he can no longer be trusted or depended upon by the employer.

Another case on dishonesty is McKinley v. BC Tel, a 2001 decision of the Supreme Court of Canada. The plaintiff was a chartered accountant who had been employed for almost 17 years when, as a result of high blood pressure and his doctor's advice, he took a leave of absence. He later indicated that he wanted to return to work but, given his medical condition, requested a position of lesser responsibility. Some three months after the Plaintiff's leave had begun and without returning to work, the defendant terminated the plaintiff's employment. The employer maintained that although it had used its best efforts to find another position for the plaintiff, none was available. At trial, BC Tel claimed that no notice was owed as the plaintiff had deliberately withheld medical information, which indicated that he could return to his old job.

The Supreme Court ruled that Mr. McKinley's conduct, although dishonest, did not justify dismissal. The Court differentiated the facts of this case from situations which involve theft, misappropriation or fraud where dismissal may be justified without any further inquiry.

However, in the case of R.T. James Whitehouse v. RBC Dominion Securities Inc. (Alberta), Mr. Whitehouse met with a prostitute in his employer's offices. Mr. Whitehouse had abandoned the prostitute on the premises where she had access to client and corporate information.

Mr. Whitehouse had lied to more senior management the following day when questioned about the incident. The Court found that the above conduct justified cause and that any perceived tolerance of this kind by the company would negatively impact the employer's relationship with other employees. Therefore, Mr. Whitehouse was fairly terminated for Just Cause.

Breach of Trust

A breach of trust occurs when someone in a position of confidence violates the trust invested by someone else. In an employment situation, it typically occurs where the employee demonstrates misconduct that promotes his/her interests instead of the employer's interests. Where the employee's misconduct was motivated by a conflict of interest, the natural trust placed in the employee will have been destroyed. However, attention needs to be paid to the specific facts to confirm if a breach of trust has occurred.

In Ng v. Canadian Imperial Bank of Commerce, a financial advisor employed by the CIBC frequently cashed cheques on behalf of her husband into her account and gave him money withdrawn from the bank, without waiting the required time for clearance of the cheques. The advisor also acted as her husband's personal banker at a time during which she knew that he had a gambling problem, while using the bank's money to help him. The court said that the decisions made by the employee while doing favours for her husband were within her understanding that they violated bank rules and procedures. As well, the employee's misconduct violated a key term of her employment contract, and therefore there was deemed just cause for termination.

Similarly, in Dowling v. Ontario (Workplace Safety and Insurance Board), a manager with the WSIB used his position to obtain financial benefits. He lowered insurance rates for certain clients in exchange for the purchase of computers for personal use at their wholesale price. In addition, he entered into secret arrangements with select clients, where he lowered the cost of insurance and split any amounts made as profit over and above the regular price with them. The employer's Code of Conduct expressly forbade the acceptance of gifts or monetary reward by an employee for a business decision. The court agreed that there was just cause for dismissal.

Insubordination

Insubordination is a form of misconduct where the employee refuses to acknowledge and accept the authority of the employer and refuses to comply with the employer's clear instructions, policies and procedures without reasonable justification. Usually, the courts will not allow an employer to fire an employee for a single incident of insubordination, unless it was of some major significance.

Daniels v. Canadian Gift & Tableware Assn. was a case involving numerous and extreme instances of insubordination. The employee, an assistant editor and co-publisher of a major consumer gift trade publication, repeatedly exhibited hostility toward her direct supervisor, refused to comply with her supervisor's instructions and treated her assistant abusively. The employee also publicly challenged her supervisor's authority on numerous occasions, going over her head to speak with board members any time she and her supervisor disagreed. The court said that the employer had just cause to dismiss the employee without notice. The employee had repeatedly undermined the reporting structure and had acted as if she had the same seniority as her supervisor even though she had no such authority. Despite numerous warnings that this kind of conduct was not acceptable, the employee continued her insubordination. Just cause was proven in this case.

Just cause was also deemed in Kontopidis v. Coventry Lane Automobiles Ltd., where a manager at an auto body shop was inexplicably absent on numerous occasions from work, despite explicit instructions from his employer to notify management when he was going to be away. The employee's absence affected the productivity of the body shop as he failed to train a new manager that had been hired. The employee also removed automobiles from the body shop without explanation. The court said that the failure to comply with explicit instructions, together with the impact of the employee's failure to notify management of repeated absence, amounted to justification for just cause dismissal.

Absenteeism/Lateness

Absenteeism is defined as occasional absences from work which an employee may attempt to justify by through communication (phone call, email, text, discussion) indicating that s/he will not be reporting to work or that s/he is not feeling well. Lateness refers to reporting for work after one's schedule of hours has begun.

Many employers have in place attendance policies which set out the procedure that an employee must follow when not coming in to work or reporting late. This will often require that the employee report his/her non-attendance before the start of the shift, and provide doctor's notes when absences are illness-related and extend beyond a certain number of days. Non-compliance with an employer's attendance policy may result in discipline and if the conduct continues, be reason for the employer as cause for dismissal.

Even in establishments where there is no formal attendance policy, repeated lateness without a legitimate reason may be regarded as a serious breach of the employee's responsibility to the employer. Where the employee cannot justify his/her persistent lateness, warnings have been issued by the supervisor and the conduct persists, the employer will be able to terminate legally.

An employer will **not** be able to establish cause for dismissal where an employee is unable to attend work due to illness. In such circumstances, an employer will need to determine whether the employee is indeed sick. To do so, an employer has the right to request that an employee provide a doctor's note where the employee has been absent on a significant number of days.

An employer would, in most cases, be required to formally warn an employee before proceeding with outright dismissal under the ground of absenteeism. The employer could not justify firing an employee who was late on only one occasion. However, chronic lateness and absenteeism may justify dismissal if the employee had been given sufficient warnings and still failed to correct this behavior without valid reasons. This was the case in *Kontopidis*, mentioned above. Because the employee was repeatedly absent from work and did not provide an explanation, the employer was justified in firing the employee without notice. The employer had provided the employee with numerous warnings and written instructions which the employee repeatedly had ignored.

However, if an employee arrives at work late for his/her shift, an employer can demand that the employee remain on duty later than the normal end time to make up for time lost due to lateness. For example, if an employee showed up at 8:10am when his/her normal start time is 8:00am, then the employer is within his/her right to require the employee to stay until 5:10pm (if the normal day's end is 5:00pm). Additionally, in the same scenario, if the employee is paid an hourly wage, the employer can ask the tardy employee to leave and return at 8:30am to start work. This condition is allowed if the hours worked is based on a minimum of 30 minute intervals.

Misrepresentation at Time of Hiring

Misrepresentation at time of hiring occurs when an employee who was hired on the basis of a skill, experience or educational achievement that s/he indicated s/he possesses, but in reality does not. The employee in such a case may be dismissed with just cause for misrepresenting the skill. For example, a person who represented that he can swim and was hired as a lifeguard may be dismissed for just cause after the employer discovers the employee's lack of ability to swim. Or if an employee also claimed that she had an MBA during the interview phase and was later discovered that this was false after being hired may be fired for just cause.

Incompetence/Poor Performance

An employee is obliged to display a reasonable level of competence in relation to the job that they are hired for. Upon hiring, an employee may also indicate her/his awareness of the duties and responsibilities of the position s/he is applying for, and her/his qualifications and/or the experience s/he possess to do the job. Under these circumstances, where it is clear that the individual demonstrates that s/he is not up to the task or has misrepresented her/his qualifications and her/his ability, the employer may have cause for termination.

Employers are obligated to advise employees if there are performance-related concerns and provide a private opportunity to address them. What would constitute a adequate warning to an employee before an employer can use continued poor performance as cause for termination? Courts have repeatedly indicated that mere expressions of disappointment with an employee's work are not sufficient. The employee must be aware of the standard of performance expected of him/her and notified that s/he has failed to meet that standard. S/he must be given a reasonable amount of time to improve performance and be warned that failure to do so could result in termination. Courts have indicated that criticism of an employee's performance must be constructive and will only be deemed so where the employer has provided practical guidance on how to improve.

Intoxication

Can an employee who comes to work under the influence of drugs or alcohol be terminated for cause? Except where the employee is suffering from alcoholism, s/he can. The foundation for terminating an employee in such circumstances is outlined as follows:

If an employee is intoxicated while at work, a serious breach of the employment contract has occurred. Not only is the employee unfit to perform the duties safely and satisfactorily, the employee is often a disruptive or discouraging influence in the workplace and an embarrassment to the employer if in contact with the clients or the public. Plus, in many lines of work, the impaired employee may present a danger to her/himself, other employees and customers which would result in potential liability problems for the employer.

An employer may be justified in terminating an employee without notice based upon a single incident of intoxication. This would likely be the case where the individual is employed in a position where the safety of co-workers and/or the public at large depend upon his decisions and his/her actions.

The mere fact that an employee exhibits signs of alcohol consumption while at work will not exclusively justify dismissal. It needs to be shown that the consumption of alcohol negatively impacted upon the employee's ability to perform his/her job.

The Courts will take a different approach to this issue if it is found that the employee is suffering from an underlying illness; namely, alcoholism. The distinction between drinking on occasion to excess and alcoholism is of course a medical, and not a legal one. Alcoholism is recognized as a disease marked not by the level of alcohol consumption but by its chronic, uncontrollable use.

Alcoholism has been found to be a "disability" and therefore one is protected from discrimination under the Human Rights Code. Termination of an employee for alcoholism will likely constitute a violation of an individual's rights under the Code.

Termination in such circumstances will therefore be unlawful and the employer will not be able to rely on the employee's disability as cause for termination.

Insolence

In the New Brunswick case, Henry v. Foxco Ltd., an employee had been working in an auto repair shop for more than seven years with a flawless record of employment up until the date of his termination. On that day, he was asked by his supervisor to work on two vans. Two hours later, the supervisor asked about the employee's progress and was told that work on the first vehicle had not been completed. The supervisor reprimanded the employee by telling him: "God, Gerald, we only get $45 or $50 per truck". The employee reacted to the criticism, in the presence of co-workers, by becoming loud and abusive and using foul language. He rejected the supervisor's suggestion that he calm down. The employee then began to taunt the supervisor to fire him. After the third such taunt, the supervisor did exactly what he was challenged to do and fired the employee on the spot.

The New Brunswick court found that the employer had cause to terminate based upon the employee's insolent behaviour. However, when appealed, the court's decision was reversed in favour of the employee. The appeals court observed that while an isolated act of insolence would not normally justify dismissal, other circumstances could have changed the ruling in favour of the employer. These could include situations where (1) the employee and superior were no longer capable of maintaining a working relationship; (2) the incident undermined the superior's credibility in the workplace and therefore his ability to supervise effectively; or (3) the employer had, as a result of the incident, suffered a financial loss, a loss of reputation or its business interests had been seriously harmed as when, for example, the incident occurred in front of customers.

In the absence of such factors, the Court indicated that the more appropriate response of an employer in these circumstances might be to proceed through progressive discipline, beginning with a warning to underline that repeat episodes of such conduct would not be tolerated.

Courts will also consider whether the misconduct in question involves profanities. The use of foul language is not cause for dismissal especially when such language is commonly tolerated in the workplace.

In determining whether insolent behaviour justifies cause for termination, the courts would also review whether the misconduct reflects a brief lapse of judgment which may be rectified with a cooling off period and an apology.

In Henry, the plaintiff was a long-term employee with a clean employment record. The misconduct represented an isolated incident. The employer was not able to establish that the incident resulted in irreparable harm to the relationship between the employee and his supervisor or weakened the supervisor's ability to manage the workplace. There was no evidence that the incident damaged the employer's financial interests or its reputation with the public. The court also found that the use of profanities had been tolerated in the workplace.

Constructive Dismissal

A constructive dismissal occurs when an employer makes a significant change to a basic term or condition of an employer's employment without the employee's actual or implied consent. It describes situations where the employer has not directly fired the employee but, by unilaterally changing the terms of employment, forces the employee to quit. Constructive dismissal is sometimes called "disguised dismissal" or "quitting with cause" because it often occurs in situations where the employee is offered the alternative of leaving or of submitting to a unilateral and substantial change to a fundamental term or condition of his/her employment. The confirmation of a constructive dismissal is based on an objective view of the employer's conduct and not solely on the employee's perception.

To demonstrate, an employee may be constructively dismissed if the employer makes changes to conditions that result in a significant reduction in salary or a significant change in such things as work location, hours of work, threats of demotion, withdrawal of specific benefits required to do the job or position. Constructive dismissal may also include situations where an employer makes the working environment intolerable through harassment or abuse of an employee or an employer gives an employee an ultimatum to "quit or be fired" and the employee resigns in response.

The employee would have to resign in response to the significant change within a reasonable period of time in order for the employer's actions to be considered as constructive dismissal.

The leading case on constructive dismissal is the Supreme Court's decision in Farber v. Royal Trust Co. Mr. Farber was a regional manager for Western Québec for Royal Trust, a real estate company. He supervised over 400 real estate agents, and administered 21 offices. With commissions, his income in 1983 had been $150,000, including a $48,000 guaranteed base salary. Royal Trust decided to undertake a major restructuring, part of which involved eliminating its regional manager positions. It offered Mr. Farber a job as the manager of the Dollard branch, a job he had held eight years earlier. It did not offer any guaranteed base salary. Mr. Farber estimated his income would be cut in half. Royal Trust offered him a $40,000 reorientation allowance and a higher commission rate than usual. The Dollard branch (at that time) was not very profitable, so Mr. Farber tried to negotiate for a more profitable branch. Royal Trust refused to vary its offer, so Mr. Farber refused to go to the Dollard branch and sued for constructive dismissal.

The court found that Mr. Farber had been constructively dismissed. In Mr. Farber's case, he had been demoted and his income had been cut in half. His demotion would have resulted in a considerable loss of status because he would have been supervising fewer employees in a smaller, less profitable region. The fact that the Dollard branch was one of the least profitable in Québec further undermined his status. The change in compensation was damaging to Mr. Farber, not only because he would earn less, but because removing his base salary entirely would subject him to greater fluctuations in income.

Temporary Layoff

An employee is on temporary layoff when an employer cuts back or stops the employee's work without ending his/her employment (e.g. laying someone off at times when there is not enough work to do). An employer may put an employee on a temporary layoff without confirming a date on which the employee will be recalled to work.

For example, a dental practice in Hope, B.C., was struggling around the time one of its receptionists was ready to return after a medical leave. The dentist couldn't afford to have her back right away and felt he could afford to pay her in a few months. He checked the province's employment standards legislation, saw the allowance for temporary layoff, and informed the receptionist she would be laid off for just less than 13 weeks.

Unfortunately for the dentist, there had been no previous layoffs and nothing in the receptionist's employment contract that allowed for a layoff. After being contacted by the receptionist's lawyer, he realized the situation and quickly offered her immediate reinstatement.

The matter went to the B.C. Supreme Court, however, which found the dentist liable for compensation from the time of the receptionist's layoff to reinstatement.

Probation

In some provinces, the legal rights of an employee are different during the employee's initial term of probation so it is important to determine if you are under probation to fully understand what your rights are.

Probation is defined as a trial period (usually 3 or 6 months) during which the employer will review and evaluate the employee to determine if s/he is suitable for ongoing employment. Under no circumstances does this status give the employer the right to discriminate or harass you; however, the conditions for dismissal may be less rigorous.

A probationary period cannot be implied or assumed into a contract of employment and automatically imposed on the employee. In order to establish an employee's probationary status, it must be done within the written offer of employment and agreed to <u>before</u> the employee starts to work. If the employee accepts a verbal offer of employment that does not specify a probationary period, then no probationary period applies. The burden is on the employer to prove an alleged probationary term.

It is generally understood that the standards of proof for cause for termination is lower for probationary employees than it is for "regular" employees who have completed their probation. However, this does not give an employer a license to treat the employee unfairly; for example, to fire the employee after 3 days of 3 month probation or for a department's production decline unrelated to the probationary employee. Any termination must be performance related as outlined in the employment contract or offer letter.

An employer may not unilaterally extend a probationary period without the consent of the employee.

An employer has the right to terminate a probationary employee without notice or severance where the employer can establish that it acted fairly and with reasonable diligence in determining whether or not the proposed employee was suitable in the job for which s/he was being tested. As long as the probationary employee is given a reasonable opportunity to demonstrate his/her ability to meet the standards the employer sets out at the time of hiring, including the ability of the person to work in harmony with others, his/her potential value to the employer in the future and other factors deemed by the employer to be essential to the acceptable performance of the position, then the employee has no legal complaint.

What is important to note is that the employment standards in most provinces allow the employer to terminate an employee on probation with no notice or pay in lieu of notice.

Here is a high level summary of current legislation in each jurisdiction:

Jurisdiction	Legislation
BC, Alberta, Ontario, Newfoundland & Labrador, Nova Scotia, Québec, Saskatchewan, NWT, Nunavut, Federal	No minimum notice required for employee dismissed with the first **three** months of employment
New Brunswick, PEI, Yukon	No minimum notice required for employee dismissed with the first **six** months of employment
Manitoba	No minimum notice required for employee dismissed with the first **one** month of employment. Otherwise, two weeks' notice is required.

Discrimination

All jurisdictions in Canada have agencies who deal with human rights complaints and legislation designed to address discriminatory practices for "protected classes" in the workplace. "Protected classes" refers to one's race, creed, colour, ethnic origin, age, gender, sexual orientation, marital status, pregnancy status, citizenship, ancestry, place of origin, family status, record of offences and disability. Many laws have identifiable elements that help you determine whether you might have been treated unlawfully.

Discrimination claims are a little different. You may have a "gut feeling" that you were discriminated against. But how can you tell if you have a valid case? There are numerous questions that you can ask yourself to help determine whether discrimination played a part in your termination.

Evidence of Discrimination

Direct Evidence. "Direct Evidence" is the best way to show that discrimination occurred. Direct evidence of discrimination includes statements by managers or supervisors that directly relate the adverse action against you to your protected class status. For example, if your employer tells you that you are being let go because you are near retirement age and the company wants to go with a younger image, you have direct evidence that your protected class status was the cause of your termination. This evidence can be in the form of verbal comments or statements written in emails, letters, instant messages (IMs), texts, memos, or notes.

Circumstantial Evidence. The likelihood of obtaining direct evidence of discrimination is extremely low. Supervisors and other company personnel are usually too sophisticated and too well-trained to openly express their biases and prejudices. In almost every case, an employee must rely on circumstantial evidence. An example could be a policy or practice when a hiring manager repeatedly posts managerial job openings only in male dominated departments. It is not as blatant unless you have evidence to the intention of the hiring manager.

A person claiming discrimination who does not have direct evidence must produce enough circumstantial evidence of discrimination to allow a jury to find that the employer acted with prejudice. The law recognizes that persons can be discriminated against even if they were not replaced by someone outside of the protected class, for example during a mass layoff.

Questions to ask yourself:

- Are you a member of a protected class? For example, if you are claiming age discrimination, are you over 40? If you are claiming disability discrimination, are you disabled?
- Were you qualified for your position? For example, if your job required you to be a licensed technician, were you licensed?
- Did your employer take unfavorable action against you? For instance, were you demoted or fired?
- Were you replaced by a person who is not in your protected class (or, in the case of age discrimination, someone substantially younger than you)?
- Were you treated differently than a similarly situated person who is not in your protected class?
- Did managers or supervisors regularly make rude or derogatory comments directed at your protected class status or at all members of your class and related to work? For example, "Women don't belong on a construction site" or "Older employees are set in their ways and make terrible managers".
- Are the circumstances of your treatment so unusual, outrageous, unjust, or severe as to suggest discrimination?
- Does your employer have a history of showing bias toward persons in your protected class?
- Are there noticeably few employees of your protected class at your workplace?
- Have you noticed that other employees of your protected class seem to be singled out for negative treatment or are put in dead-end jobs?

- Have you heard other employees in your protected class complain about discrimination, particularly by the supervisor or manager who took the adverse action against you?
- Are there statistics that show favoritism towards or bias against any group?
- Did your employer violate company policy in the way s/he treated you?
- Did your employer retain less qualified, non-protected employees in the same job?

Once you establish an action or pattern of discrimination, consider the reason that your company gave for terminating you. In court, an employer has the opportunity to offer a legitimate, non-discriminatory reason for its conduct. This is not very difficult for an employer to do. All that the law requires is that the employer states a legitimate reason. It does not have to prove that it is the true reason. A company can almost always come up with some reason for the action that it took. Once the employer articulates this reason, your proof of discrimination is gone and you will have to offer additional evidence, as discussed below.

If the employer cannot offer a valid reason for your termination, you have proven a case of discrimination. However, don't count on this happening. You may think, "my employer can never come up with a good reason for firing me!" You need to remember that your employer doesn't need a "good" reason, just any reason besides your protected status. The vast majority of employers can do this and do this regularly.

Assuming that your employer can offer any explanation at all for terminating your employment, you must next consider whether you can prove that the reason is just a cover-up for discrimination. There are several ways to do this.

Can you show that the stated reason is:

- Factually untrue?
- Insufficient to have actually motivated your discharge?
- So riddled with errors that your employer could not have legitimately relied upon it?
- Is false because you have direct or circumstantial evidence that demonstrates that your protected status is more likely to have motivated your employer than the stated reason?
- Inconsistent with a pattern of warnings, terminations or disciplinary action of others?

If you can demonstrate any of the above, you may be able to prove that the employer's stated reason is just a smoke screen for discrimination. The law requires you to show not only that the stated reason is false, but that the unlawful factor was the real reason, or that the employer's stated reason and your protected status both played a role in your termination.

Racial Discrimination

Let's look at a simple hypothetical example to illustrate discrimination based racial bias. Darryl is of minority race and has been at ABC Company for two years. Darryl feels discriminated against because of his race in relation to opportunities for promotion and job assignments. Generally, it seems like minorities are not being promoted as frequently as non-minorities in the company. Darryl wants to complain about how the races are being treated differently, but he wants to be discreet about it.

So Darryl goes to his supervisor and talks about how hard it is for people to move up at ABC, but doesn't use the word "race". He discusses how he knows he does a good job, and some co-workers don't perform as well, yet those co-workers get promoted and get better assignments. (Darryl is referring to the white co-workers, but he doesn't openly say that.) The supervisor speculates that the plant manager has it in for Darryl and they talk about some minor incidents that have happened and he agrees that those incidents might have caused the plant manager to dislike him. (Darryl knows that the plant manager also might have reason to dislike the white co-workers who still get promotions and good assignments, but he doesn't mention that.)

At no point does Darryl clarify that his complaint is based on how the races are treated differently. Darryl avoids saying "race discrimination". In addition, Darryl is also a bit scared of being too aggressive in raising the race issue as he fears losing his job.

Within six months, Darryl has been fired. The company does not like complainers. The company fears that Darryl is setting them up for a discrimination lawsuit. How did they justify his termination?

After the discussions, the supervisor began closely scrutinizing Darryl's work, watching his time, writing him up whenever justifiable (even though in the past most little things were overlooked). Eventually, Darryl is placed on formal discipline for poor performance or rule violations or attendance (minor infractions mostly). After another short time, Darryl is terminated for violating the terms of his discipline by committing additional poor performance or rule violations.

Darryl contacted a lawyer because he feels he has been wrongfully terminated because he got disciplined for infractions that others don't get disciplined for. The lawyer asks him about incidents that happened at work that might have caused the employer to want to be rid of Darryl. He recalls that he made the verbal complaint to the supervisor six months ago. He describes the circumstances.

Darryl might have two potential cases, one for discrimination and one for retaliation. Both cases have their challenges and problems.

Darryl's lawyer feels that Darryl committed several errors in how he made his complaint, errors that weaken his potential retaliation case. If a court concludes that Darryl's complaint was not a "discrimination" complaint, then his retaliation claim may get dismissed. If only Darryl had been less modest with his accusations. For example:

- Darryl did **not** say he felt discriminated against because of his race. It would have been to his advantage to state the legal category that might apply to his complaint that he was making, rather than be evasive because the employer will argue that he did not in fact make a race discrimination complaint and therefore did not gain protection against retaliation.

- Darryl did **not** state any facts in his complaint which directly tend to show that discrimination might be occurring. He could have talked about whites getting treated better, but he did not. It's not necessarily enough even if he had mentioned "race". Courts like to see examples of race-related mistreatment in order to objectively understand that a complaint is made in good faith. A good solid complaint will mention "race" and will use race-related examples.

- Darryl said damaging things during the complaint process about how he agreed that the plant manager might have it in for him due to some incidents in the past. This makes it look like Darryl did not believe he was being discriminated against due to race, but rather because of ongoing problems stemming from old events including long-simmering personality conflicts. So Darryl undermined both his potential retaliation claim and his potential race discrimination claim.

- Darryl did not complain to Human Resources or to some designated high-level manager. It's best to get the problem into the hands of Human Resources or people with more power to fix it than front-line supervisors, especially if front-line supervisors are the source of the problem.

There are big problems in Darryl's case now. Those problems could cause the case to get tossed out of court on the technicality that he didn't say enough of the right issues and he said too much of the wrong issues in his complaint. So what could have been a thriving retaliation case is now a more questionable case that may or may not be worthwhile depending on many other facts and circumstances.

In addition to the errors above, Darryl missed an opportunity. He did not complain in writing. It's best to make a written complaint using relevant facts. Darryl missed an opportunity. Verbal complaints allow the employer to dispute what he claims he said in his complaint, but he is still allowed to testify to his own recollection, however, a written complaint would end any speculation about what Darryl said.

Unfortunately, the problems Darryl faces in this example are not unique to racial discrimination. All such cases involve complaints and so any case could have the same problems as Darryl faces unless followed through properly.

Gender Discrimination

Gender discrimination occurs when actions or policies limit advancement due to gender, pregnancy, child bearing capacity, sterilization, fertility or related medical conditions. Examples include interview questions that focus on whether you are married or pregnant or plan to have a family. Some company policies such as classifying a job as "male" or "female"; paying different wages based on gender; or having separate paths for promotions or occupations based on gender.

Sexual Harassment

Sexual harassment, seen as a form of gender discrimination, is defined as being a recipient of unwelcome conduct of a sexual nature that negatively affects the work environment or leads to job-related consequences for the recipient of the harassment. It could amount to just cause for dismissal on the basis that it is conduct that is destructive to the employment relationship. A factor which significantly influences a court in deciding whether sexual harassment amounts to just cause for dismissal is whether the employer has a clear policy or procedure on sexual harassment which is enforced in the workplace on a daily basis. Was the employee told and understand that sexual harassment was completely unacceptable within the workplace.

Sexual harassment may occur when:

- Someone says or does things to you of a sexual nature which you do not welcome. This includes behaviour that a person should know you do not expect, want or welcome including sexual comments, jokes, pictures and/or physical contact such as brushing up against you.

- A person having authority or power over you (manager, supervisor, etc.) makes sexual suggestions or demands that you do not want or welcome.

- A person having authority or power denies you something important, such as a promotion or review, punishes you or threatens to do something to you for refusing a request of a sexual or non-platonic nature.

A particularly tough battle occurs when you complain about sexual harassment and end up quitting your job. In such a situation, the company's conclusion might be that you did not properly go through the complaint process about sexual harassment before quitting and therefore you can't sue over the employer's failure to stop the harassment. For example: a woman who quit due to ongoing sexual harassment did not properly complete the complaint process. She quit her job too soon and therefore she loses her case in court.

In the case Pond vs. Canada Post, heard before the Canadian Human Rights Tribunal ("CHRT") followed as such:

Pond was an employee who worked at Canada Post. She complained that her immediate supervisor sexually harassed her by using a pornographic statuette as the basis for making offensive comments about her. The supervisor in reference to this statue said in front of other employees and Pond that: "Women are only good for two things: secretarial work and house work.". On other occasions and in front of other employees, the supervisor would make numerous comments of a sexual nature about Pond's sex life. Furthermore, she argued that the supervisor's permission and encouragement to male employees to post posters of naked women in the workplace also constituted sexual harassment. The CHRT held that the statuette and the posters in combination with the comments constituted sexual harassment.

In order to win a claim for sexual harassment, your evidence needs to show a pattern of behaviour and that you have not been participating in it yourself. Therefore, if your work environment regularly shares raunchy jokes and you have willingly contributed to the discussions, then you would have a very difficult case as your participation can be seen as consent.

Age Discrimination

Age discrimination affects workers at both ends of the age spectrum. However, it is very difficult to prove in a court.

Age discrimination most commonly impacts people over the age of 50 as they are generally at the higher end of the wage scale, closer to taking their pension and require higher health benefits. What they don't realize is that studies have shown that a 50+ employee is less expensive to hire and train, has lower absences and turnover rates, is more flexible with their schedules, costs less in damage or theft liabilities, and is more efficient and more productive than younger workers are.

The case of Kearns v. Dickson Trucking Ltd. is one example in which age discrimination was successfully proven. However, the evidence in that case was overwhelming and there was no other reasonable explanation for the termination. The complainant, a 69-year-old salesman, was the best in the organization and there were no complaints at any time about his performance. He was terminated on the basis of "a lack of potential in the area serviced by him", however, the first time this issue was ever raised was in the letter of termination. His position was not declared redundant but rather was filled by a younger person. Mr. Kearns was awarded damages for lost wages and for hurt feelings and self-respect.

Age discrimination can happen to young employees as well. Most often, employers tend to discriminate against young people during the hiring process as they may fear the stereotype that young people are not reliable, party too hard, won't want to work long hours and won't be dedicated to being with an employer for a long period. Some other examples of age discrimination based on youth occurs when someone makes a "joking" statement directed at the young employee like "is this bring your kid to work day?".

While some younger employees say they've had their age held against them, older workers still bear the brunt of discrimination.

Duty to Accommodate/Disabilities

Employers have a duty to accommodate disabled employees to the point of "undue hardship." Undue hardship consists of several factors: financial cost, health & safety requirements and outside sources of funding. (Some provinces have more factors.)

There are various disabilities that are protected from discrimination: mental, physical (mobility, blindness, deaf, etc.), disease (AIDS, Cancer, etc.), obesity, depression, colour blindness, speech impediment, fear of flying, panic attacks and addiction. Courts, tribunals and human rights commissions have become increasingly active in promoting the protection of disabled employees under human rights legislation.

For example, in Keays vs. Honda, Kevin Keays was employed with Honda Canada Inc. ("Honda") for 14 years. Mr. Keays developed Chronic Fatigue Syndrome ("CFS") and initially took a disability leave in October 1996, returning in December 1998. After the long-term disability insurer denied further compensation, Mr. Keays returned to work despite his protests and that of his doctors that he remained disabled. After his return, and as a result of the CFS, Mr. Keays had to take a number of days off work, which became a contentious issue between Honda and Mr. Keays.

Although there is no dispute that Honda initially accommodated Mr. Keays' absences, Honda later asked Mr. Keays to provide a medical note for each absence. This caused friction between the parties. In March 2000, Honda also "coached" Mr. Keays, a form of discipline which Mr. Keays disagreed with. In early 2000, Mr. Keays asked Honda to remove the "coaching" from his record and to remove the requirement that he provide a medical note for each absence. Honda denied this request. Mr. Keays then hired a lawyer to deal with the issue. In response, Honda asked Mr. Keays to meet with an occupational medicine specialist. The pretext for this meeting was based on Honda's position that "we no longer accept that you have a disability requiring you to be absent… In order for Dr. Brennen to get to know you and understand completely your condition, we advised that we would arrange for Dr. Brennen to meet with you".

Mr. Keays advised, through his lawyer, that he would not meet with Dr. Brennen unless the purpose and parameters of the assessment were clarified. Honda responded by terminating Mr. Keays for insubordination.

The court found Honda discriminated against Mr. Keays and operated in bad faith citing Honda's failure to accommodate Mr. Keays' disability, which is a breach of the Ontario Human Rights Code, and therefore an "independent actionable wrong".

Employees who are addicted to drugs and alcohol are considered to be disabled. Employers usually are expected to go to considerable lengths to provide time off, modified duties and access to assistance to accommodate such employees.

In Fantom Technologies Inc., an employee with a drug and alcohol addiction was required to take substance abuse treatment under a last-chance agreement ("LCA"). These agreements state that, if there is any repetition of the problematic behaviour, the employee is automatically dismissed. LCAs also commonly state that the employee will have no right to contest or arbitrate the firing, except on the narrow ground as to whether the employer has proven that the problematic behaviour has in fact been repeated. As well, any further lateness or absences would be grounds for termination, without any right to grieve.

The employee was subsequently late and absent on several occasions and, as per the agreement, he was terminated. A lawsuit was filed and the arbitrator determined that both the last chance condition and the 'cannot-grieve' clause were discriminatory, and therefore invalid:

"…a condition was imposed upon [the employee] because of his handicap, which subjected him to a review process particular to him, and not imposed upon his fellow employees. And the fact that he agreed to it, does not render the Agreement any less unenforceable."

The employee was ordered to be returned to work. The arbitrator noted that the employer had not presented any evidence that the employee's absenteeism was so bad that it could no longer be tolerated by the employer.

National Origin/Ethnicity

Discrimination towards people of any ethnicity should never be tolerated. While most people are familiar with more blatant forms of racial discrimination such as not promoting people who are visible minorities, there are also more subtle forms. Employers cannot ask where you were born; however, they are allowed to ask if you are authorized to work in Canada. While the latter question can be asked for perfectly legitimate reasons, it can also be used to find out your citizenship.

Another form of discrimination occurs if an employer implements speaking English only rules in the workplace. There are times when it may be a business necessity (i.e. dealing with customers); however, an employer cannot enforce such a rule when you are on a meal or coffee break.

Religion

Some religions have practices and rituals that need to be attended to during the work shift. Employers need to accommodate these activities as long as it does not impose any undue burden on the business activities such as altering work schedules or relaxing dress codes. However, there are times when it may be necessary for safety reasons to side with the employer (i.e., in construction jobs that require the use of a hard hat).

Religious discrimination complaints most commonly arise when employees lose their jobs after they refuse — for religious reasons — to work on certain days. This scenario represents the highest number of religious discrimination cases. However, it is important to recognize that the court will look at the _effect_ of a particular rule, rather than its _intent._ If a rule has a discriminatory effect, the employer must take reasonable steps to accommodate, unless accommodation would create undue hardship. The responsibility of showing undue hardship falls to the employer.

In O'Malley v. Simpsons-Sears Ltd. (1985), Theresa O'Malley, a long-time employee of the respondent, became a Seventh Day Adventist. She could no longer work between sundown Friday and sundown Saturday (her Sabbath), in accordance with the tenets of her new faith. The respondent's policy required all full-time employees to work during that time period, on a rotating basis. Mrs. O'Malley therefore lost her full-time status, leading to the human rights complaint on religious grounds. The court recognized that the company's policy of opening for business on Saturdays stemmed from sound business objectives and <u>not</u> from any desire or intent to discriminate against certain employees.

However, a similar situation can go the other way. In Drager v. I.A.M. & A.W. (1994), Daniel Drager was a Seventh Day Adventist, who, like Theresa O'Malley, was required by his religion not to work from sundown Friday to sundown Saturday. While his union suggested alternatives to the occasional times when Mr. Drager would be asked to work on Friday night, the employer insisted that Mr. Drager would have to either obtain a dispensation from his church, make arrangements with other workers to exchange shifts, or move to another city and work in a larger plant where he would be less likely to be asked to work Friday shifts. The court found that accommodation had not been offered by the employer. The employer had rejected the union's suggestions for resolution on the basis that it should not have to incur any expenses in the accommodation process.

In another case, Jones v. C.H.E. Pharmacy Inc. (2001), the religion-based conduct at issue was the refusal of an employee to participate in decorating the store where he worked for Christmas. Mr. Jones is a Jehovah's Witness, and, in accordance with his faith, does not participate in the celebration of Christmas. Jones' faith allowed him to stock shelves with Christmas merchandise but forbade him from decorating the store for Christmas. For sixteen years, his employer accommodated his religious beliefs. On November 10, 1988, his supervisor asked him to hang a garland. Jones complied, but felt sick inside. A few days later, the manager asked him to hang a Santa Claus decoration. He refused, claiming that his religious beliefs prohibited him from doing so. Five days later, he refused the same supervisor's request to set out poinsettias. That same day, he was called into a meeting with the owner of the store who told him to set out poinsettias or face immediate dismissal.

Jones left the office, cleaned out his locker, and filed a human rights complaint. In the hearing, the employer claimed that the requirement to set out poinsettias was not discriminatory, since the flowers were considered merchandise, which Jones was allowed to stock, and not decorations.

The B.C. Human Rights Tribunal found that the employer knew that Mr. Jones' religious beliefs prevented him from participating in any celebration of Christmas, including decorating the store. Rather than attempting to accommodate those beliefs, the employer gave Jones an ultimatum: decorate or be fired. Setting out poinsettias at the front of the store was both displaying

Christmas decorations, because poinsettias are festive, and stocking merchandise, because the poinsettias were for sale. However, although the store was selling the flowers, they served to decorate the store and to entice customers to shop there. Mr. Jones, whose faith prohibits him from displaying decorations, was therefore discriminated against with respect to a term or condition of employment because of his religion when he was fired for refusing to set out poinsettias. It would not have incurred hardship to accommodate Mr. Jones. The supervisor who had asked Mr. Jones to set out poinsettias admitted that he did the job himself in a few minutes.

Workplace Bullying or Mobbing

Bullying is usually seen as acts or verbal comments that could 'mentally' hurt or isolate a person in the workplace. Sometimes, bullying can involve negative physical contact as well. Bullying usually involves repeated incidents or a pattern of behaviour that is intended to intimidate, offend, degrade or humiliate a particular person or group of people. It has also been described as the assertion of power through aggression.

Mobbing is an extreme form of workplace bullying that devastates the lives of its target. It refers to a social interaction, through which one individual is attacked by a group of individuals on almost a daily basis and for periods of many months, forcing the person into an almost helpless position. Some of the worst cases of mobbing go on for long periods of time and can actually continue for many years causing severe, sometimes irreparable psychological, emotional and physical health damage. In the worst cases this abuse has lead to suicide and even incidents of workplace violence. Not infrequently, mobbing can spell the end of the target's career, marriage, health, and livelihood. From a study of circumstances surrounding suicides in Sweden, it was estimated that about twelve percent of people who take their own lives have recently been mobbed at work.

Examples include:

- Spreading malicious rumours, gossip, or innuendo that is not true.
- Excluding or isolating someone socially.
- Intimidating a person.
- Undermining or deliberately impeding a person's work.
- Physically abusing or threatening abuse.
- Removing areas of responsibilities without cause.
- Constantly changing work guidelines.

- Establishing impossible deadlines that will set up the individual to fail.

- Withholding necessary information or purposefully giving the wrong information.

- Making jokes that are 'obviously offensive' by spoken word or e-mail.

- Intruding on a person's privacy by pestering, spying or stalking.

- Assigning unreasonable duties or workload which are unfavourable to one person (in a way that creates unnecessary pressure).

- Underwork - creating a feeling of uselessness.

- Yelling or using profanity.

- Criticising a person persistently or constantly.

- Belittling a person's opinions.

- Unwarranted (or undeserved) punishment.

- Blocking applications for training, leave or promotion.

- Tampering with a person's personal belongings or work equipment.

There is a "fine line" between strong management and bullying. Comments that are objective and are intended to provide constructive feedback are not usually considered bullying, but rather are intended to assist the employee with their work.

People who are the targets of bullying may experience a range of effects. These reactions include:

- Shock.
- Anger.
- Feelings of frustration and/or helplessness.
- Increased sense of vulnerability.
- Loss of confidence.
- Physical symptoms such as inability to sleep or loss of appetite.
- Psychosomatic symptoms such as stomach pains or headaches.
- Panic or anxiety, especially about going to work.
- Family tension and stress.
- Inability to concentrate.
- Low morale and productivity.

If you feel that you are being bullied, discriminated against, victimized or subjected to any form of harassment:

- Firmly tell the person that his/her behaviour is not acceptable and request that they stop. You may ask a supervisor to be with you when you approach the person.
- Keep a factual journal or diary of daily events. Record:
    - ✓ The date, time and what happened in as much detail as possible
    - ✓ The names of witnesses.
    - ✓ The outcome of the event.

    Remember, it is not just the character of the incidents, but the number, frequency, and especially the pattern that can reveal the bullying or harassment.
- Keep copies of any letters, memos, e-mails, faxes, etc., received from the person.
- Report the harassment to the person listed in your workplace policy, your supervisor, or an HR manager. If your concerns are minimized, report to the next level of management.
- Do not retaliate! You may end up looking like the instigator. This may cause confusion and inconsistencies for the people responsible for evaluating and responding to your situation.

Most Canadian jurisdictions have a "general duty provision" in their Occupational Health & Safety legislation, which requires employers to take all reasonable precautions to protect the health and safety of all employees. Jurisdictions in Canada that have specific workplace violence prevention regulations include Alberta, British Columbia, Saskatchewan, Manitoba, Nova Scotia and Prince Edward Island, as well as Federally regulated workplaces.

In 2002 the province of Québec enacted the Psychological Harassment at Work Act, which provides that every employee has a right to a work environment free from psychological harassment. Employers must take reasonable action to prevent psychological harassment and, whenever they become aware of such behaviour, to put a stop to it.

Under the Ontario Occupational Health and Safety Act 1979, "all employers must take every precaution reasonable in the circumstances to protect the health and safety of their workers in the workplace. This includes protecting them against the risk of workplace violence". Under the act, workplace violence is defined as "...the attempted or actual exercise of any intentional physical force that causes or may cause physical injury to a worker. It also includes any threats which give a worker reasonable grounds to believe he or she is at risk of physical injury". However, the Ontario Occupational Health and Safety Act does not specifically cover the issue of psychological harassment. The Bill-29 amendment protects "workers from harassment and violence in the workplace" and includes protection from psychological abuse and bullying behaviors in the Ontario workplace.

Saskatchewan made workplace bullying illegal in 2007 by passing The Occupational Health and Safety (Harassment Prevention) Amendment Act. The act broadened the definition of harassment to include psychological harassment.

How to Tell You are Being Terminated

Most people are completely blindsided when they are terminated. But termination is not a process that happens overnight. It takes some time to get the paperwork ready and coordinate the parties that need to know (i.e. HR, IT, Security, etc.). Here are some typical signs that you may be marked for termination other than the obvious like losing a major account or screwing up a major project.

Has Your Area of Control Been Reduced? Any reorganization in which you no longer have the full level of control as before is a sign that you're getting moved out. If your manager tells you he's reassigning some of your responsibilities to another employee to lighten your heavy load, don't fall for it. It's just a diplomatic way for your manager to say he no longer believes you can do the job.

Have You Been Left Out of Key Meetings and Decisions? If you are respected and accomplished, you're asked for your opinion. So when you're suddenly no longer asked to weigh in on key issues, especially that affect your area or that you have been engaged in before, it can signify that your coworkers don't see you as strategic, your subordinates have lost confidence in you or you've become an barrier to getting things done and they'd sooner move ahead without you.

Are You Being Treated Like a Telemarketer Calling During the Dinner Hour When You Try to Get Buy-In? Not being able to get approval for your plans, individual projects or budget can indicate that your peers or management no longer support you. It shows you're not in tune with your colleagues or your company's needs. Or that your secret successor has been chosen. You can't be effective or successful without buy-in.

Do You Have to Constantly Fight to Get Anything Done? If colleagues are always arguing with you in meetings and they either don't listen to or rebuff your ideas, it indicates that your objectives are not the company's objectives or that you are being set up to fail.

Do You Find That Your Top Priorities No Longer Match Up With Your Manager's? This is a clear indication that you and your manager are drifting apart and, unless you get back in alignment with him/her, s/he may decide to let you go. Similarly, if you find your lines of communication with your boss are vanishing—or worse, s/he assigns you to report to someone else—it means you no longer matter in his/her strategy. If you were, s/he'd devote a portion of his/her valuable time to you.

Does Your Supervisor Minimize Your Accomplishments? If you're doing back flips and your peers are saying they didn't notice or refuse to recognize, that's pretty bleak. It shows a lack of respect and that your colleagues don't see what you're doing as worthwhile or they sense that you will not be in the fold too long.

Does Your Boss Ask You to Work On "Special Projects"? Special projects are a euphemism for busy work. When you're assigned to special projects only, it means the boss has lost so much confidence in your ability to lead that s/he's trying to get you off the high-profile projects you had been working on until s/he can find a replacement for you. For example, if you are asked to work on a special project that involved investigating opportunities for a new product line in Eastern Europe but the company has no plans for expansion into Eastern Europe any time soon, and you weren't given a staff or a travel budget. This is a sure sign that you are in line to be thanked for coming out and let go.

Did You See a Confidential Search Ad That Describes Your Job to a Tee? You see (or worse a friend notices) a job posted on an online website that describes your job exactly in a company that sounds suspiciously like yours.

Are People Avoiding You At All Costs? Eye-contact is difficult to make with someone if you know his or her head is on the chopping block. Small talk is just as tough. It's best just to avoid that person altogether. So if people are no longer doing that fun "stop 'n' chat" in the hall or the coffee room empties or suddenly quiets down to an awkward silence when you enter, then guess what?…you may just be a marked man or woman for termination.

Are You Being Given Impossible Jobs With No Chance Of Success? This one is underhanded; which is why it's so popular. You are being set up for failure. The company needs a legitimate reason to give you the boot, especially if you've done everything right and are the key to your team. Enter the impossible project. If you've been given a thankless task, at least be thankful for the obvious tip-off that you're about to get the boot.

Are Your Responsibilities Redefined So That You Have Less Responsibility Than the Boss' Kid? Being "streamlined" of your responsibilities is a sure-fire sign that there's something unpleasant on the way. After all, you don't fire someone who's got a ton of important work to do, with loads of people underneath him/her. So, be mindful if you are given a new job title with less work, less budget, less people (or no people) and yet you have a hard time finding anything of any real value to do all day. Not long after this, you may be out.

Has Your Office, Cubicle or Working Space Recently Been Downsized? When employees are in the firing line, it's a lot easier to move them around and downsize their environment without worrying about their morale. If you are reading this in your new 6ft by 6ft cubicle with no lights on a 5 year old PC with a 200MB hard drive and dot matrix printer to match, you're not exactly a valued employee any more.

Do People Whisper More or Does the Conversation Change as You Approach? If you're marked for termination, you'll be the last one to know about it. And being the mature responsible people that they are, your co-workers will be quite happy to whisper about your impending doom in a corner of break room while sipping their coffees. Until you show up, when suddenly the conversation will change abruptly to something really original…like the weather.

Have You Recently Been Asked to Take Some Time Off? As we know, companies in North America are not prone to encouraging vacation time (compared to Europe, where they get tons of time off). If you are encouraged to take vacation but it is not to use up your annual allotment before end of the fiscal year before you lose it or for a genuine reward for a huge project you've just finished, then you are in trouble. When the boss tells you to take a break, they're more than likely telling you that they'd rather not have you in the office.

Are You Noticing Paper Trails Between Yourself and Your Superiors? Suddenly, you now notice everything is happening via emails instead of casual conversations. There's a reason for that. HR requires written/printed evidence of everything if there's to be a firing. A paper trail is necessary to determine that your manager did everything by the book, and to record every single one of your screw-ups. So, if you've gone from getting a few emails per week, to a daily deluge of paper and a full inbox, these are warning signs that you're being watched very closely.

Have You Recently Been Promoted to a Position of Less Responsibility? If the company promotes you into a newly created role, with less responsibility and no direct reports, then you may be faced with position elimination. It's hard to fire someone. It's easy to eliminate a position. You can get rid of anyone, even protected classes (older folks, pregnant women etc) if you simply eliminate a position. If you were formerly "Manager of Client Services" and are now "Director In Charge Of Special Project Development" (and there have never been any special projects), you may as well collect your personal effects from your cubicle now.

What To Do If You Are Targeted For Termination.

Here are some things to do that are essential to survive this process whether termination occurs or not.

Document, Document, Document!

Be sure to collect (hard and soft copies) of all documents (emails, memos, status reports, etc.) that confirms that you have done your work and have completed it on time. Ensure that you are not collecting documents that you are not authorized to have in your possession as this will backfire in any future claim. It shows an employee in a light of acting in bad faith and with dishonourable intentions and is therefore highly cautioned against. The reason for gathering hard copies is in case you are terminated and your network access is immediately removed as in the vast majority of cases. As well, network activity is monitored so you don't want them to see that you are emailing confidential company information to an external source even if it is yourself.

Create a Journal

Keep a log or journal of all pertinent events such as dates, times, locations and participants of activities that you have completed successfully. Don't bother tracking other people's issues as it will look that you have spent your time targeting other people. When you need to defend yourself, pointing the finger at others is not an effective nor respectable strategy.

Create a Narrative of Events.

Include items such as:

- When you started work.
- How you performed early on.
- When your employment took a turn for the worse.
- To what do you attribute that turn.
- Basis as to why you attribute it to that cause.
- Significant events to date following that turn.
- Relevant comments made and by whom to whom.

Remember to make notes on a same-day basis at home. Do not make notes at work because that may either tip people off that you are preparing for legal action or co-workers may be disturbed thinking that you are writing about them.

Create a List of Witnesses

It is easier to make a list of potential witnesses while you are still employed. Make sure you list names, addresses and telephone numbers and any unsolicited relevant comments that they may have made.

Network

If you feel strongly that you are targeted for termination, then start looking for a new job now. Don't wait until you are fired as it is easier to find a job when you are still employed. This way, when interviewing for other job opportunities, you don't have to give a reason as to why you are no longer employed.

Do Your Job

Although you may be under a great deal of stress with the prospect of losing your job, keep doing it at the best performance level you can. Don't make it easy for your employer to fire you. This practice will not only make it difficult for an employer to terminate you, it will keep your good reputation, dignity and self respect intact by staying professional throughout this ordeal. Look at it as an exercise that is well worth the effort in the long run for your career growth especially when your work environment is in a state of flux. Learning to cope with stress in the workplace is one of the best career builders in today's economic environment.

Mend Fences

Make sure that your relationships with your co-workers are positive and they still see you as a team player. You don't want to give them reason to provide unfavourable information about you to your employer. Plus you will need good references in case you proceed with legal action. Always try to think about how your actions might affect things for you and others beyond the immediate moment.

Be Mindful of Upcoming Dates

Sometimes, companies will schedule terminations prior to an important date (i.e. the start of a new fiscal year, before a shareholder's meeting, prior to scheduled bonuses, etc.). Be aware of these types of dates and be prepared for them. As well, over the past decade, many corporations have an unwritten policy about which days of the week to let people go. The most popular days are Tuesdays and Wednesdays so if your supervisor schedules a last minute meeting on those days with little description of the topic and you can't find him/her all day to inquire, be prepared. Few companies fire people on Fridays anymore as studies have proven that anger and retaliation (i.e. going "postal") occurs most often when people are terminated on Fridays.

Avoid Traps

Managers are looking for a key excuse to terminate so don't make it easy for them. Therefore, don't be late, don't violate company rules, don't take long lunches, don't make mistakes on the job, don't make personal phone calls, don't have long chats with co-workers, etc. Focus on your work, be professional and don't give in to the pressure of their scrutiny.

Maintain Your Focus

Don't disengage because of the stress or the feeling that you have no options. Make sure that you are fully effective in your job and perform like nothing is wrong. Don't withdraw from discussions. Don't act like you are about to be fired because instead of getting people's support, you will end up with your co-workers distancing themselves from you so that they are associated with a "marked" man/woman.

Do Not Confront Your Boss

One of the worst things you can do is ask your boss if s/he is going to fire you. You are just reminding him/her that s/he can. It will put your supervisor in a defensive position. It will also show him/her that you are already mentally prepared to go which is advantageous to him.

Do Not Be Self Destructive

Do not file complaints or stress-related claims that have no written concrete evidence as it will make you look foolish. You don't want to look desperate or dramatic. If you feel that you want to proceed with this, you may want to consult a lawyer first.

Do Not Go On Vacation

Don't demand to have a vacation suddenly to avoid the situation at work. More terminations are planned while employees are on vacation because it gives management and HR opportunities to hold all the meetings they want about you. As well, it gives them the opportunity to sift through your desk and computer files to find an excuse to terminate you. Obviously, if you had booked a legitimate vacation prior to this situation, don't cancel it.

Do Not Just Quit

Some people feel so much stress that they quit. While tempting, don't do it until you get an objective opinion such as consulting a lawyer. You could be sacrificing income and benefits and any severance owed to you. You could also screw up a good case. Commonly, many people are paranoid and totally misread signals and never realize that they were not targeted for termination after all.

Do Not Make Illegal Media Recordings

It is illegal to make secret media recordings with your boss. If you wish to record a conversation, you must notify him/her prior to turning on the recorder. If you record them without prior consent, you will jeopardize your case (the tape is not admissible anyway), you will provide them grounds for dismissal, or you will permanently damage your reputation and/or relationships in the office.

Do Not Access Information Without Authority

When people feel that they are targeted for termination, they feel that it is within their right to find out what the plans are. In that regard, they sometimes access other people's files, go through papers on their boss's desk, go through drawers not belonging to them or try to access computer files that they are not authorized to read. These acts are all grounds for dismissal and will torpedo your case.

Collecting Your Evidence

Regardless of how righteous you are in your case, the evidence that you produce will be paramount to your success. Here are some key tips on collecting this evidence.

Building Your Case

To build a winning case, the onus is on you to gather as much truthful and relevant evidence, written and oral, as you can. After all, if you go to court, the burden of proof will be on your shoulders as you will have to prove that the employer willing engaged in misconduct in regard to your termination. Even if you don't end up in court, you need to support a case that a judge or arbitrator could find credible in order for your employer to consider settling the claim in your favour.

Organizing Your Documents

Collect and put in chronological order all of the documents that you can find concerning your employment every pay stub, every email, every review. Try, within your company's rules, to get copies of:

- Performance evaluations.
- Disciplinary warnings or reprimands.
- Letters of thanks or praise (from managers, customers, or co-workers).
- Internal memos.
- Company bulletins.
- Attendance record.
- Any document stating the reason for your dismissal.
- Handbooks, manuals, or other documents describing work rules, policies, and procedures.
- Pension benefits and retirement plan information.
- Documents related to your unemployment compensation claim.
- Copies of work assignments including special projects.
- Job description.
- Awards, accolades and/or accomplishments.
- Volunteer and/or charity participation through the company.
- Organizational charts, diagrams, floor plans, etc.

Do not take documents or access information to which you have no right and are not entitled. If you are a union member, ask your union to assist in acquiring documents that are otherwise difficult to obtain, but to which you are legally entitled.

Identifying Your Witnesses

If you think co-workers or others observed your unfair treatment, make a list of their names, home addresses, email addresses and home telephone numbers, along with a summary of what you expect them to say - good or bad. The "bad" or unfriendly witnesses are especially important to know about so that your lawyer can evaluate the damage they might do to your case. You don't want any surprises.

Ask friendly witnesses to give you a written statement of anything they saw or heard in person regarding your situation as soon as you decide to take action against your employer. Memories fade over time. Make sure the witnesses state only the facts of which they are personally aware and give specific examples of what they have seen themselves or what they were told directly. General statements such as, "Everyone knew that the manager was out to get her," are not helpful to your case. Get statements that specify the "who", "what", "when", and "where" of the biased behaviour such as your manager's berating you or interfering with your ability to perform. If possible, have the written statement signed in front of a Notary Public.

Keep in mind that you shouldn't count on witnesses in your company that won't put their observations in writing. Many employees will be fearful of reprisals from the employer if they side with you. So don't assume that just because everyone tells you that they agree with you that they will testify on your behalf.

The most useful witness statements are fact-focused and objective. They should be detailed enough so that whoever reads them - the court, an attorney, or a mediator - will see the "big picture".

If you know of employees who were mistreated in the same way you were, ask them for statements about the way they were treated. If your supervisor, for example, made insulting and demeaning remarks to you and other workers, get statements from the other co-workers that quote or paraphrase the remarks, give the dates on which they were made, and name any others who were present.

Common Mistakes Employers Make

You might assume that even the biggest employers should be well-versed on how to deal with employee issues. But that is not the case. Most companies, regardless of the size, have been found to be sloppy in the way that they manage the rights of their employees. Be aware of these mistakes and ensure that you are not negatively impacted by them.

1. You warned them about the harassment but they didn't do anything about it.

    It is your employer's legal and moral obligation to take effective, direct and corrective action designed to put an immediate stop to the harassment as soon as it is reported. When they do not follow through, they open themselves to a wrongful dismissal lawsuit.

2. After you reported the harassment, they would not let the issue rest.

    Some companies overreact to charges of harassment. In that regard, they may call you into countless meetings to tell your story repeatedly. You end up getting frustrated, angry, intimidated and/or humiliated which makes your employer cynical and try to dissect your story. At this point, you will usually want to be left alone after filing the complaint. Often these post-complaint sessions become as harassing as the initial cause for the complaint.

3. They would not tell you what you did wrong.

    In reaction to increasing privacy concerns, some employers try to protect the identity of complainants against an employee. In doing so, they tend to not provide you with enough information to understand what you did wrong. Therefore, you cannot fix the performance problems effectively as the issues are not clarified.

4. They wouldn't follow up on the information you gave them.

    Sometimes, if an employer needs an investigation to lead to a particular outcome for their own sake, they tend to neglect to follow up on leads that do not result in their favour. This act shows disinterest in truly resolving the issue and disrespect to the complainants. This also has the potential to expose their vulnerability to a lawsuit if this development ever became publicly known.

5. Your supervisor constantly criticized you.

    When an employment relationship begins to deteriorate, the weaknesses in your performance become the target. This is reinforced through constant criticism and negativity either publicly and privately towards you. The employer is sending a strong subliminal message that you are no longer welcome. It is clear that the employer is invested in driving you to quit by trying to deflate and discourage your confidence about future prospects at the company.

6. Your supervisor was never consistent or clear about what was expected of you.

    Whenever it becomes apparent that your supervisor refuses to give you objectives or targets, it shows that they are not investing in your future at the company. It implies that s/he has a different agenda.

7. They were setting you up to fail.

    Employees know when something is going on. You are given vague instructions, if any, and you are quickly condemned for doing it incorrectly. The level of support for you vs. your co-workers is blatantly lower. Your supervisor's response to your mistakes is very different compared to the ones towards your co-workers. Your supervisor sets unattainable performance goals. A jury will look at whether the goals set for you were realistic and achievable and whether any changes were justified.

8. They terminate you without hearing your version of events.

    Sometimes, employees are terminated prior to being able to provide their side of the story. If they refuse to hear you out, then that only reinforces the suspicion that the employer was only interested in using the complaint as an excuse for termination rather than assessing the situation objectively.

9. They terminated you without following their own procedures.

    One of the biggest concerns for an employee whether they are being treated fairly in regard to discipline. If your employer fails to follow its typical personnel practices in dealing with you, it may establish that you were targeted by the use of differential treatment. That failure of consistent treatment among all employs may serve favorably for your case.

10. They fired you just after you received a positive performance review.

    When this occurs, it undermines your employer's allegation that you are a poor performer. Performance reviews are to be taken seriously by employers. A jury would hold them to whatever was documented during those reviews. That is why it is key that you do not sign any review that you do not agree with, ever.

Disciplinary Action

Most terminations are preceded with some sort of disciplinary action whether in the form of verbal warnings or written ones. Receiving a warning or a reprimand is one of the most difficult and stressful experiences on the job. That is why many people unknowingly sabotage themselves when responding under such duress. If you know how to handle the disciplinary action (whether justified or not), you may avoid layoff terminations. You can survive employee discipline if you respond positively and constructively. Always be prepared and professional in any response you may give.

Even if you feel that the discipline is unwarranted, do not argue, raise your voice or be belligerent with your supervisor about the fairness or wisdom of the warning. If the matter becomes a struggle, your boss will interpret your actions as argumentative and that you are unwilling to be a team player. By behaving in an professional manner, you may be surprised how easily you can diffuse the potentially volatile situation. That may seem hard to do when you are feeling under such great stress but tune your perspective to focus on a "bigger picture" that includes a confident understanding of your rights.

After the discussion, think about the content of the discussion without being defensive or blinded by ego. For example, if you are being disciplined for lateness, don't think that because Jimmy does it, it is okay for you. Regardless of how any other employee conducts him/herself, you should always make the best effort to follow the established rules. You don't want to make it easy for management to select you in times of layoffs or cost cutting.

If your actions that are being disciplined are not your fault, for example, if a health problem is the reason for your tardiness, then it is still your responsibility to supply your employer with sufficient information to show it is a health issue and not a behavioural issue. Depending on the severity of your situation, you may require to provide a note from your doctor to verify your condition.

If a verbal warning is more subjective (i.e. bad attitude), it may be harder to manage. You may need to show your supervisor respect regardless of your actual feeling towards him/her. Keep disrespectful opinions to yourself when speaking to your supervisor or coworkers. Make sure you apply this to both verbal and nonverbal communication. Nothing shows disrespect more than a scowl, a heavy sigh, crossed arms, rolling eyes or stares. Body language is the hardest thing to be aware of but one of the most noticeable forms of communication and belligerence.

Be very careful who you trust at the workplace. Many people feel comfortable to bad-mouth their boss or teammate to their "work" friends. Be mindful of what you are saying and to whom. Sometimes another co-worker overhears this conversation and will report it to someone else. Other times your friend may accidentally discuss what you said in another conversation. If your negative comments spread, there will be no way to resolve that issue if you are disciplined about it. Even if you aren't formally disciplined, you will create negative relationships that you may depend on. Like the old adage, you can't unring a bell.

If you have been unable to resolve the verbal warning(s), your supervisory may move it to the next disciplinary level by issuing you a written warning. Be sure to keep calm and professional. If you become enraged and challenge your supervisor for escalating the issue, you will easily convince your supervisor that you cannot work with him/her. Take time to reflect before you act.

If you need clarification, then ask for it. In many cases, a representative from Human Resources will be present. If you need further information (e.g. when the offense occurred, what specifically you have allegedly done, etc.), this is the perfect opportunity to ask questions as long as you are calm and thoughtful. If you have concrete information that can be beneficial to your defense, you can ask permission to say something in your defense. If the warning is based on misinformation, then you need to say so at this opportunity. Otherwise, silence can be interpreted as consent and a later response can be seen as suspicious by your supervisor.

Don't be pressured to sign any disciplinary documents that you don't agree with. You are not obligated to sign such documents unless you are in agreement. Once you sign, you will have great difficulty retracting that signature at a later date without diminishing your credibility.

PIPs

Performance Improvement Plans are often referred to as a "PIP". Usually, the plan outlines that your performance must improve within a certain period of time, otherwise, you will be terminated.

The goals and time frame must be realistic and objective. If you feel that the PIP is too subjective, then it is possible that you may negotiate clearer standards. If there are particular obstacles that prevent you from meeting certain PIP goals, you should outline them so that they are taken into account and not held against you. However, do not needlessly nitpick on the issues especially if it is reasonably clear. You will just reinforce the already prevailing negative perception of you.

Once the action on the PIP begins, you will probably meet with your supervisor on a regular basis to discuss your progress. Let your supervisor drive this process. Do not badger him to have a meeting if he misses one unless your PIP states that you have the responsibility to take the lead. Allow the issues between you and your supervisor to take lower priority if he chooses. Do not remind him that you are a problem employee by continually asking him "how am I doing?". And do not ask him if he is going to fire you. While it may be tempting because you are nervous of the next step, you will only be remind him that he can fire you. Resist the urge to put yourself in the line of fire. Remain calm and poised.

Suspensions and Involuntary Leaves

Most employers will terminate an employee for repeated negative behaviour. However, some employers will address the issue with a suspension as a final warning. When you return, you must strictly comply with the required standards otherwise you are guaranteed to be terminated. What if you return and your behaviour is exemplary? How long does the suspension remain an issue on your record? There are no laws as to a statute of limitation on the suspension.

An involuntary leave is more severe. It is usually applied when an employee is charged with serious misconduct. If an employee is charged with sexual harassment, suspected of theft or embezzlement or abusive conduct of peers are usually sent home with pay while the investigation proceeds. At any time, the leave can be converted to an unpaid leave if the employee is not cooperative with the investigation, abandons employment or is deemed to be guilty.

If this is your situation, remember that you are still an employee of the company. If you wish to keep your job, then you must be mindful to follow whatever directions your employer has given you even if it is a call-in requirement during certain times of the day or participate in the investigation. If you do not do so, then it can be interpreted as job abandonment and will merit termination. If you have a good wrongful termination case brewing, you do not want to torpedo it by engaging in conduct that justifies termination.

Handling a Termination Meeting

If you are summoned to a termination meeting, you must attend it otherwise you will immediately be terminated for insubordination. Usually, there will be more than one person attending this meeting (usually someone from HR) along with your supervisor. This additional person acts as a witness that all procedures where properly handled. Therefore, be mindful of your behavior. Do not lose control or curse out your manager. **Be professional at all times**.

Keep It Together!

You have a right to ask the reason if one is not provided. Keep your head clear because you will need to recall the reason given (if any). If the reason stated can later be proven as false, then this will help your case as it may infer that the real reason was an unlawful one. Sometimes if you wait long enough for the firing manager to drone on, s/he may give inconsistent reasons which will also help your case. Try traditional Japanese negotiation tactics by using silence. The Japanese believe that silence is golden and the mouth is the root of all trouble. You should use silence and let their mouth fill in the gaps. You may find it very useful as an information gathering tool as well as a protection tactic.

If you realize in the meeting that the reason is overtly false, you have the right to point that out in a professional and respectful manner. For example, if they provide a reason that you were over budget when telling you why you are being fired, you can simply say that "I have a copy of my reconciliation that shows I was not over budget. May I provide you with that document?". If this case were to escalate to the courtroom or arbitration, your act of offering the employer proof of your innocence would show a jury that you gave the employer an opportunity to correct the error. If the supervisor refuses to do so, a jury may see you as a victim to an uncaring and overtly arrogant employer.

Do Not Admit Or Agree to Any Wrongdoing!

If an employer offers you the option of resigning instead of being terminated, don't commit to an answer in this meeting. Request a day or two to think it over and decide what is best for you. Remember to keep your communications short, impersonal and professional.

The employer may provide you with an agreement to accept a severance package. Do not sign it there. If an employer is coercing you to sign it there, do not surrender. You have the legal right to request some time (a week minimum) to return a signed severance agreement. This will give you the opportunity to consult a lawyer and determine if the package offered is fair. If you require more than a week, feel free to contact the HR department near the week's end for an extension. Most will oblige for a few days extension as they do not want to be seen as making you sign a document under duress.

At this meeting, the employer may provide you with a cheque for your remaining pay, earned vacation pay and severance. You may take this cheque but do not cash it until you have decided that you don't want to pursue legal action. Cashing the cheque is a sign of consent and will impact you negatively if you plan to go forward with legal action. Consult a lawyer or check with Service Canada as to what minimums you are entitled to in order to ensure that you are being treated equitably. As well, you may be able to negotiate for more money or benefits (i.e. extension of health benefits, career placement service, training, etc.)

Security Escort

Don't be offended if you are escorted to your desk after the meeting to clean it out as well as escorted to the exit. This is legal and the company is trying to ensure that little disruption to the work environment occurs. Employees will be impacted enough by seeing you walk out with your belongings. The company will not want further morale reductions as a result from your play-by-play to your co-workers. It is in your best interest to say as little as possible.

Do Not File an Internal Grievance Immediately

Many employers offer employees the opportunity to file internal grievances. It is not recommended to file one immediately as it may hinder your legal action. When you tell your story, you want to do it as few times as possible. The more you tell it, the more it varies. This will create holes in your story that the employer's lawyer will walk right through. Plus, there is no guarantee that the employer's representative will be as diligent in recording your details. You want to ensure that your side of events is consistent with all people you discuss it with. As this person will be a witness for the employer if your case goes to trial so it may compromise your position if your story varies from person to person. If you are not consistent, the court will side with the employer's version of events.

Do Not Write to Upper Management

Some people feel that if upper management knew what was going on that they would rectify the issue. So they write a letter to the President of the company to explain the situation. Usually these letters are rambling, embellished or angry in tone. Letters like this will only hinder your situation and reinforce the contention that you deserved to be terminated.

Should I Sign a Release?

An employer who dismisses an employee without cause is obliged to provide notice of termination (e.g. two weeks' notice) or pay in lieu notice (i.e. the salary equivalent to two weeks' notice). Minimum notice periods/payments for federally and provincially regulated employers are listed in the Notice of Termination Appendix later in this book. In addition to notice, employees with five years or more of service and who are either part of a mass termination or were employed by an employer with a payroll of $2.5 million or more will be entitled to severance pay.

These payments are outlined by federal or provincial law and must be made within seven days of termination or by the employee's next pay date. Further remedies however, may and often do require the initiation of a lawsuit for wrongful dismissal or a complaint to the provincial Human Rights Commission if discrimination is at issue.

At termination, the employer may offer the employee a 'termination package'. The termination package outlines the payments, benefits or other offers such as a letter of reference the employer is prepared to provide upon termination. Termination packages are often made conditional upon the signing of a Release by the employee. The Release is a contract which spells out the payments and any other elements to be provided by the employer in exchange for a release by the employee of any further legal claims he may have against the employer with respect to his employment and/or termination of employment. Put simply, if an employee signs the release, s/he is accepting the employer's offer in full and final satisfaction of any claims s/he may have and will therefore not be able to pursue any further legal action against the employer.

The release typically contains the type of jargon familiar to lawyers but not to most employees confronted with the document. Given what is a stake, employees are always advised to refrain from signing a release until they have obtained legal advice. The value of the offer is dependent upon a whole host of factors such the damages for wrongful dismissal the employee can obtain as well as the other remedies s/he can pursue. Few employees have the legal expertise to make a proper assessment of the offer contained in a release on his/her own. Pressure to sign on the spot should immediately raise suspicions that the employer is seeking to have the employee agree to an unfair deal and should be resisted at all costs. You have the right to simply say "no, I will exercise and reserve my right to legal counsel before signing any document of a legally binding nature".

No action is required by an employee and specifically, no forms must be signed in order to obtain employment standards notice or severance payments from an employer. An employer therefore has no right to a signed release in exchange for employment standards payments. Unfortunately, this will not stop some employers from making such payments conditional upon a release in order to avoid or at least discourage legal action on the part of a terminated employee. There is therefore no benefit to an employee in signing a release under these circumstances as the employer is obliged to make payment of employment standards entitlements even if the employee refuses to sign.

Post – Termination Emotions

One of the biggest stresses after being terminated is to react emotionally. It is hard not to take things personally but, in all honesty, it is really just a business transaction. Don't fall into the trap of building your self-worth around your job because it is not healthy nor is it accurate. Be mindful of and try to avoid these emotional pitfalls:

1. **Seeing Yourself as a Failure in Life**. You are not a failure in any way. Even if you were fired for just cause, it means that this job or company was not a good fit for you. Many people blame themselves by saying:

    a. I should have seen this coming.
    b. I've let my family down.
    c. If I played my cards right, I would still have my job.
    d. Being fired doesn't happen to people like me.
    e. I should have worked harder.
    f. I should have kissed my boss's butt.

While these feelings are normal and understandable, they are fruitless and a waste of your energy. A bad attitude, especially when it comes to your self-image, is the last thing that you need right now. Pick a set period of time to mourn and beat yourself up (say about a day or two tops) if you must and then put it behind you forever and move forward. You will be unable to negotiate an equitable severance package or land a new job with this attitude. And you will stress your friends and family further.

Remember, almost everyone has been fired including: Jerry Seinfeld, Larry King, Michael Bloomberg, Robert Redford, Walt Disney, Bill Belichick, and the list goes on. And everyone will tell you that it was the best thing that ever happened to them. Getting hired doesn't teach you anything. Getting fired does.

2. **Focusing on Revenge.** Many people feel hurt and maligned when they are fired. In order to regain their self respect, they feel the urge to exact revenge to "teach them a lesson". This is the wrong approach and is guaranteed to jeopardize any chance of a successful negotiation.

> This is the worst possible action you can take. It can only backfire on you by damaging your reputation, derailing your career, and, in some cases, bring criminal charges against you. It will also justify why you were selected for termination. There is nothing truer than the old adage that "the best revenge is living well". Focus on the positive emotions and actions and you will be a lot happier.

3. **Being Engulfed By Behavior That Prevents You From Moving Forward.**

   a) **Isolation:** After termination, many people tend to isolate themselves from others. Start to network right away either through job search groups or outplacement services or taking a training course. Isolation is most likely to cause you to sink into depression and despair which will cause you to make irrational decisions, if any. It is this fear that many companies enact a policy not to fire employees on a Friday. The terminated employee tends to isolate themselves over the weekend which has led to the ex-employee returning to the office on Monday in a violent rage or committing suicide.

   b) **Denial:** Don't be in denial about your current state whether it be financial, emotional, or occupational. You are better off to know where you stand right away so that you can make educated decisions. Talk to someone you trust to get another perspective of your situation – good and bad. You will be surprised how well you will benefit from it.

   c) **Paralysis:** The shock of being terminated can put some people in a mental and emotional state of paralysis preventing them from moving forward. Establish an action plan and task list (e.g. update resume by the 12th, post resume to job sites on the 13th, call headhunters during the week of the 20th, etc.) Establish daily, weekly and monthly objectives. If you are not that organized or not a self-starter, ask friends for help. Make sure your goals are small and keep a record of the ones you have accomplished.

Don't feel overwhelmed by what you need to do but be sure to feel fulfilled by what you have done.

4. **Don't Focus On Your Fears, Focus On Your Future.** Picture yourself successful, happy and in your ideal job. By visualizing your potential, you will work towards achieving it. If you continue to focus on your fears ("I can't do that", "I won't have any money", "I'll never get another job", etc.), you increase the chances of it coming true. It is like driving a car – wherever you look is where your car will veer. Don't see yourself as a victim but as a victor.

5. **Don't Be A Whiner.** Fact is, millions of people have worse problems than you do. Sure you lost your job but countless people suffer terminal diseases, threats of physical violence, and lack of food or shelter to name but a few. Would you want to trade places with them? I would think not. They have dire problems, you do not. Put everything in perspective and be grateful that you aren't worse off.

Tips For Managing Your Emotions

Here are some things that you should do in order to keep your negative emotions from blinding you from moving forward.

1) Involve your life partner in your severance decisions. They are your best support system and can give you an objective perspective on the situation. Keep communicating with them. Be sure to understand what they are feeling as well as they are apt to share some of your emotions with you. Don't assume that they can be the tower of strength for you at all times.

2) Get plenty of exercise and plenty of sleep. Whether it is walking or going to the gym, exercise is proven to relieve stress and make you feel good about yourself. Sufficient sleep will provide the rest you need to be clear headed and make effective decisions.

3) Do not increase your diet for sweets, caffeine or tobacco. Not only are these items not healthy for you, they are known to create agitation and stress even though at the time of consumption it feels like the opposite.

4) Do not spend too much time with your former co-workers. It can be depressing hearing about how life goes on without you at the company plus it may make them feel uncomfortable, at least at the beginning. Plus it may put them in an awkward spot if their employer knows about it since the employer may assume that you are trying to get confidential information from them.

5) Do not sit at home all day. Try to get a regular activity that will take you out of your house like meeting friends for lunch or seeing headhunters or going to the library to

research careers. If you sit at home watching television all day, you will erode your self-worth and derail your focus. Even if there are days that you choose to stay home, don't spend the entire day in your pajamas. Put your clothes on first thing in the morning and complete your normal grooming process as you would if you were on a regular schedule.

6) Find a friend that you can lean on to be a sounding board. But remember; don't dwell on the same thing every time you chat with him/her. If you are not making progress in your discussions, you will lose that trusted supporter.

7) Join a networking or support group. There are lots of them in this economic climate. HAPPEN is a popular networking group for people searching for new employment opportunities. There are also online groups on LinkedIn.com. They may even lead you to a connection to a new job.

Should I File A Complaint?

If terminated for cause and without any payment whatsoever, it is a natural instinct to contact your provincial Ministry of Labour. The Ministry of Labour will be able to provide information as to the statutory severance and termination payments owing if appropriate cause cannot be proven. However, there are several reasons why filing a claim with the Ministry of Labour could prove to be a disaster.

What You See Is Not What You Get

Assume that during the initial communication with the Ministry of Labour one is advised that they are entitled to 20 weeks' severance/termination pay commensurate with a 12-year employee in a company with a payroll in excess of $2.5 million. Assuming an annual salary of $52,000.00, this payment represents $20,000.00. Common sense would dictate that if you bring a claim with Employment Standards and there is found to be no validity to the employer's allegations of cause, that one would be entitled to payment of $20,000.00. This assumption is wrong. The Employment Standards Act contains a provision which limits the amount of any Order for wages (which term includes severance and termination pay) to $10,000.00. Therefore, unless the employer voluntarily pays severance/termination, the Labour Board only has authority to order it to pay up to $10,000.00.

Adding Insult To Injury

To make matters worse, if an employee files a claim with Employment Standards for severance or termination pay, there is also a provision of the Act which would then prevent the employee from bringing a civil action for wrongful dismissal. Given that wrongful dismissal damages are almost always significantly greater than Employment Standards minimums (base payments), one can see the significant complications in filing an Employment Standards claim. Not only would the employee be limited to $10,000.00, but the employee would also be giving up a right to common law damages which can be tens of thousands dollars more than base damages.

With that in mind, one should understand that filing an Employment Standards claim should only be made in very limited circumstances. It is important in all cases to seek legal advice before any action is taken.

Damages for Wrongful Dismissal

Take, for example, a waiter, 52 years of age, with just under five years of service who is receiving an hourly rate of $11.00 for a 40-hour workweek. In addition to his base salary, the employee earns tips and is enrolled in the employer's group benefits plan. The individual is entitled to two weeks' paid vacation. According to the Ontario Employment Standards Act, that individual would be entitled to a minimum of four weeks' notice. The employer offers to provide termination pay in the amount of 4 weeks' base salary or $1,760.00 and nothing more.

Secondly, the employee has a right to more than base pay upon termination. Under the Act, the employee is also entitled to continuation of benefits over the notice period and vacation pay calculated as a percentage of the termination pay owing. In the above example, the individual would be entitled to vacation pay at 4% of $1760.00 or $70.40. The employee would also be entitled to any wages and vacation pay owing at the time of termination. Tips and gratuities or any non-performance related bonuses (e.g. Christmas bonus) are not included in the salary calculation of termination pay.

Employment Standards Act

Seek legal advice on the offer before you sign. If the offer is reasonable, it will likely be there after you have obtained advice. The more pressure that is put on you by the employer to sign, the greater is the likelihood that the offer is unreasonable. It is understood that seeing a lawyer is as much fun as going to see a dentist. However, in both cases they are necessary "evils".

Many people assume that any severance package received is reasonable, and that their employer would never try to take advantage of them. Such theories ignore the fact that the employer is running a business and it makes business sense to pay less rather than more.

An employer cannot offer less than minimum statutory payments or base payments. But what if the employer adds a few weeks to the "base" payment? To the layman, it may appear that the employer is being generous, when in fact it is not. To use an example, take a ten-year employee who is entitled to severance and termination pay in the equivalent of 18 weeks (Severance of one week for every year plus termination maximum of 8 weeks). In that situation, the employee is entitled to 18 weeks' pay at an absolute minimum and without signing a release. If the employer seeks a signed release form in exchange for 20 weeks, the employee would receive only two weeks over Employment Standards minimum payments and in exchange for giving up rights to common law damages which could represent 12 months' pay or more. Common law entitlements are based on several factors including the person's age, position, years of service, and the availability of alternate employment taking into consideration the employee's education and training. Unlike statutory notice, common law notice is not fixed but is based on what a

Court believes is reasonable in the circumstances. In monetary terms, an employee could be leaving tens of thousands of dollars on the table.

It should be understood that Employment Standards minimum payments are payable without an employee having to sign any release whatsoever. In other words, the employer would be obligated, in the above example, to pay 18 weeks pay and the employee would retain the right to bring a civil claim.

Where the offer fails to meet or barely meets entitlements under the Act, a signed Release will never be binding upon the employee. However, where an offer exceeds entitlements under the Act, a signed Release will likely absolve the employer from any further obligation to the departing employee. Given the serious consequences which may result, individuals who are presented with a termination package and are asked to sign a release, are strongly advised to obtain independent legal advice before signing such an agreement. Only by doing so, you will be able to evaluate the employer's offer in relation to your rights and determine the best course of action including whether you might be better off bringing a civil action against the employer for wrongful dismissal. Besides, once you sign, you can't retract it unless you can prove without a doubt that you signed under duress or if the amount signed for was less than your rights afforded by your province's employment standards legislation. If you are not sure, seeking an employment lawyer's advice before you sign rather than after you sign is always in your best interest. And ensure that the lawyer you consult with is an experienced labour lawyer, not your cousin the real estate lawyer. It can make all the difference between a good settlement and the best settlement.

Types Of Claims For Legal Action

Bad Faith

In its decision in Wallace v. United Grain Growers, the Supreme Court of Canada observed that the involuntary loss of one's job can be a traumatic event and that when employment is terminated, the employee is vulnerable and in need of protection. Thus, employers are held to an obligation of good faith and fair dealing in the manner of dismissal. Where there has been a breach of that duty, the Courts may order compensation in addition to damages for wrongful dismissal.

While Wallace specifically stated that injured feelings and emotional upset resulting from the fact of the dismissal do not provide a basis for compensation, injuries such as humiliation, embarrassment and damage to one's self-esteem or sense of self-worth caused by the manner of termination may be worthy of compensation. The following are but a few examples of conduct by an employer which, according to Wallace, could result in bad faith damages:

1. False allegation that termination was due to the employee's inability to do his job.
2. False allegation that termination was for cause.
3. Spreading word through the industry that the employee was terminated for dishonest conduct.
4. Refusal to provide a letter of termination after termination.
5. Firing an employee immediately upon return from disability leave.
6. Replacing an employee shortly after he had been told that he was being laid off due to a shortage of work.

Other cases provide further examples of the type of conduct that would constitute bad faith on the part of the employer and justify increased damages. In Noseworthy v. Riverside Pontiac-Buick Ltd., the Ontario Court of Appeal recognized that additional damages were warranted based upon a finding that the employer had confronted the plaintiff with false allegations of forgery and threatened to lay criminal charges if the employee did not sign a letter of resignation.

In Antonacci v. Great Atlantic & Pacific Co. of Canada, the trial judge found that bad faith damages were justified because of unfounded allegations against the employee of poor performance, harassment, intimidation and threats that cast a shadow on him that would make it virtually impossible for him to find another position.

In Prinzo v Baycrest Centre for Geriatric Care, the Ontario Court of Appeal found that the plaintiff was entitled to bad faith damages as a result of phone calls from the employer prior to the plaintiff's termination and while she was on disability leave, inferring that she was exaggerating or faking illness and letters to the plaintiff falsely suggesting that her doctor had indicated she was fit to return to work. This conduct caused the plaintiff loss of self-esteem and disability for several months following her dismissal.

Bad faith damages will be available where it can be shown that the employer's conduct demonstrates intent, malice or blatant disregard for the employee. It is employer conduct which amounts to callous or insensitive treatment of the employee.

Mental Distress

Rarely will there be a termination of employment which does not cause an employee to suffer emotionally and psychologically from the loss of work and associated loss of income, the loss of self-esteem and the disruptions to one's life which result. The question considered here, is under what circumstances an employee might sue for damages which result from the loss of employment.

A key case on aggravated damages in an employment context is Vorvis v. Insurance Corp. of B.C. In Vorvis, the plaintiff had returned to school to study law, after a successful career as a sales manager. Upon graduation, he went to work for the defendant and over the course of seven years, received a promotion and several merit pay increases.

Difficulties arose for the plaintiff upon the defendant's decision to hire a new general counsel who became the plaintiff's immediate supervisor. The mandate of the general counsel was to improve the productivity of the corporation's legal department. The general counsel became increasingly dissatisfied with the pace of the plaintiff's work, and instituted weekly productivity meetings to review the plaintiff's performance. The trial judge noted that these meetings became "an inquisition" and "as the pressure increased the plaintiff became tense, agitated and distressed, finally requiring medical attention and a tranquilizer".

A little more than a year after the general counsel's hire, the plaintiff was terminated simply because the plaintiff no longer fit into counsel's plans for the legal department.

The plaintiff sued seeking damages for wrongful dismissal and damages for mental distress caused by his termination. The courts, at all levels, concluded that the mental distress experienced by the plaintiff as a result of his termination, did *not* give rise to aggravated damages in addition to the damages he sought for wrongful dismissal.

To succeed with a claim for aggravated damages where an employee has been terminated, there must be evidence of a wrong committed by the employer separate and apart from its failure to provide appropriate notice. According to Vorvis, in the absence of such an "actionable wrong", the employer's conduct, even though offensive and hurtful to the plaintiff, would not give rise to aggravated damages.

In Rahemtulla v. Vanfed Credit Union, the plaintiff was dismissed from her position as a bank teller on the basis of unfounded accusations of theft. She suffered severe emotional distress as a consequence of her summary dismissal and the accusations of the defendant. The Court held that the accusations of theft, even if motivated by a desire to extort a confession and solve the mystery of the missing funds, amounted to an act with reckless disregard as to whether or not shock would ensue from the accusation. The Court found that the plaintiff did not have to show that the defendant's conduct was caused by malicious intent to cause harm or any motive of spite. The Court further found that the employer's conduct was outrageous and observed:

"While the financial institution has the right to dismiss a suspect employee without investigation, the proper conduct of its affairs does not require that it be given the right to make reckless and very possibly untruthful accusations as to the employee's honesty which will foreseeably inflict shock and mental suffering. Considering all of these circumstances, I am satisfied that Mr. Flack's conduct can fairly be described as flagrant and outrageous".

The Court awarded the Plaintiff $5,000.00 for mental distress.

An employer by communicating an employee's termination in a reckless fashion, may cause the employee mental distress. Such communications may also constitute intentional infliction of mental suffering. In Bohemier v. Storwal International Inc., the employee had been employed for 35 years when his termination notice was delivered on a Friday evening by taxi. The letter expressed no gratitude for service, offered no proposal to aid in obtaining new employment and did not specify the basis for payment in lieu of notice. The Court, in awarding damages for mental distress, held:

"The evidence discloses that the usual practice of Storwal on dismissals was to call the employee into the office of a superior at the end of the last day of work. There is no explanation of why this was not done in the case of the plaintiff. Hughes believes that it was due to inadvertence and that the plaintiff left the plant before his superior had an opportunity to speak with him. The reason for departing from the usual practice does not matter. Someone in authority at Storwal must have arranged that the notice be delivered by taxi cab. In my opinion, it was reasonably foreseeable that such an action would aggravate the mental suffering of the plaintiff that would inevitably caused by the act of dismissal and the inadequate period of notice."

Overtime

The parties may also enter into an agreement whereby overtime is not compensated by overtime pay but by paid time off at one and one-half times the number of overtime hours worked.

The Act requires employers to keep records of the hours worked by an employee during the course of a week and to retain such records for at least three years following that employee's termination. It is a fact however, that many employers do not keep these records. Employees are therefore advised to maintain detailed records of their hours worked over the course of their employment. Don't wait until you need the records to start recording them from memory. You need to maintain these records in a timely manner. In such circumstances, the log kept by the employee will be the best evidence available for determining overtime compensation owing.

While employees and employers can contract to provide for overtime compensation on terms which exceed the entitlements under the Act (Employee's Rights section for overtime regulations), they cannot agree to waive or forego entitlement to overtime. Any such agreements are not enforceable.

An employee may seek to enforce his or her right to overtime by one of two means. The employee may either:

1. Bring a claim for overtime. A claim for overtime will be limited to losses incurred in the six months preceding the filing of the claim and is capped at $10,000.00; or

2. Bring a civil action for overtime pay owing. In Kumar v. Sharp Business Forms Inc. in the decision of the Ontario Superior Court of Justice, the Court ruled that the provisions of the Act, including those regarding overtime, are implied terms of every contract of employment and the failure of the employer to pay overtime owing, constitutes a breach of contract, damages for which are recoverable by way of a civil action. An individual may seek damages for overtime extending over a two-year period prior to the filing of the claim. In the decision of Abdelshahid v. Schiffenhaus Canada Inc., an Ontario Court awarded civil damages for loss of overtime pay.

In Matioski v. Lake of Woods Business Incentive, an employee worked lots of overtime, a fact the employer did not dispute. However, the employer argued that the employee had agreed that he would not be paid for overtime, but would instead receive time off in lieu. That is permitted if the employee agrees, time off equal to time and half can be taken rather than OT pay.

The trouble in this case was that the employee was dismissed before he could take the time off in lieu which he has accumulated. So now what happens? Well, the law deals with that possibility too:

If the employment of an employee ends before the paid time off is taken under subsection (7), the employer shall pay the employee overtime pay for the overtime hours that were worked in accordance with subsection 11 (5)

Clearly, the employee is entitled to be paid his OT, since he can no longer take it as time off. The problem for the employee in this case is that he did not keep clear records of how much OT he actually worked. He guessed it to be in the range of 1300 hours over 5 years, but he couldn't prove that. Of course, the employer has a legal obligation to keep track of hours worked, including overtime hours and the court here rules that the employer breached that legal requirement. The central purpose of that section is to ensure that employers pay attention to their employees' working hours and don't later try and play dumb about hours worked. So therefore, given that the employer admits the employee worked lots of OT, and that it nevertheless failed to track that OT, that it ought to have an obligation to pay the employee at least some OT. Right?

Wrong.

The Plaintiff has the onus of proving the number of hours worked on a balance of probabilities... I cannot say that the evidence of the Plaintiff regarding hours of overtime he worked meets this standard. While it is regrettable that proper records were not kept by either party, this court cannot accept estimates without some assurance of relative accuracy.

Although it was against the law that the employer did not keep these records, the employee must prove how much OT he worked, and if he can't, the employer is off the hook. That's the case even though everyone agreed that the employee worked lots of OT for which he was not paid! In this case, the court ordered the employer to pay a token $1 to the employee.

Inducement

Sometimes, an employee who is not looking for another position, while happily and securely employed in long term employment, may be approached by an employer who wishes to hire him/ her away. Sometime later, after inducing that employee to leave, the new employer terminates that employee's employment.

In Antidormi v Blue Pumpkin Software Inc., a decision of the Ontario Superior Court, the plaintiff had been employed as a Channel Sales Manager for a large software developer. She was one of the company's highest achievers, winning awards and bonus incentives for her sales efforts. At the time the case arose, she was on track to earn salary and commissions for the year well into the six figure range.

A few months after joining the company, the plaintiff was contacted by a former colleague with news of an employment opportunity with Blue Pumpkin ("BP"), an American company seeking to build its sales team and develop the Canadian market. The colleague advised that she would be submitting the plaintiff's name to BP's V.P. Sales for consideration even though the plaintiff indicated that she was doing really well where she was and enjoying it there.

In the follow-up phone conversation with the plaintiff, BP's V.P. Sales addressed the plaintiff's concerns about the company and its products. A meeting was agreed to even though the plaintiff indicated that she was not interested in changing jobs. At the meeting in Toronto, the V.P. Sales shared his vision for Canada and told the plaintiff that BP's executives recognized Canada as having the potential to be its fastest growing market and were committing the necessary resources to facilitate its growth.

In the V.P.'s words, "the sky was the limit". He represented that if the plaintiff proved herself in the Canadian market, she could fast track and pursue her goal of working in the global marketplace.

The plaintiff did not accept the offer to join BP immediately. After researching the company, the plaintiff went out to California to meet with BP's senior management including the company's CEO who expressed complete confidence in his V.P. Sales and confirmed that this was a long-term opportunity. Upon further reassurances that she would enjoy job security as long as she performed and that building the Canadian territory would take at least three to five years, the plaintiff agreed to leave her current employer of some 19 months and join BP.

At the start, the plaintiff's position was that of Account Executive. Within a few weeks, she was made Territory Manager – Canada and Latin America. Throughout her employment with BP, the plaintiff's performance was outstanding and consistently at or above assigned objectives. The V.P. Sales repeatedly expressed satisfaction with BP's work and further indicated that he anticipated she would have a solid and immediate impact on BP's performance in Canada. Approximately five months after the plaintiff commenced employment with BP, the V.P. Sales was replaced by the company's V. P. Worldwide Sales. About a month later, the plaintiff was advised that she was being terminated as management had changed its focus. When the plaintiff protested about the promises which had been made to her and the impact of the termination would have upon her family, BP would only say that the plaintiff might have to change her lifestyle.

At trial, the Court determined that the plaintiff would never have left the stable and lucrative position with her former employer but for the misrepresentations from BP about job prospects and job stability. The plaintiff had been employed by BP for six months at termination. The Court took BP's misrepresentations into account in awarding the plaintiff reasonable notice of 10 months. BP's conduct at termination and following the plaintiff's termination led to an increase in the notice period to 12 months. Based on the plaintiff's salary and expected bonuses/commissions over the notice period, damages were fixed at $320,000.00.

Incentive by a prospective employer to leave one's present job may extend the notice period that would otherwise be awarded, and could well result in a period of notice exceeding the length of employment itself.

The same situation can be applied to independent contractors who are lured to a permanent position and are soon terminated. In this situation, they are enticed to give up their business with a reasonable expectation of lasting employment, and therefore, income.

What Happens if a Business is Sold?

If a business is sold to a new owner, there are rules that the new owner must follow regarding existing employees. Generally, an employee should not lose any rights or money because the business was sold.

Employee Rights Under a New Owner

If the employee keeps his/her job, the employee is usually entitled to maintain his/her seniority with respect to all the benefits and rights that were enjoyed before the business was sold.

Employee Rights If Fired or Constructively Dismissed by the New Owner

If an employee is fired or constructively dismissed, the new employer will be responsible for giving the employee a reasonable notice period, or pay, instead of notice. Under the law, a "constructive dismissal" happens when the employer does not officially fire the employee but instead imposes a fundamental change in the employee's working conditions or benefits. For example, the new employer may significantly reduce pay or benefits, or demote an employee.

Often, the new employer is also responsible for giving employees severance pay. If you work for a business that is sold and lose your job without proper notice or pay in lieu of notice, or lose significant rights or benefits in your job, this may be considered wrongful or constructive dismissal. You may be able to sue both the former and new employer.

Resignation

If you resign, are you entitled to termination pay or other entitlements or have you forfeited those as well as eligibility to Employment Insurance? In certain cases, especially when you are feel you have no choice, you may be entitled to payment and be eligible for Employment Insurance. The following are some common situations.

"I Quit!!"

What if I quit as a result of the workplace stress? If I yell "I quit" and walk out, is it binding?

Consider the following situation. A dentist (the employer) hires a consultant to evaluate the operation of his dental practice. In a report critical of the dentist's business operations, the consultant recommends changes, which include removing some of the duties previously performed by the office manager (the employee). Shortly after learning of the recommendations, the office manager writes to her employer as follows:

"If your intention was to hurt and destroy me – you've done a good job. Because of you, and your wife, the consultant and your staff, you've all succeeded! I'm resigning immediately. Enclosed, is the key to the office".

After the note and the key are delivered, the dentist indicates that he needs an explanation and arranges to meet with the office manager. A long and emotional conversation then ensues. According to the dentist, the employee maintains her desire to resign during their conversation. The office manager on the other hand, states she was told to take a few days off and they would work things out. On that basis, the employee alleges that she withdrew her resignation. The following day, the employer advises his staff that the employee resigned. Upon learning what the staff had been told, the employee contacts the employer and is told, "I think we should part company." The employee sued for wrongful dismissal.

There was no dispute that the office manager's employment had come to an end. The legal issue was whether the employee had resigned her employment. What was at stake was entitlement to notice and Employment Insurance benefits. If the employee "resigned" she would not likely be entitled to notice or EI benefits.

Courts will find that a resignation has occurred only where the conduct in question is clear and unequivocal. A resignation will not be found simply on the basis of actions or words expressed by an employee in the "heat of the moment" and in response to highly charged emotional circumstances.

The law recognizes spontaneously made statements may not constitute a valid resignation. Neither should an employer seize upon the extreme utterances of an emotionally charged employee. An employee who proclaims "I quit" in the heat of the moment may have done anything but.

An indication from the employee that she is not satisfied with her employment and is looking for other work, or is thinking of quitting does not necessarily constitute a resignation. Similarly, a situation where an employee resigns, but soon thereafter withdraws the resignation will not likely constitute a resignation. This may be so even if an employer subsequently accepts the resignation.

There is also a legal distinguish between a resignation which is voluntary and a refusal by an employee to accept a significant change made by the employer to the terms of employment, such as a significant demotion or a reduction in pay. In this case, the employment relationship may have been terminated by the conduct of the employer and not the employee's resignation, and the employee's right to notice and Employment Insurance may not have been eliminated.

The court found that the circumstances of the case did not support a resignation and the individual was entitled to damages for wrongful dismissal. The Court based its decision on the following:

1. While the resignation was a product of an emotional and stressful time in the employee's life, it was not a spontaneous outburst in circumstances which undermined the fact that it was tendered voluntarily. The delivery of the note and the key, taken alone, represented an indisputable resignation by the employee.

2. However, the employer did not accept the resignation. Instead, he wanted to discuss the matter further with the employee and such discussions took place.

3. While the employee started to resign, she never did so explicitly. Instead she agreed to meet with the employer to discuss the issues which gave rise to her concerns.

4. When all of the circumstances surrounding the "resignation" and the conduct of the parties which followed are taken into consideration, the court concluded: "the plaintiff did not voluntarily resign from her employment".

Given the very serious consequences which can happen to an individual who resigns his or her employment, both in respect of entitlement to notice and EI benefits, those contemplating resignation are strongly urged to seek legal counsel before pursuing such action.

Constructive Dismissal

Employees should also remember that resignations arising from pressure to accept different terms or leave the company could simply be a camouflaged termination. So when is quitting a constructive dismissal?

- If you were fired even if you had already quit.

- If your employer does something that makes it virtually impossible for you to continue on the job.

- If your employer changed some working conditions that led to your quitting (i.e. can't be something that bothered you since the start of your employment). This change must be recent enough that a cause and effect relationship or direct correlation can be established between the change(s) and quitting.

- A change in working conditions is so demeaning or upsetting or unfair. Note: If you are thin-skinned or the change(s) is done for business reasons in which most employees have accepted the change(s) without complaint, then you won't have a strong case.

For example, in Viens v. Suburban Distributors, an employee was called into his employer's office one day and asked to take a twenty percent pay cut or be laid off. The court found that this was a constructive dismissal.

However, courts have also, on occasion, drawn a distinction between a reduction in base salary and other benefits. In Otto v. Hamilton & Olsen Surveys, the employer unilaterally cut its employees' paid vacation time from six weeks to four, and also ceased its five percent contribution to the R.R.S.P. plans of its employees. The total loss to the two employees who quit and claimed constructive dismissal as a result were between 6.49 percent and 8.00 percent of their total compensation.

The trial judge found that they were constructively dismissed, but the Alberta Court of Appeal disagreed. The Court of Appeal was convinced by several factors. Firstly, the benefits removed were not base salary but just collateral benefits. Salaries were maintained. Second, the company had a practice of regularly increasing the benefits package during good economic times. Third, the company did not decrease the compensation package in bad faith, but instead decreased it because of an economic downturn. Finally, the employer actually had one of the most generous compensation packages in the industry, even after the cuts.

Resigning After Receiving Notice of Termination

An employee who has been given a written notice of termination can resign and continue to keep the right to severance pay. To keep this right, the employee must give the employer *two weeks'* written notice of his or her resignation. The resignation must also take effect during the *statutory notice period*–the period of written notice that is required to be given by the employer.

If an employer provides longer notice than is required, the statutory part of the notice period is the last part of the period that ends on the date of termination.

For example:

Heather has worked for seven years, and is entitled to seven weeks' notice of termination under the Employment Standards Act ("ESA"). Heather's employer gives her 10 weeks' notice. Heather must give her employer at least two weeks' written notice of her resignation. As long as Heather's resignation takes effect during the statutory notice period, in this case the last seven weeks of the 10-week notice period, she continues to be entitled to severance pay.

Termination Law

A number of expressions are commonly used to describe situations when employment is terminated. These include "let go," "discharged," "dismissed," "fired", "ousted", "cut" and "permanently laid off."

Recent studies have confirmed that the loss of a job is the fourth single most devastating event to an individual's emotional well being - just after death of a child, parent and divorce. The symptoms of depression which affect many who unexpectedly lose their employment - sleeplessness, anxiety, lack of appetite, indecision and irritability - closely resemble a person in mourning.

For many, the initial shock and humiliation quickly develops into a sense of abuse and outrage. The desire to strike back at your former employer, who so callously and foolishly destroyed your family's economic security, is to be expected and overwhelming.

Once the fog clears, many terminated employees question whether their former employer followed the law and did not infringe on the employee's rights. Here are some common areas that people question and how the law interprets them.

Job Role Discontinuance/Elimination

An employer should be allowed to make good faith re-organizations to grow with its business demands. What an employer is not allowed to do, however, is to pretend that the reason was job discontinuance or lack of work when really it was terminating a problem employee. If the employee can show that the real reason was the intent to cut him from the work force because he was a nuisance, then the complaint will be allowed.

For example, if an employee has a job function of "project manager" and the company decides to do away with this and create a position of "senior project manager", then there will be an examination of the real life job functions of the two positions to see if there is a real difference.

Several situations may indicate that a lack of work or job discontinuance is not dominant reason for a layoff including:

1. Where, shortly after an employee's termination, a replacement worker is hired to fill the employee's position and the duties performed by the replacement worker are substantially the same as those performed by the employee.

2. Where a decision to dismiss an employee comes right after a decision to re-organize the workplace, thus indicating that the reorganization was specially engineered so as to justify the employee's dismissal.

3. Where the employer first tells the employee that they have been dismissed for cause, and then later alleges it was because of a layoff.

4. Where the employee is replaced temporarily while he or she takes a leave of absence (or is otherwise re-assigned), and the employer later refuses to reinstate the employee claiming that there are no vacant positions.

5. Where the employee's old position becomes vacant and open for application within a reasonable time following the layoff but the employee is not offered the position.

In order to make a finding that the layoff resulted from a discontinuance of a function, the duties performed by the employee must no longer be performed in the workplace where he or she was employed. Where a set of activities is merely handed over in its entirety to another person, or the duty is simply given a new and different title so as to fit another job description, the discontinuance of a function test will not be met.

Where these responsibilities are subsequently contracted-out to individuals who engage in exactly the same work, on the same premises, with the same equipment, and pursuant to the same instructions, the Canada Labour Code deems this activity acceptable.

There were two relevant cases where the employer was found to have acted in bad faith. In Nihal Mathur vs Bank of Nova Scotia, the employer alleged that his termination was due to a decision to merge two positions to one, for which he was not the successful candidate. Mathur challenged this action on the basis that it was disguised attempt to terminate him and the redundancy decision was not one made in good faith. The court ruled in favour of Mathur's claims and, as a result, Mathur received due compensation.

The second case was one dealing with eliminating a project manager role and creating senior project manager role with alarmingly similar responsibilities. In Mahavir Mathur vs. Bank of Nova Scotia, Mathur was laid off due to discontinuance of function. The court found that the Bank acted in bad faith and Mahavir was reinstated.

Conflict of Interest

Conflict of interest is one of the most rapidly developing and complicated areas of just cause for dismissal. Seeking employment with another company or considering starting one's own business in competition with their employer will not amount to just cause for termination in most cases.

Whether an employer has just cause to terminate an employee in circumstances of a potential conflict of interest will depend upon the nature of the employment relationship, the details of the potential conflict and the circumstances surrounding the actions of the employee. Courts have increasingly recognized the very far reaching duties of management and senior level employees to avoid engaging in any conduct which could possibly amount to or be perceived as a potential conflict of interest.

Conduct Outside of Work

One of the most controversial grounds of just cause for termination involves the actions or activities of an employee outside of normal working hours. A court may conclude that such conduct could amount to just cause for termination if it occurs in the course of an event or activity that is somehow work related, is serious in nature and tends to reveal a less than honest or trustworthy character of the individual. For example, a judge held that a serious assault of a fellow employee with whom the individual was involved in a romantic relationship, outside of business hours, amounted to just cause for termination.

Unless there is some link or connection that is established between the misconduct in question and the individual's employment or employment relationship, conduct outside of working hours will not normally constitute just cause for termination.

Cause Discovered After Firing

It is a common misconception that an employer is not permitted to rely upon misconduct unknown to it at the time of termination as just cause for termination of the employment relationship. This is known in law as "after acquired cause" or "expost facto justification for dismissal".

A common example of cause discovered after firing involves falsification of expense reports or theft of an employer's property. Such misconduct, if proven, could constitute just cause for dismissal, even though the employer was not aware of it at the time of termination.

Misstating Education, Qualifications, and Experience

Most court decisions involving misstatements or misleading information provided by employees at the hiring stage relate to the job candidate's education, qualifications and experience. An employee may be terminated for just cause as a result of misrepresentations made to the employer during pre-employment interviews and discussions.

The courts, in recent years, have emphasized the relationship of trust between an employer and an employee which begins at the point that the employee submits his or her resume to the employer, indirectly vouching for the accuracy of the information submitted to the employer. In many instances, it is difficult to draw the line between the typical "sales pitch" made by an employee in the course of job interviews verses misrepresentations (e.g. lying about working for IBM or earning an MBA, etc.) which may subsequently support a termination for just cause without notice and without compensation.

Not Providing Essential Information

In most cases, a person's failure to provide information to an employer during the hiring process will not amount to lying or falsifying information. This is due to the fact that courts historically have taken the position that an individual is not legally required to bring information to the attention of the employer where that information has not been requested.

In the case of senior management and executive employees, it is possible that a court may conclude that they have a duty to advise the employer of information which may affect their decision to hire the individual such as conflict of interest.

Damages for Injury to Reputation

The only recognized legal basis on which to award any damages for injury to reputation would be for loss of an opportunity to enhance one's reputation, which are limited to people such as actors and artists, where a very real benefit of their employment includes the opportunity to enhance their reputation and popularity within their profession.

In only the rarest situations will a wrongfully terminated employee have a valid claim for damages for defamation. Generally speaking, a written or verbal statement is defamatory if it harms the reputation of a person so as to lower him/her in the opinion of the community.

Spying on Employees Without Cause

In Colwell v. Cornerstone, Colleen Colwell had been working for the company for more than seven years, when she learned a secret camera had been installed in the ceiling of her office almost a year earlier by her boss, Trent Krauel, Cornerstone's vice-president in finance.

Shocked, she immediately had the camera removed. But Colwell felt psychologically violated and emotionally distraught, and sought medical attention. She was prescribed sedatives. In the next few weeks, she and Krauel had several meetings to discuss this.

He claimed the camera was installed to detect theft by maintenance staff.

There had been several incidents of theft on the premises in the year prior to this secret camera installation, he claimed. He did not intend to spy on her, he stated, rather he was concerned her office would be used by the thieves to "review the loot".

He assured her he trusted her, wanted her to remain in her position, and that she was not a suspect. To Colwell, these explanations seemed suspicious.

To top it off, Krauel maintained his right to install the camera secretly in her office. He was sorry she was upset, but he owed her no apology.

Colwell was upset and disbelieving. Money was never kept in her office and no theft had taken place there. Worse, since she was responsible for the maintenance staff, why had she never been told they were under suspicion? Krauel's explanation reinforced her sense of violation.

Blind to the impact on Colwell, Krauel asked her to stay on for six months, while Cornerstone tried to complete a business deal that Colwell was involved with. He said the company would "look after her" at the end of the six months.

Colwell could not bear the thought of continuing to work for Krauel, given how he had betrayed her sense of trust. In a last-ditch effort to resolve the situation, Colwell went to the president of Cornerstone, with an offer to train her replacement in exchange for a letter of recommendation and a severance package. He did not respond.

Colwell resigned and sued both Cornerstone and Krauel for constructive dismissal. The judge found for Colwell. He had little patience for Krauel, describing his explanations as "preposterous" and "unbelievable".

He concluded that the secret installation of the camera, Krauel's lack of apology or repentance, and his declaration he had a right to install the camera in Colwell's private office without advising her, coupled with his preposterous explanation, the court said, made it impossible for Colwell to continue in her employment. The judge wondered "what was the real reason for installing the camera?" He could draw no conclusion. Krauel's conduct amounted to more than "bad faith" and "unfair dealing" and Colwell was justified in leaving the "poisoned environment".

What right do employers have to spy on their employees? Monitoring and surveillance are powerful tools against workplace theft. However, employers must have a reasonable apprehension of abuse by employees to justify their use. Employers have the right to install cameras in the workplace, however, that right is limited by the obligation to exercise it in good faith and fairness.

Reinstatement

There is no right to reinstatement. There are however instances surrounding a termination which may entitle an employee to reinstatement. This is because both provincial and federal statutes provide for such a remedy in specific circumstances.

Consider the following situations:

1. An employee, aged 65, is let go after the employer has hired a replacement even though the employee has expressed no interest in retirement.

2. An employee goes on parental leave and while away, is replaced. Upon advising the company that she is ready to return to work, the employee is told her job has been given to someone else.

3. An employee complains that he has not received the vacation pay to which he is entitled only to have the employer respond by advising him that if he doesn't like it, he can look for work elsewhere.

4. A bank advises an employee that she is being dismissed without cause. In response to inquiries from the employee as to the reason for the dismissal, the bank indicates it was not satisfied with her performance.

5. An employee complains about safety violations in the workplace. Her campaign to have the employer adhere to safety standards results in her termination.

6. An employee is terminated after explaining that she cannot work late because she has been unable to arrange babysitting for her children.

7. An employer refuses to return an employee to his job after he has recovered from a work-related injury.

8. A dispute between an employer and an employee over his right to bereavement leave, after the death of a parent, leads to termination.

In each of the above cases, there are grounds for a statutory claim seeking reinstatement or re-employment. The following statutes govern the above examples:

a) Where employment is governed by federal human rights legislation, the right to be employed free from discrimination is governed by the Canadian Human Rights Act. Both provincial and federal human rights legislation allow an employee to seek reinstatement where discrimination as a protected class can be established (e.g. age, family status, etc.).

b) The Employment Standards Act covers examples 2, 3 and 8 where an employee, who goes on a leave of absence, is entitled to return to his/her job upon the completion of the leave. Failure by the employer to return the employee to their former position or a similar position is a violation for which the employee can seek reinstatement. The same will apply where the employee has been terminated as a result of his/her efforts to enforce his/her legal rights.

c) Canada Labour Code (example 4) - Federally-regulated employers such as banks are governed by the CLC. When an employee of a federally-regulated company has been unjustly dismissed, his/her options for resolution may include reinstatement.

d) Occupational Health and Safety Act (example 5) - An employee cannot be terminated for insisting to safe working conditions. In these circumstances, an employee who has been terminated can request reinstatement.

e) Workplace Safety and Insurance Act (example 7) - An employer has a reemployment obligation to an employee who has recovered from a workplace injury. Unlike the previous examples, however, an employer who fails to comply with its reemployment obligation faces only financial penalties for non-compliance.

Does an employee who has been terminated have a right to reinstatement? If the circumstances of the termination fit within the legal guidelines set out above, the answer could be yes. In these cases, even where the employee does not want to return to the place of employment, s/he may have a claim for additional payments if s/he gives up her/his right to reinstatement.

Provincial Termination Laws

Here is how the laws apply in each province/territory:

Alberta

Source: employment.alberta.ca

Termination Notice

Termination notice is not required:

(a)   To terminate the employment of an employee for just cause.

(b)   When an employee has been employed by the employer for 3 months or less.

(c)   When the employee is employed for a definite term or task for a period not exceeding 12 months on completion of which the employment terminates.

(d)   When the employee is laid off after refusing an offer by the employer of reasonable alternative work.

(e)   If the employee refuses work made available through a seniority system.

(f)   If the employee is not provided with work by the employer by reason of a strike or lockout occurring at the employee's place of employment.

(g)   When the employee is employed under an agreement by which the employee may elect either to work or not to work for a temporary period when requested to work by the employer.

(h)   If the contract of employment is or has become impossible for the employer to perform by reason of unforeseeable or unpreventable causes beyond the control of the employer.

(i)   If the employee is employed on a seasonal basis and on the completion of the season the employee's employment is terminated.

Employer's Termination Notice

To terminate employment an employer must give an employee written termination notice. The following table denotes the minimum time requirements associated with employers lawful obligation to notify an employee of termination.

Length of Employment	Notice Required
Less than 3 months	None
3 months but less than 2 years	1 week
2 years but less than 4 years	2 weeks
4 years but less than 6 years	4 weeks
6 years but less than 8 years	5 weeks
8 years but less than 10 years	6 weeks
10 years or more	8 weeks

Termination Pay

Instead of giving a termination notice, an employer may pay an employee termination pay of an amount at least equal to the wages the employee would have earned if the employee had worked the regular hours of work for the applicable termination notice period.

An employer may give an employee a combination of termination pay and termination notice, in which case the termination pay must be at least equal to the wages the employee would have earned for the applicable termination notice period that is not covered by the notice.

If the wages of an employee vary from one pay period to another, the average of the employee's wages for the 3-month period immediately preceding the date of termination of employment is to be used to determine the employee's termination pay.

You're entitled to all your wages, overtime, general holiday pay and vacation pay owed within three days of your last day of employment. If you're fired for just cause, you're entitled to all wages, overtime, general holiday pay and vacation pay within 10 days of your firing.

Earnings Not to Change After Termination Notice Given

Neither the wages, wage rate, nor any other term or condition of employment may be reduced by an employer between the time termination notice is given and the date employment terminates, whether or not work is required to be performed during that period.

During the period between the dates a termination notice is given and termination of the employment, the employee remains employed by the employer unless;

(a)   the employer gives the employee termination pay, or

(b)   the employer terminates employment of the employee;

      (i)   for just cause;

     (ii)   if the employee is laid off after refusing an offer by the employer of reasonable alternative work;

    (iii)   if the employee refuses work made available through a seniority system;

    (iv)   if the employee is not provided with work by the employer by reason of a strike or lockout occurring at the employee's place of employment, or

     (v)   if the employment contract is or has become impossible for the employer to perform by reason of unforeseeable or unpreventable causes beyond the control of the employer.

Temporary Layoff

If an employer wishes to maintain an employment relationship without terminating the employment of an employee, the employer may temporarily lay off the employee.

Termination Pay After Temporary Layoff

On the 60th consecutive day of temporary layoff, an employee's employment officially terminates and the employer must pay the employee termination pay on that day.

Severance Pay

In general, if any of the following apply, you may have a claim for severance above any minimum entitlement:

- Re-employability is not easily achieved.

- You are earning an above average income (50K plus).

- You are in a middle management role.

- You were solicited or lured from your previous employer.

- You are in a skilled or specialized job.

- You are older (45 plus).

As an employee you become eligible for termination notice following three months of continued employment. Length of notice is calculated based on your length of time of employment. This provision only allows a maximum of 8 weeks' notice or pay or combination of both even if you have worked over 8 years with the employer.

What Are the Exceptions to Termination Notice?

You aren't entitled to termination notice if:

- You're fired for just cause.

- You're a construction worker.

- You're covered by other laws (academic staff).

- You're a municipal police officer.

- You were hired for a definite term or task of less than 12 months. (This doesn't apply to oil well drilling or geophysical exploration.)

- Your boss made a reasonable offer of another job and you said "no."

- You refused work available through a seniority system.

- You're laid off because of a strike or lockout at your workplace.

- You have an agreement where you can say "yes" or "no" to temporary work.

- There's a lack of work your employer couldn't foresee or control.

- You're a seasonal worker and your work is finished at the end of the season.

- You're on temporary layoff and don't come back to work within 7 days after your boss asks you to in writing.

- Your job is clearing land and involves cutting, removing, and disposing of trees and/or brush.

Temporary Layoffs

Your boss doesn't have to give notice or pay compensation if you're laid off temporarily.

If the lay-off is temporary, you must be called back to work within 59 days. Otherwise, your job is over on the 60th day, and your boss must give you termination pay on that day according to your length of service. But there are some exceptions.

- If, after your layoff began, you and your boss agreed that you would get wages or an amount instead of wages. In this case, you're eligible for termination pay only when the agreement ends.

- If your boss is making payments towards your pension or insurance plan, or a similar benefit. After your job ends, you're eligible for termination pay when the payments stop.

- If you're unionized and your contract has recall rights. Your job ends and you get termination pay when the recall rights expire.

Your employer must ask you to return to work in writing after a valid temporary layoff. If you don't report back to work within 7 days of that written request, your employer can let you go without further notice or termination pay.

If you're let go while on temporary lay-off, you're still entitled to termination pay.

There are special rules for school workers and school bus drivers:

- If the summer break is longer than 59 days, the temporary layoff of school workers and school bus drivers can be longer. This means your employer doesn't have to give you termination pay because there's a summer break. But you must work until the end of one school year and be given the option of working again when the next school year begins.

- The temporary layoff provisions don't apply to workers who get paid by their employer during the summer break.

Sale of a Business

If a business is sold, and the employee continues to be employed by the new owner, the length of employment for the purpose of notice includes the period of employment both with the previous, as well as the current owner.

When considering the termination notice for the employee, the employer must consider this total period of employment.

When Notice is Not Required

There are a number of circumstances where an employer is not required to give notice of termination. Probably the most important of these circumstances is termination for "just cause." Examples of just cause include:

- willful misconduct,

- disobedience, or

- deliberate neglect of duty.

Other circumstances that permit an employer to terminate employment without giving notice include:

- The employee was hired for a definite term or task of less than 12 months, at the end of which the employment terminates (the 12-month limit for term or task does not apply to oil well drilling or geophysical exploration).

- The employee was laid off after refusing an offer by the employer of reasonable alternative work.

- The employee refuses work made available through a seniority system.

- The employee is not provided with work because a strike or lockout is taking place at the employee's place of employment.

- The employee is employed under an agreement by which the employee may elect either to work or not to work for a temporary period when requested by the employer.

- The contract of employment is or has become impossible for the employer to perform by reason of unforeseeable or unpreventable causes beyond the control of the employer.

- The employee was hired on a seasonal basis and at the end of the season the employment is terminated.

- The employee is on temporary layoff and does not return to work within seven days after being requested to do so, in writing, by the employer.

- The employee is in the construction industry.

- The employee is employed in the cutting, removal, burning or other disposal of trees and/or brush for the primary purpose of clearing land.

When an employee's employment is terminated for just cause, the employer must pay all wages, overtime, general holiday pay and vacation pay due the employee within ten days following the date of termination. The employer must be able to support their position to justify that there was just cause for dismissal without notice.

Constructive Dismissal

Some employers attempt to make working conditions so intolerable for their no longer wanted employees in the hopes that they will quit on their own to save the company the effort and money involved in termination procedures. Most frequently this involves cutting salaries and/or reducing benefits, but it may also include relocating employees to smaller offices, eliminating their secretarial support, or other measures.

When such changes are made, an employee may elect to view them as "constructive dismissal." This means that the employer's actions have been so inconsistent with the agreed-upon employment contract that they can be seen to contravene the contract.

When determining what actions constitute constructive dismissal, the Courts again examine the question of degree. Cutting a salary in half, for example, can normally be seen as a clear contravention of the employment contract. However, particularly in this economic climate, it cannot be said that *any* reduction in salary or benefits constitutes constructive dismissal, and in recent practice the Courts have tended to draw the line at cuts of approximately 20 percent.

Wrongful Dismissal

When an employer terminates employment without just cause and without reasonable notice (or pay in lieu of notice), or when there is a clear case for claiming constructive dismissal, the employee may choose to seek compensation for breach of contract.

The Courts consider wrongful-dismissal actions as "damage" claims, rather than "debt" claims, and the wrongfully dismissed employee is obliged to reduce the effect of the damages caused - by doing his or her best to find another job.

Settlements are based on net damage. If the employee finds a position at half the pay he or she was previous earning, for example, the former employer will be required to pay the difference.

While employment contract law seems clear, both employers and employees should keep in mind that the law only sets out minimum standards, and is therefore open to interpretation.

Employees who are not members of unions cannot base their expectations for employment on the conditions granted to their fellow unionized workers. Each contract for employment is separate and individual. What constitutes wrongful dismissal in a collective bargaining unit may not constitute it in a non-unionized environment.

Employers who risk wrongful dismissal claims are taking a financial gamble. The cost of a successful claim by a former employee who has not found other work can be expensive not only financial but in reputation as well.

Employers who want to terminate the contract of an employee are well advised to seek legal assistance before they begin the process. On the other hand, employees who feel they have been wrongfully - or constructively - dismissed are wise to take similar action.

Group Termination

Alberta has no provisions regarding notice of group termination or mass layoffs.

To File a Complaint:

http://www.employment.alberta.ca/SFW/1697.html

British Columbia

Source: www.labour.gov.bc.ca

Termination Notice

Once you get your notice of termination, your employer can't change any condition of your job, including your wage rate, unless you give written consent. Your vacation, leave, strike or lockout, or absence due to illness can't be used as part of the notice period. The notice period is based on your years of service.

Length of Employment	Notice Required
Less than 3 months	None
3 months but less than 1 year	1 week
2 years but less than 3 years	2 weeks
3 years but less than 4 years	3 weeks
4 years but less than 5 years	4 weeks
5 years but less than 6 years	5 weeks
6 years but less than 7 years	6 weeks
7 years but less than 8 years	7 weeks
8 years or over	8 weeks

Termination Pay

The amount the employer is liable to pay becomes payable on termination of the employment and is calculated by:

     (a) totalling all of the employee's hourly wages earned during the last 8 weeks,

     (b) dividing the total by 8, and

     (c) multiplying the result by the number of weeks of termination notice required.

In calculating (a), use only regular wages and number of hours worked in a typical week (i.e. don't include bonuses, overtime or extra hours worked).

For the purpose of determining the termination date, the employment of an employee who is laid off for more than a temporary layoff (see below) is deemed to have been terminated at the beginning of the layoff for legal purposes.

No Notice or Compensation Required

No compensation is required if an employee is given advance written notice of termination equal to the number of weeks for which the employee is eligible. This notice must be in writing.

An employee can also be given a combination of written notice and compensation equal to the number of weeks of pay for which the employee is eligible.

An employee must be able to work during the notice period. If an employee is on vacation, leave, temporary layoff, strike or lockout, or unavailable for work due to medical reasons during the notice period, the employer must either suspend the notice period until the employee returns to work or pay that employee compensation in lieu of notice.

Once written notice has been given, the employer may not alter any condition of employment, including the wage rate without the employee's written consent.

Notice or compensation is not required if:
- The employee has not completed three consecutive months of employment.
- The employee quits or retires.
- The employee is dismissed for just cause.
- The employee works on an on-call basis doing temporary assignments, which he or she can accept or reject.
- The employee is employed for a definite term.
- The employee is hired for specific work to be completed in 12 months or less.
- It is impossible to perform the work because of some unforeseeable event or circumstance (other than bankruptcy, receivership or insolvency).
- An employer whose principal business is construction employs the employee at one or more construction sites.
- The employee refuses reasonable alternative employment.

- The employee is a teacher employed by a board of school trustees.

Temporary Layoff

A fundamental term of an employment contract is that an employee works and is paid for his/her services. Therefore, any layoff, including a temporary layoff, constitutes termination of employment unless the possibility of temporary layoff is;

- Expressly provided for in the contract of employment;
- Implied by well-known industry-wide practice (e.g. logging, where work cannot be performed during "break-up"); or
- Agreed to by the employee.

In the absence of an expressed or implied provision in an employment agreement that allows temporary layoff, the Act alone does not give employers a general right to temporarily lay off employees.

Where a temporary layoff is permitted by the terms and conditions of employment, the Act applies to limit it to:

- A layoff of up to 13 weeks in a period of 20 weeks, or
- A period of time in which an employee covered by a collective agreement has the right to be recalled.

If an employee's hours are reduced, a week of layoff is a week in which an employee earns less than 50 percent of his or her weekly wages at the regular rate, averaged over the previous eight weeks.

A temporary layoff becomes a termination when:

- It exceeds 13 weeks in any period of 20 consecutive weeks, or
- The recall period for an employee covered by a collective agreement is exceeded.

When a temporary layoff becomes a termination, the beginning of the layoff is the termination date and the employee's entitlement to compensation for length of service is based on that date.

Group Terminations

Where an employer intends to terminate 50 or more employees at a single location within a two-month period, the employer must give written notice of group termination to each employee affected. The length of notice depends on the number of employees affected.

If the amount of written notice is less than the required termination pay, employees must be paid the difference. The notice of group termination must be given as follows:

(a) At least 8 weeks' notice, if 50 to 100 employees will be affected;

(b) At least 12 weeks' notice, if 101 to 300 employees will be affected;

(c) At least 16 weeks' notice if 301 or more employees will be affected.

If an employee is not given notice, the employer must give the employee termination pay instead of the required notice or a combination of notice and termination pay.

The B.C. Employment Standards Act does not remove an employer's right to terminate an employee. The Act requires that employees who are terminated to receive written notice or compensation based on length of service.

Wrongful Dismissal

Some employees who are terminated sue for wrongful dismissal through the courts. This is different than a complaint made to the Employment Standards Branch. Those who wish to consider an action for wrongful dismissal should seek legal advice. The Employment Standards Branch does not provide this advice.

If an Employee Quits

An employee who voluntarily quits his or her employment is not entitled to written notice of termination or compensation for length of service. Final wages, including any outstanding wages such as annual vacation pay, statutory holiday pay and overtime either worked or in a time bank, must be paid to the employee within six days after the employee's last day of work. The Act does not require the employee to give notice to the employer.

If an employee does give notice, the employer may accept or refuse the notice. If the employer refuses the notice, or terminates the employee during the notice period, the employer must pay compensation equal to the lesser of:

- The remaining amount of notice the employee has given; or
- The employee's statutory entitlement under the Act.

Constructive Dismissal

Sometimes, even if you quit, the law will say that the employer forced you to quit and actually fired you. This is called "constructive dismissal". To prove it, you would have to show that you had no reasonable choice, other than quitting. That's hard to show. Constructive dismissal may apply if the employer has changed any important part of your job without your consent, such as your pay, your job duties, or your job title.

To File a Complaint:

http://www.labour.gov.bc.ca/esb/self-help/sh-start.htm

Manitoba

Source: www.gov.mb.ca

Termination Notice

The amount of notice employers must provide employees depends on the length of time that employee has worked for them.

Period of employment	Notice period
less than 1 year	one week
at least 1 year and less than 3 years	two weeks
at least 3 years and less than 5 years	four weeks
at least 5 years and less than 10 years	six weeks
at least 10 years	eight weeks

Employers can still either allow the employee to work out this notice period, or pay wages in lieu of notice, for the same number of weeks.

Termination/Severance Pay

The amount of severance is based on the last regular bi-weekly rate of pay, excluding allowances. Generally, the applicable work week for the classification applies. If employee's weekly hours vary between summer and winter, severance pay is based on an average of normal hours of work over the fiscal year.

No-Notice Period

When the period of employment has been less than 30 days, employers have the right to end the working relationship without notice.

Group Terminations

Employers who intend to terminate a group of 50 or more employees within four weeks must provide more notice than for an individual termination.

Number of Employees	Notice Required
50 to 100	10 weeks
101 to 299	14 weeks
300 or more	18 weeks

Wrongful Dismissal

While there is no direct reference to "wrongful dismissal" or "constructive dismissal" in the Manitoba Labour Code, terminations that are deemed "unfair" are:

No employer or other person acting on behalf of an employer may suspend, terminate or restrict or threaten to suspend, terminate or restrict the employment of an employee, or layoff or threaten to lay off an employee, or otherwise discriminate against an employee,

(a) Because garnishment proceedings are taken or might be taken against the employee.

(b) Because the employee files or might file a complaint under this Code or assists in the initiation of a complaint, prosecution or other proceeding under this Code.

(c) Because the employee requests or receives information or advice from an officer or requests or demands anything that the employee is entitled to under this Code.

(d) Because the employee gives or might give information or evidence in respect of an investigation, prosecution or other proceeding under this Code.

(e) Because the employee makes or might make a statement or disclosure that may be required of the employee under this Code.

(f) Because the employee refuses to work or attempts to refuse to work on a Sunday, if he or she is permitted to refuse under the Code.

To File a Complaint:

http://www.gov.mb.ca/labour/standards/forms.html

New Brunswick

Source: www.gnb.ca

Termination Notice

Every employer in New Brunswick, when dismissing an employee for cause, must do so in writing setting out the reasons for such action. Otherwise the dismissal without notice is not valid even if cause exists. The dismissal then becomes a termination without notice and the employer must pay the employee the wages the employee would have earned during the notice period.

Every employer in the Province of New Brunswick when terminating or laying off an employee must give:

Period of employment	Notice period
6 months and less than 5 years	two weeks
at least 5 years	four weeks

An employer may pay the employee the wages the employee would have earned during the applicable notice period instead of providing written notice.

An employer can lay off an employee without notice where:

1. The layoff is for a period not exceeding six (6) days.
2. There is lack of work due to any reason unforeseen by the employer at the time notice would have been given.

An employer can lay off or terminate an employee without notice where:

1. The termination of employment is due to the completion of a definite assignment the employee was hired to perform over a period not exceeding twelve (12) months.
2. The employee has completed a term of employment fixed in the employment contract, unless the employee is employed for a period of three (3) months beyond that period.
3. The employee retires under an established retirement plan.
4. The employee is doing construction work at a work site in the construction industry.
5. The termination or layoff results from the normal seasonal reduction, closure or suspension of an operation.

6. The employee has refused reasonable alternative employment offered by the employer instead of being terminated or laid off.

Temporary Layoff

In addition, an employer can lay off an employee without notice where:

- The layoff is for a period not exceeding six days.
- There is lack of work due to any unforeseen reason.

Wrongful Dismissal

An employer shall not dismiss, suspend, lay off, penalize, discipline, or discriminate against an employee if the reason is related to:

a. The request of an employee for a leave of absence provided for under the Act.

b. An employee making a complaint or giving information against the employer with respect to the Act.

c. An employee giving information or evidence against the employer with respect to the alleged violation of any provincial or federal act or regulation.

d. The dismissal, suspension, layoff, penalty, discipline or discrimination is an attempt by the employer to evade any responsibility imposed upon him/her under the Act or any other provincial or federal act or regulation.

Constructive Dismissal

Where an employer unilaterally makes a fundamental or substantial change to the employee's contract of employment (a change that violates the contract's terms) the employer is committing a fundamental breach of the contract that results in its termination and entitles the employee to consider himself/herself constructively dismissed.

Group Terminations

New Brunswick is one of the few jurisdictions that do not increase the notice period with the size of the affected group. Only six weeks' notice needs to be given where 10 or more terminations are anticipated and only then if the group to be dismissed represents at least 25 per cent of the total workforce in the establishment.

How to file a complaint:

http://www.gnb.ca/0308/02-e.asp

Newfoundland and Labrador

Source: www.hrle.gov.nl.ca

Termination notice

An employer shall not terminate an employee unless written notice of termination is given by or on behalf of the employer directly to the employee

An employer shall not temporarily lay off an employee unless written notice of the temporary lay-off is given by or on behalf of the employer to the employee within the period required.

Period of employment	Notice period
At least 3 months and less than 2 years	one week
At least 2 years and less than 5 years	two weeks
At least 5 years and less than 10 years	three weeks
At least 10 years and less than 15 years	four weeks
At least 15 years	six weeks

No Notice Required

No termination notice is required when:

a) The employee has committed misconduct or been so neglectful of duty that the interest of the employer is adversely affected.

b) The employer pays to the employee wages equal to the normal wages covering the period of notice that the employer would otherwise be required to give. Normal wages includes the amount for overtime wages that might have been earned by the employee on the basis of the overtime practised in the period of 1 month before his or her termination.

c) The employee is laid off for a period not exceeding 1 week.

d) The employee is employed for a firm non-renewable term or for a specific task, where the term or task does not exceed 12 months and the employment is not terminated before the completion of the term or task.

e) The employee rejects an offer by the employer of reasonable alternative employment of a similar nature requiring similar skill, effort and ability that would enable the employee to earn during a similar number of working hours a total wage comparable to that earned by the employee for services rendered.

f) The employee has reached the age of retirement according to the established practice of the undertaking in which the employee is employed.

g) The employer is required to terminate the contract of service on account of:

i. Destruction of or major breakdown to plant machinery or equipment.

ii. Climatic or economic conditions that are beyond the foreseeable control of the employer and that necessitate declaration of redundancy.

h) The contract of service between the employer and the employee has existed for less than 30 days.

Group Terminations

Where an employer intends to terminate the contracts of service of 50 or more employees within a 4 week period, the employer shall give to each employee written notice of intention to terminate the contract of service.

The employer shall either,

a) For the duration of the notice period continue to employ the employees on whom notice of intention to terminate has been served; or

b) Pay the employee wages equal to the normal wages covering the period of notice that the employer would otherwise be required to give.

The period of notice of intention to terminate the contracts of service required is as follows:

Number of Employees	Notice Required
50 to 199	8 weeks
200 to 499	12 weeks
500 or more	16 weeks

Temporary Layoff

A temporary layoff is a period of lay off up to 13 weeks in duration in any 20 consecutive week period. Notice of temporary lay-off has to be given, either one to six weeks notice depending on the length of service of the employee. No notice is required, however, if the lay-off is for less than one week.

If the layoff exceeds 13 weeks, the employment is terminated. At the time of the original "layoff" the employee should have received one to six weeks notice. The temporary lay-off provisions do not provide employees with additional notice periods.

Wrongful Dismissal

The Human Rights Commission does not handle wrongful dismissal complaints unless the reason for the dismissal is a protected ground, such as age, race, sex, disability, etc.

How to File a Complaint:

http://www.hrle.gov.nl.ca/lra/labourstandards/default.htm

Northwest Territories

Source: www.ece.gov.nt.ca

Termination Notice

No employer shall terminate the employment of an employee who has been employed by that employer for a period of 90 days or more, unless the employer:

a) Gives the employee a written notice of termination indicating the date the notice is given and the date on which the employment is terminated; or

b) Pays the employee termination pay.

This does not apply to an employee

a) Who is temporarily laid off;

b) Who is employed in an activity, business, work, trade, occupation or profession that is exempted by regulation;

c) Whose employment is terminated for just cause;

d) Whose employment is terminated because the employee has refused an offer by the employer of reasonable alternative work with the employer; or

e) Who is on temporary layoff and does not return to work within seven days after being requested to do so in writing by the employer.

A notice of termination must be given to an employee in advance of the date of termination by a period of at least two weeks plus one additional week for each year of employment over two years, to a maximum of eight weeks.

Period of employment	
under 3 years	two week
3 years to less than 4 years	three weeks
4 years to less than 5 years	four weeks
5 years to less than 6 years	five weeks
6 years to less than 7 years	six weeks
7 years to less than 8 years	seven weeks
8 years or more	eight weeks

The period of notice required shall not coincide with the annual vacation of an employee whose employment is being terminated. If an employee has been employed by the same employer more than once, the separate periods of employment shall be deemed to be one period of employment; if not more than 90 days have elapsed between each period of employment.

An employer shall not, between the date that the notice of termination is given and the date of termination of employment:

a) Reduce an employee's wages or rate of wages; or

b) Alter any term or condition of an employee's employment.

Termination Pay

An employer shall, between the date that the notice of termination is given and the date of termination of employment, pay wages and provide benefits to an employee to whom the notice is given in an amount not less than the wages and benefits to which the employee would have been entitled, if the employee had worked his or her usual hours of work in that period, whether or not work is required or performed.

If termination pay is given to an employee, the amount of the termination pay must be equal to the wages and benefits to which the employee would have been entitled, if the employee had worked his or her usual hours of work for each week of the period for which notice would otherwise be required.

An Employment Standards Officer may declare that an employer has terminated the employment of an employee, if the Employment Standards Officer is satisfied that:

a) The employer has substantially altered a condition of the employee's employment; and

b) The purpose of the alteration is to discourage the employee from continuing in the employment of the employer.

Group Termination

A group termination occurs when an employer terminates 10 or more employees at one place of employment within a four week period. Termination includes a layoff with no recall date or a lay-off of 26 weeks or more. The employer must give notice of group termination.

The minimum notice for a group termination is:

Applies to Employees Terminated Within …	Number of Employees Terminated	Notice Required
4 week period	25-49	4 weeks
	50-99	8 weeks
	100-299	12 weeks
	300 or more	16 weeks

Wrongful/Constructive Dismissal

The NWT Employment Standards Act does not currently address specifics in the matters of wrongful dismissal or constructive dismissal. Contact the Department of Education, Culture and Employment to inquire about your situation and potential remedies.

To File a Complaint:

http://www.ece.gov.nt.ca/Divisions/Labour/index.htm

Nova Scotia

Source: www.gov.ns.ca

Termination Notice

An employer shall not discharge, suspend or lay off an employee, unless the employee has been guilty of willful misconduct or disobedience or neglect of duty that has not been condoned by the employer, without having given at least:

Period of employment	Notice period
At least 3 months and less than 2 years	one week
At least 2 years and less than 5 years	two weeks
At least 5 years and less than 10 years	four weeks
At least 10 years	eight weeks

This applies in all cases except when:

(a) A person whose period of employment is less than three months.

(b) A person employed for a definite term or task for a period not exceeding twelve months.

(c) A person who is laid off or suspended for a period not exceeding six consecutive days.

(d) A person who is discharged or laid off for any reason beyond the control of the employer.

(e) A person who has been offered reasonable other employment by his employer.

(f) A person who, having reached the age of retirement for the held position.

(g) A person employed in the construction industry.

Every employer required to give notice of termination shall give notice in writing addressed to each person whose employment is to be terminated and shall serve the notice personally or by registered mail.

An employer cannot fire or suspend an employee whose period of employment is 10 years or more unless the employer has just cause. If fired without just cause, the employee could be entitled to be reinstated to his/her position.

An employer can lay off an employee whose period of employment is ten years or more. The employer would be required to give the employee eight weeks' written notice of the lay off or eight weeks' pay in lieu of that time.

No Notice Required

If an employee is guilty of willful misconduct, disobedience, or neglect of duty, the employer can end the employee's employment without notice.

Severance Pay

You will want to speak to a lawyer in regard to severance pay awarded through the courts. The Labour Standards Code & Regulations do not provide for severance.

Group Termination

Amount of notice required for employees who are terminated as part of a group termination.

Applies to Employees Terminated Within	Number of Employees Terminated	Notice Required
4 weeks	10-99	8 weeks
	100-299	12 weeks
	300 or more	16 weeks

Wrongful Dismissal

Where the period of employment of an employee with an employer is ten years or more, the employer shall not discharge or suspend that employee without just cause.

To file a complaint:

http://www.gov.ns.ca/lae/employmentrights/process.asp

Nunavut

Source: www.justice.gov.nu.ca

Termination Notice

Notice of termination means a written notice of termination of employment given by an employer to an employee. An employer who wishes to terminate the employment of an employee by notice of termination shall give the employee written notice of termination of not less than:

Period of employment	
At least 3 months to less than 3 years	two week
3 years to less than 4 years	three weeks
4 years to less than 5 years	four weeks
5 years to less than 6 years	five weeks
6 years to less than 7 years	six weeks
7 years to less than 8 years	seven weeks
8 years or more	eight weeks

The period of notice required shall not coincide with the annual vacation of the employee whose employment is being terminated.

Where notice of termination is given, the employer,

(a) Shall not reduce the wages or rate of wages or alter any term or condition of employment of the employee to whom notice is given; and

(b) Shall, between the date that the notice of termination is given and the date of termination of employment, pay wages and benefits to the employee to whom the notice is given in an amount not less than the wages and benefits to which the employee would have been entitled if the employee had worked his or her usual hours of work in that period, whether or not work is required or performed.

Temporary layoff means an interruption of the employment of an employee by an employer for a period:

a) Not exceeding 45 days of layoff in a period of 60 consecutive days, or

b) Exceeding 45 days of layoff, where the employer recalls the employee to employment within a time fixed by the Labour Standards Officer.

Where an employer temporarily lays off an employee and the layoff exceeds a temporary layoff;

a) The employment of the employee shall be deemed to have terminated on the last day of temporary layoff; and

b) The employer shall pay the employee termination pay.

Where an employee has been employed by the same employer more than once, those periods of employment shall be deemed to be one period of employment if not more than 90 days have elapsed between each period of employment.

Termination Pay

An employer who wishes to terminate the employment of an employee by paying termination pay in place of giving notice of termination shall pay the employee termination pay in an amount equal to the wages and benefits to which the employee would have been entitled if the employee had worked his or her usual hours of work for each week of the period for which notice would otherwise be required.

The above does not apply to an employee;

a) Who is temporarily laid off;

b) who is employed in an activity, business, work, trade, occupation or profession that is exempted by regulation;

c) Whose employment is terminated for just cause;

d) Whose employment is terminated because the employee has refused an offer by the employer of reasonable alternative work; or

e) On temporary layoff who does not return to work within seven days after being requested to do so in writing by the employer.

Group Termination

Where an employer wishes to terminate the employment of 25 or more employees at one time or within any period not exceeding four weeks, the employer shall, in addition to any notice required, give the Labour Standards Officer written notice of not less than:

Applies to Employees Terminated Within …	Number of Employees Terminated	Notice Required
4 week period	25-49	4 weeks
	50-99	8 weeks
	100-299	12 weeks
	300 or more	16 weeks

Wrongful Dismissal

The Nunavut Labour Standards Board does not currently address specifics in the matters of wrongful dismissal or constructive dismissal. Contact the Labour Standards Board to inquire about your situation and potential remedies.

Constructive Dismissal

Where an employer has substantially altered a condition of employment and the Labour Standards Officer is satisfied that the purpose of the alteration is to discourage the employee from continuing in the employment of the employer, the Labour Standards Officer may declare that the employer has terminated the employment of the employee.

To File a Complaint:

http://www.workrights.ca/content.php?sec=6

Ontario

Source: www.labour.gov.on.ca

Termination Notice

Under the Employment Standards Act, 2000 (ESA) a person's employment is terminated if the employer:

- Dismisses or stops employing an employee due to the bankruptcy or insolvency of the employer.

- "Constructively" dismisses an employee and the employee resigns, in response, within a reasonable time.

- Lays an employee off for a period that is longer than a "temporary layoff".

In most cases, when an employer ends the employment of an employee who has been continuously employed for a minimum of three months, the employer must provide the employee with either written notice of termination, termination pay or a combination (as long as the notice and the termination pay together equal the length of notice the employee is entitled to receive).

An employer is not required to give an employee a reason why his or her employment is being terminated. There are, however, some situations where an employer **cannot** terminate an employee's employment even if the employer is prepared to give proper written notice or termination pay. For example, an employer cannot end someone's employment, or penalize them in any way, if any part of the reason for the termination of employment is based on the employee asking questions about the ESA or exercising a right under the ESA, such as refusing to work in excess of the daily or weekly hours of work maximums, or taking a leave of absence specified in the ESA.

Qualifying for Termination Notice or Pay in Lieu

Certain employees are not entitled to notice of termination or termination pay under the ESA. Examples include: employees who are guilty of willful misconduct, disobedience, or willful neglect of duty that is not trivial and has not been condoned by the employer. Other examples include construction employees, employees on temporary layoff, employees who refuse an offer of reasonable alternative employment and employees who have been employed less than three months.

Temporary Layoff

For the purposes of the termination provisions of the ESA, a "week of layoff" is a week in which the employee earned less than half of what he or she would ordinarily earn (or earns on average) in a week.

A week of layoff does not include any week in which the employee did not work for one or more days because the employee was not able or available to work, was subject to disciplinary suspension, or was not provided with work because of a strike or lockout.

Employers are not required under the ESA to provide employees with a written notice of a temporary layoff, nor do they have to produce a reason. They may, however, be required to do these things under a collective agreement (union) or an employment contract.

Under The ESA, a "Temporary Layoff" Can Last:

- Not more than 13 weeks of layoff in any period of 20 consecutive weeks; **or**

- More than 13 weeks in any period of 20 consecutive weeks, but less than 35 weeks of layoff in any period of 52 consecutive weeks, where;

    - The employee continues to receive substantial payments or contributions to any aspect of benefit program from the employer; **or**

    - The employee is entitled to receive supplementary unemployment benefits whether s/he receives them or not; **or**

    - The employer recalls the employee within the time frame set out in an agreement with an employee who is not represented by a trade union.

If an employee is laid off for a period longer than a temporary layoff as set out above, the employer is considered to have terminated the employee's employment. Generally, the employee will then be entitled to termination pay.

Written Notice of Termination

Under the ESA:

- An employer can terminate the employment of an employee who has been employed continuously for three months or more if the employer has given the employee proper *written notice* of termination and the notice period has expired; **or**

- An employer can terminate the employment of an employee *without* written notice or with *less* notice than is required if the employer pays *termination pay* to the employee.

When an employee is terminated, the written notice required under the ESA is generally determined by how long someone has been employed by an employer. Notice of termination of employment, once given, cannot be withdrawn without the consent of the employee.

The following chart specifies the periods of statutory notice required.

Length of Employment	Notice Required
Less than 3 months	None
3 months but less than 1 year	one week
1 year but less than 3 years	two weeks
3 years but less than 4 years	three weeks
4 years but less than 5 years	four weeks
5 years but less than 6 years	five weeks
6 years but less than 7 years	six weeks
7 years but less than 8 years	seven weeks
8 years or more	eight weeks

Notice can be provided in person or by mail, fax or e-mail, as long as delivery can be verified.

Requirements During the Statutory Notice Period

During the statutory notice period, an employer must:

- Not reduce the employee's wage rate or alter a term or condition of employment;
- Continue to make whatever contributions would be required to maintain the employee's benefits plans; and
- Pay the employee the wages he or she is entitled to, which cannot be less than the employee's regular wages for a regular work week each week.

Regular Rate

This is an employee's rate of pay for each non-overtime hour of work in the employee's work week.

Regular Wages

These are wages other than overtime pay, vacation pay, public holiday pay, premium pay, termination pay and severance pay and certain contractual entitlements.

Regular Work Week

For an employee who usually works the same number of hours every week, a regular work week is a week of that many hours, not including overtime hours.

Some employees do not have a regular work week. That is, they do not work the same number of hours every week or they are paid on a basis other than time. For these employees, the "regular wages" for a "regular work week" is the average amount of the regular wages earned by the employee in the 12 weeks in which the employee worked immediately preceding the date the notice was given.

An employer is not allowed to reduce an employee's wages by scheduling an employee's vacation time during the statutory notice period unless the employee **after** receiving written notice of termination of employment agrees to take his/her vacation time during the notice period.

Termination Pay

An employee who does not receive the written notice required under the ESA must be given termination pay in lieu of notice. Termination pay is a lump sum payment equal to the **regular wages** for a **regular work week** that an employee would otherwise have been entitled to during the written notice period. An employee earns vacation pay on his or her termination pay. Employers must also continue to make whatever contributions would be required to maintain the benefits the employee would have been entitled to had he or she continued to be employed through the notice period.

Regular Work Week Example

Ellen has worked for three and a half years. Now her job has been eliminated and her employment has been terminated. Ellen was not given any written notice of termination. Ellen worked 40 hours a week every week and was paid $12.00 an hour. She also received four percent vacation pay. Because she worked for more than three years but less than four years,

Ellen is entitled to three weeks' pay in lieu of notice.

1. Ellen's regular wages for a regular work week are calculated as:

   $12.00 an hour $\times$ 40 hours a week = $480.00 a week

2. Her termination pay is calculated as:

   $480.00 $\times$ 3 weeks = $1,440.00

3. Then her vacation pay on her termination pay is calculated as:

   4% of $1,440.00 = $57.60

4. Finally, her vacation pay is added to her termination pay and is calculated as:

   $1,440.00 + $57.60 = $1,497.60

Based on Ellen working for 3.5 years, her resulting entitlement adds up to $1,497.60.

Non Regular Work Week Example

Joe has worked at a nursing home for four years. He works every week, but his hours vary from week to week. His rate of pay is $12.00 an hour, and he is paid six per cent vacation pay.

Sadly for Joe, his employer eliminated his position and did not give Joe any written notice of termination. Joe was ill and off work for two of the 12 weeks immediately preceding the day his employment was terminated. Joe earned $1,800.00 in the 12 weeks before the day on which his employment ended.

Joe is entitled to four weeks of termination pay.

1. Joe's average earnings per week are calculated as:

   $1,800.00 for 12 weeks $\div$ 10 weeks (Joe was off sick for two weeks therefore these weeks are not included in the calculation) = $180.00 a week

2. His termination pay is calculated as:

   $180.00 $\times$ 4 weeks = $720.00

3. Then his vacation pay on his termination pay is calculated as:

   6% of $720.00 = $43.20

4. Finally, his vacation pay is added to his termination pay:

   $720.00 + $43.20 = $763.20

In the end, Joe would be entitled to $763.20.

When Termination Pay is Paid

Termination pay must be paid to an employee **either** seven days after the employee is terminated or on the employee's next regular pay date, whichever is **later**.

Group Termination

Special rules for notice of termination may apply when the employment of 50 or more employees is terminated at an employer's establishment within a four-week period. This is often referred to as group or mass termination.

The amount of notice employees must receive in a mass termination is not based on the employees' length of employment, but on the number of employees who have been terminated. An employer must give:

- 8 weeks' notice if the employment of 50 to 199 employees is to be terminated.
- 12 weeks' notice if the employment of 200 to 499 employees is to be terminated.
- 16 weeks' notice if the employment of 500 or more employees is to be terminated.

Exception to the Group Termination Rules

The group termination rules do not apply if:

1. The number of employees whose employment is being terminated represents 10% or less of the employees who have been employed for at least three months at the establishment, <u>and</u>
2. None of the terminations are caused by the permanent stoppage of the employer's business at the establishment.

Temporary Work After Termination

An employee can work for the employer on a temporary basis in the 13-week period **after** his or her employment has been terminated, without affecting the original date of the termination. When the temporary work has ended, the employer is not required to provide any further notice of termination to the employee.

If an employee works beyond the 13-week period after the termination date, the employee becomes entitled to written notice of termination as if it had never been given. The employee's period of employment will then also include the period of temporary work.

Exemptions to Notice of Termination or Termination Pay

The notice of termination and termination pay requirements of the ESA do not apply to an employee who:

- Is guilty of willful misconduct, disobedience or willful neglect of duty that is not trivial and has not been condoned by the employer.

  Note: "willful" includes when an employee intended the resulting consequence or acted recklessly knowing the effects their conduct would have. Poor work conduct that is accidental or involuntary is generally not considered willful.

- Was hired for a specific length of time or to do a specific task. However, such an employee will be entitled to notice of termination or termination pay if:

  - The employment ends before the term expires or the task is completed; or

  - The term expires or the task is not completed more than 12 months after the employment started; or

  - The employment continues for three months or more after the term expires or the task is completed.

- Is employed in construction, this includes employees who are doing off-site work in whole or in part who are commonly associated in work or collective bargaining with employees who work at the construction site.

- Has refused an offer of reasonable alternative employment with the employer.

- Has refused to exercise his/her right to another position that is available under a seniority system. This usually means the employee gives up the right to displace or "bump" another employee in order to keep working.

- Is on a temporary lay-off.

- does not return to work within a reasonable time after being recalled to work from a temporary layoff.

- Is terminated during or as a result of a strike or lockout at the workplace.

- Has lost his or her employment because the contract of employment is impossible to perform or has been frustrated by an unexpected or unforeseen event or circumstance, such as a fire or flood that makes it impossible for the employer to keep the employee working.

  Note: This does not include bankruptcy or insolvency or when the contract is frustrated or impossible to perform as the result of an injury or illness suffered by an employee.

Wrongful Dismissal

An employee cannot sue an employer in court for wrongful dismissal **and** file a claim for termination pay or severance pay with the ministry for the same termination or severance of employment. The employee must choose one or the other and may wish to obtain legal advice concerning their rights.

Greater Right to Termination Notice, Pay in Lieu, and Severance Pay

The ESA provides minimum standards only. Some employees may have rights to notice termination pay **and** severance pay. Employees may wish to obtain legal advice concerning their rights.

Severance pay is compensation that is paid to a qualified employee who has his or her employment "severed." It compensates an employee for loss of seniority and job-related benefits. It also recognizes an employee's long service.

In Ontario, severance pay is not the same as termination pay, which is given in place of the required notice of termination of employment.

A person's employment is "severed" when their employer either:

- Dismisses or stops employing the employee, *including* an employee who is no longer employed due to the bankruptcy or insolvency of his or her employer; or
- "Constructively" dismisses the employee and the employee resigns in response within a reasonable time; or
- Lays the employee off for 35 or more weeks in a period of 52 consecutive weeks; or
- Lays the employee off because all of the business at an establishment closes permanently; or
- Gives the employee written notice of termination and the employee resigns after giving two weeks' written notice. The resignation would take effect during the statutory notice period.

Employee Resigns After Receiving Notice of Termination

An employee who has been given a written notice of termination can resign and continue to keep the right to severance pay. To keep this right, the employee must give the employer **two weeks'** written notice of his/her resignation. The resignation must also take effect during the statutory notice period–the period of written notice that is required to be given by the employer.

If an employer provides longer notice than is required, the statutory part of the notice period is the last part of the period that ends on the date of termination. For example:

Kate has worked for seven years, and is entitled to seven weeks' notice of termination under the ESA. Kate's employer gives her 10 weeks' notice. Kate must give her employer at least two weeks' written notice of her resignation. As long as Kate's resignation takes effect during the statutory notice period, in this case the last seven weeks of the 10-week notice period, she continues to be entitled to severance pay.

An employee qualifies for severance pay when his/her employment is severed and s/he:

- Has worked for the employer for five or more years, including all the time spent by the employee in employment with the employer, whether continuous or not and whether active or not **and**
- His or her employer:
    - Has a payroll in Ontario of at least $2.5 million; **or**
    - Has severed the employment of 50 or more employees in a six-month period because all or part of the business closed.

To calculate the amount of severance pay an employee is entitled to receive, multiply the employee's regular wages for a regular work week by the sum of:

- The number of completed years of employment; **and**
- The number of completed months of employment divided by 12 for a year that is not completed.

Regardless of the outcome, the maximum amount of severance pay required to be paid under the ESA is 26 weeks. For example, if Harold worked for his employer for 30 years, the maximum severance pay would be the equivalent of 26 weeks, not 30 weeks per the ESA maximum.

A regular work week example

Marie regularly works 40 hours a week and is paid $15.00 an hour. Her employer has a payroll of more than $2.5 million. Her employer gives Marie seven weeks' notice of termination and Marie works for the notice period. At the end of the notice period, Marie's employment is severed. On that date, Marie has been employed for seven years, nine months and two weeks.

Here's how to calculate Marie's severance pay entitlement.

1. Calculate Marie's regular wages for a regular work week.
   Susan usually works 40 hours a week × $15.00 = $600.00
2. Number of Marie's completed years = 7

3. Divide the number of complete months Jan was employed in the incomplete year by 12. Marie worked 9 complete months ÷ 12 = 0.75

4. Add the number arrived at in Step 2 (7) to the number arrived at in Step 3 (0.75),
    7 + 0.75 = 7.75

5. Multiply Marie's regular wages for a regular work week ($600.00) by the number arrived at in Step 4 (7.75).
    $600.00 × 7.75 = $4,650.00.

In the end, Marie is entitled to $4,650.00 in severance pay.

Employee paid on a basis other than time worked example:

Drew works as a commission salesperson at his employer's high-tech retail store, one of the biggest in the city. He is paid commissions on sales made and not on the basis of time worked.

Drew's employer decides to downsize and Drew is given eight weeks' written notice of termination of employment. He works the notice period and his employment is severed. On the date his employment is severed, he has been employed for 9 years, 6 months and 3 weeks.

Drew's employer has a payroll of more than $2.5 million. In the last 12 weeks of his employment, Drew has received $7,723.00.

To calculate Drew's severance pay entitlement.

1. Calculate Drew's "regular wages for a regular work week". The average of the regular wages he received in the weeks he worked during his last 12 weeks of employment.

    $7,723.00 ÷ 12 = $643.58

2. Number of completed years = 9.
3. Divide the number of complete months Drew was employed in the last year he was employed by 12.

    (Drew worked 6 complete months ÷ 12 = 0.5)

4. Add the number arrived at in Step 2 (9) and the number arrived at in Step 3 (0.5)
    9 + 0.5 = 9.5
5. Multiply Drew's regular wages for a regular work week ($643.58) by the number arrived at in Step 4 (9.5) $643.58 × 9.5 = $6,114.01.

After all is said and done, Drew is entitled to $6,114.01 in severance pay.

An employee must receive severance pay either seven days after the employee's employment is severed or on what would have been the employee's next regular pay day, whichever is **later**.

Exemptions from Severance Pay

An employee is not entitled to severance pay if s/he:

- Has refused an offer of "reasonable alternative employment" with the employer; or

- Has refused "reasonable alternative employment" that is available to the employee through a seniority system; or

- Is severed and retires on a full pension (not including Canada Pension Plan benefits); or

- Has his/her employment severed because of a strike, as long as the employer can show that the economic effects of the strike caused the closing of part or all of the business; or

- Is employed in construction, including employees who are working off-site and who are commonly associated in work or collective bargaining with employees who work at the construction site; or

- Is employed in the on-site maintenance of buildings, structures, roads, sewers, pipelines, mains, tunnels or other works; or

- Is guilty of willful misconduct, disobedience or willful neglect of duty that is not trivial and was not condoned by the employer; or

- Has lost his/her employment because the contract of employment is impossible to perform or has been frustrated by an unexpected or unforeseen event or circumstance. This does not include bankruptcy or insolvency or when the contract is frustrated or impossible to perform as the result of an injury or illness suffered by an employee.

Reprisals

Employers are prohibited from terminating or penalizing employees in any way for:

- Asking the employer to comply with the Employment Standards Act, 2000 (ESA) and the regulations.

- Asking questions about rights under the ESA.

- Filing a complaint under the ESA.

- Exercising or trying to exercise a right under the ESA.

- Giving information to an employment standards officer.

- Taking, planning on taking, being eligible or becoming eligible for a parental, pregnancy, personal emergency, declared emergency, family medical leave, organ donor, or reservist leave.

- Being subject to a garnishment order (i.e., to have a certain amount deducted directly from wages to satisfy a debt).

- Participating in a proceeding under the ESA.

- Participating in a proceeding under section 4 of the Retail Business Holidays Act. This section of the act regards tourism exemptions that allow retail businesses to open on holidays.

- Refusing to take a lie detector test.

To File a Complaint:

http://www.labour.gov.on.ca/english/es/forms/claim.php#claim_form

Prince Edward Island

Source: www.gov.pe.ca

Termination Notice

Under the Employment Standards Act, an employer must tell an employee in writing that s/he will fire or suspend or lay off that employee. This is called giving notice. "Notice" is the letter telling the employee that s/he will no longer work for the employer after a given date. It can also refer to the period of time between receipt of the letter and the official date of termination.

How much notice an employer must give an employee depends on how long the employee was employed.

Period of employment	Notice period
at least 6 months and less than 5 years	two week
at least 5 years and less than 10 years	four weeks
at least 10 years and less than 15 years	six weeks
at least 15 years	eight weeks

If the employer does not want to give the employee notice, the employer must give the employee pay in place of notice. This means that the employer must pays the employee as much pay as that employee would have received had the employee worked for his/her notice period.

No Notice Required

There are times when an employer does not have to give an employee notice or pay in lieu of notice when ending the employee's job. In order to end an employee's job without notice or pay in lieu of notice, the employer must show that s/he:

- Had made his/her expectations clear to the employee, and

- Has warned the employee to change his/her behaviour, and

- Has warned him/her that not improving his/her behaviour could lead to him/her being fired, or

- When an employee works for employer for less than 6 months, or

- When the employer offers the employee other reasonable employment.

This kind of action would be acceptable if, for example, the employee was late for work repeatedly. Of course, there are times, such as when an employer can prove that s/he had a good reason to fire the employee because, for example, the employee committed theft. Then the employee can be fired without warning or notice.

When an employer has given the employee proper notice that their job is coming to an end, the employer:

- May not change the employee's rate of pay or any other condition of employment, such as benefits, and

- May not require the employee to use remaining vacation during the notice period unless the employee agrees, and

- Must pay the employee all the wages s/he is entitled to receive.

Group Termination

All provinces, except Prince Edward Island, employers must alert the government about group terminations. As well, all provinces except PEI, have enacted some forms of additional protections for the employee who faces lay-off in group termination situations.

Applies to Employees Terminated Within ...	Number of Employees Terminated	Notice Required
2 months	10-99	4 weeks
	100-299	12 weeks
	300 or more	16 weeks

Severance Pay

At the present time, PEI has no legislation that speaks to the issue of severance pay.

To File a Complaint:

http://www.gov.pe.ca/cca/index.php3?number=1025374

Québec

Source: www.cnt.gouv.qc.ca/

Termination Notice

An employer must give the employee a written notice of termination of employment before terminating his/her employment or laying him/her off for a period of more than 6 months. At the end of a contract for a fixed term or if the employee has completed the task for which he had been hired, the employer is not required to give this notice.

The time periods for giving the employee notice vary according to their length of uninterrupted service.

Period of employment	
3 months to one year	One week
1 to 5 years	Two weeks
5 to 10 years	Four weeks
10 years or more	Eight weeks

An employer is not required to give a notice of termination of employment to an employee credited with less than 3 months of uninterrupted service.

If the employer does not give the employee the notice of termination of employment within the stipulated time periods or gives it within a period of insufficient length, the employer will have to pay the employee compensation equal to the wages that the employee would normally have earned between the date when the notice should have been given to him and the date when his employment ends, excluding overtime. For example:

Vincent has worked as a mechanic for 6 years. He was laid off 3 months ago. Today, he received by mail a letter from his employer informing him that his employment will end definitively in 4 weeks' time.

Is this legal? No. The notice that Vincent received when he was laid off is of no effect. The employer will have to pay Vincent a compensatory indemnity equal to 4 weeks of wages.

The notice of termination of employment is of no effect and of no value if it is given to the employee while he is laid off, except in the case of a seasonal job, the length of which does not ordinarily exceed 6 months per year.

Some employees are excluded from receiving a termination notice. They are:

- Employees with less than 3 months of uninterrupted service.

- Employees who have committed a serious offence.

- Employees dismissed or laid off due to superior force (example: fire).

- Employees whose contract for a fixed term ends.

- Employees who have completed the precise task for which they had been hired.

Group Termination

A group termination or collective dismissal occurs when an employer terminates the employment of ten employees or more in the same establishment in the course of two consecutive months. In addition, the layoff, for a period of six months or more, of not fewer than ten employees also constitutes a collective dismissal. The notice required is as follows:

Number of employees	Time periods
10 to 99	8 weeks
100 to 299	12 weeks
300 and over	16 weeks

Some employees are excluded from the application of the provisions related to the Notice of Collective Dismissal. They are:

- Employees with less than 3 months of uninterrupted service.

- Employees laid off for less than 6 months.

- Employees of an establishment whose activities are seasonal or intermittent.

- Employees whose contract for a fixed term or for a specific task expires.

- Casual employees or students who work for the government.

- Employees of an establishment affected by a strike or a lockout.

- Employees having committed a serious offence.

Wrongful Dismissal

A recent trend in Québec's civil court decisions has also done away with a predetermined ceiling in awarding damages representing a reasonable notice of termination. The ceiling, until this recent trend, was for 12 months' salary. Although this ceiling has been set aside by many decisions, Québec civil courts still tend to be less generous than Common Law courts in awarding damages representing reasonable notice of termination.

In Québec, employees with three years or more of continuous service who believe that they were dismissed without just or sufficient cause may file a complaint with the Labour Standards Commission seeking, among other remedies, reinstatement. The complaint must be filed within 45 days of the dismissal. The ability to seek reinstatement is an important right and gives Québec employees significant leverage in negotiating termination packages.

A recent trend has developed where, if a Labour Commissioner finds that reinstatement is not warranted, a severance indemnity will be awarded, in addition to back pay for the period between the date of the dismissal and that of the award. A rule of thumb generally used by Labour Commissioners is one month of salary per year of continuous service. As a result, Labour Commissioners can award significant monetary awards. The employer is faced, if a Labour Commissioner finds in favour of an employee, with either reinstating the employee with back pay or not reinstating the employee but having to pay for a substantial severance indemnity in addition to any back pay that might have been ordered if the employee had been reinstated.

Furthermore, the Labour Standards Act also identifies specific situations in which an employer will be assumed to have improperly dismissed an employee or to have taken retaliatory measures against an employee, including the following:

- Mandatory retirement. Demanding someone retire based on age (e.g. at 65) violates the Charter of Human Rights and Freedoms.

- Termination after an employee avails himself of a statutory right. Therefore, if you lodge a complaint that your rights are being infringed upon, you cannot be fired for it.

- Termination after an employee supplies information to the Commission regarding the application of labour standards or testifies in an action relating thereto. If you complain to a governing body that the labour code is being violated by your employer at your workplace, you should be safe from retaliation including termination by your employer.

- Termination following a seizure by garnishment against the employee. For example, if the government orders your employer to garnish your wages to pay owed child support, your employer cannot fire you for this cause.

- Termination related to an employee's pregnancy. If you become pregnant, your employer cannot fire you because of their concerns in regard to additional health costs and absences from work (parental leave, doctor's appointments, etc.)

- Termination to avoid application of the Act or one of its regulations. Your employer cannot terminate you on the grounds that they are unaware or unwilling to follow the regulations set out in the Employment Standards Act.

- Termination because an employee refused to work beyond his normal working hours because of obligations related to the custody, health or education of his/her minor child, provided s/he took all reasonable steps available to fulfill such obligations in another manner.

- Termination related to an absence due to illness or accident for a period not exceeding seventeen weeks over the twelve preceding months for an employee who has three months or more of uninterrupted service with his employer.

If an employer terminates an employee with a claim of just cause but never provided adequate warnings, the terminated employee has a strong case for wrongful dismissal. If such a case is won in court by the terminated employee, the employer risks additional financial damages because unproven allegations of cause have been linked to a breach of the duty of good faith and fair dealing.

To File a Complaint:

http://www.cnt.gouv.qc.ca/en/in-case-of/dismissal-not-made-for-good-and-sufficient-cause/index.html

Saskatchewan

Source: www.gov.sk.ca

Termination notice

Except for just cause other than shortage of work, no employer shall fire or lay off an employee who has been in his service for at least three continuous months without giving that employee at least:

Period of employment	Notice
At least 3 month to 1 year	one week
1 year to less than 3 years	two weeks
3 years to less than 5 years	four weeks
5 years to less than 10 years	six weeks
10 years or more	eight weeks

Termination pay

Upon termination, the employee is entitled to annual vacation pay with respect to all total wages (less previous vacation pay already allotted) earned by the employee. This applies whether or not an employee has completed a full year of employment.

Where an employer fires or lays off an employee, they shall pay to the employee, in respect of the period of the notice given, the sum earned by the employee during that period *or* a sum equivalent to the employee's normal wages for the period of the notice (not including overtime), whichever is greater.

When an employer discharges or lays off an employee without having given the notice required, they shall pay to the employee, in respect of the minimum period of notice required, a sum equivalent to the employee's normal wages for that period, not including overtime.

Where the wages of an employee, not including overtime, changes from week to week, his/her average wages for the past four weeks (four weeks wages not including overtime divided by four) will be used to determine the average weekly wage for calculation purposes.

Group Termination

A group termination occurs when an employer terminates 10 or more employees at one place of employment within a four week period. "Termination" includes a lay-off with no recall date or a lay-off of 26 weeks or more. The employer must give notice of group termination.

The minimum notice for a group termination is:

Number of employees	Time periods
10 to 49	4 weeks
50 to 99	8 weeks
100 and over	12 weeks

Wrongful Dismissal

If an employee claims that s/he has been wrongfully dismissed and demands pay in lieu of notice, there is no set guideline to determine the amount payable. While it has been recommended that an employee would be entitled to one month's pay for every full year of service, this amount is generally overstated in most cases in Saskatchewan.

On the other hand, there can be special factors in a few cases that make the notice period much greater that this general recommendation. For example, if the CEO of a very large corporation was dismissed after only one year of service, s/he would likely be entitled to a sum far greater than one month of pay due to seniority, potential loss of other financial benefits or specific "golden parachute" clauses in his/her employment contract. A "golden parachute" is a clause that some managerial or executive personnel request upon hiring to allow them a specified amount of compensation in case of termination.

Another example would be where an employer persuaded an employee to leave a secure long term position elsewhere to begin working with them. The court will also consider other factors such as the age and education of the individual and how difficult it might be to find a similar position elsewhere.

To File a Complaint:

http://www.publications.gov.sk.ca/prdtermlist.cfm?t=1596&cl=2

Yukon

Source: www.gov.yk.ca

Termination Notice

Termination notice is required after the employee completes 6 consecutive months of employment with the employer.

The amount of notice differs depending on the length of time the individual was employed. The notice **must** be in writing and if the employer fails to do so, the employee may be entitled to one week's wages for each week of notice to which he or she was entitled. The graduating scale of notice is as follows:

Period of employment	Notice
At least 6 months to less than 1 year	one week
1 year to less than 3 years	two weeks
3 years to less than 4 years	three weeks
4 years to less than 5 years	four weeks
5 years to less than 6 years	five weeks
6 years to less than 7 years	six weeks
7 years to less than 8 years	seven weeks
8 years or more	eight weeks

The termination requirements do not apply to:

1. An employee who has **not** completed 6 months of consecutive employment.
2. An employee discharged for just cause.
3. An employee whose employer has failed to abide by the terms of the employment contract.
4. An employee being temporarily laid off (less than 13 weeks).
5. An employee unable to perform an employment contract due to an unforeseeable event or circumstance.
6. An employee who has refused reasonable alternative employment.
7. An employee working in the construction industry.

8. An employee working in a seasonal or intermittent undertaking operating less than 6 months in a year.

9. The termination of an employment relationship due to the completion by the employee of a project or assignment that the employee was hired to perform over a period not exceeding 12 months, whether or not the exact period was stated in the employment contract.

10. An employee who is still employed after completing the term of employment that was fixed in the employment contract, unless the employee is employed for a period of more than one month after the completion of that term.

The Employment Act of the Yukon specifically prohibits the employer from giving notice of termination when the employee is on annual vacation.

Termination Pay

An employer shall, between the date that the notice of termination is given and the date of termination of employment, pay wages and provide benefits to an employee to whom the notice is given in an amount not less than the wages and benefits to which the employee would have been entitled, if the employee had worked his or her usual hours of work in that period, whether or not work is required or performed.

If termination pay is given to an employee, the amount of the termination pay must be equal to the wages and benefits to which the employee would have been entitled, if the employee had worked his or her usual hours of work for each week of the period for which notice would otherwise be required.

Group Terminations

A group termination occurs when an employer terminates 25 or more employees at one place of employment within a four week period. The employer must give notice of group termination.

The minimum notice for a group termination is:

Applies to Employees Terminated Within …	Number of Employees Terminated	Notice Required
4 weeks	25-49	4 weeks
	50-99	8 weeks
	100-299	12 weeks
	300 or more	16 weeks

Wrongful/Constructive Dismissal

The Yukon Employment Standards Act does not address specifics in the matters of wrongful dismissal or constructive dismissal at the present time. Contact the Department of Education, Culture and Employment to inquire about your situation and potential remedies.

To File a Complaint:

http://www.community.gov.yk.ca/labour/comp.html

Legal Action

Legal Advice

Are you wondering if you should speak to a lawyer? If you feel that your rights have been violated then you may want to go that route. Here are some tips that will assist you on your next step.

Hiring an Attorney

Should I hire my tax lawyer or the lawyer who handled my real estate transaction? No. You need a specialized employment and labour lawyer, especially one that has extensive experience working with employees. Some labour lawyers specialize on the employer's side of the disputes. If possible, you should lean towards a lawyer that focuses on the issues of the employee. And make sure that they do not have a conflict with the company that you are planning to sue. For example, if you work(ed) for XYZ Company and the lawyer works for XYZ on various labour issues, then there is a conflict of interest. In this case, a reputable lawyer will not take your case. Ask the lawyer *before* you present your case to him/her if there is a conflict.

How Do I Know if I Need an Attorney?

Firstly, just because you were fired or laid off does not mean you have a case. Assess your circumstances realistically and check what proof (documents, journal entries, witnesses) you have at your avail. What are you trying to get out of it? If you are doing this for pride, then this may not be justification for the stress and expense of this process.

Most lawyers will charge for an initial consultation so make sure that this investment is worth it. Plus, if you proceed, you will probably have to provide an initial retainer fee (average $1,500 – 3,000). And the fees can easily go above the retainer fee if the case goes to court.

Review one of the templates provided in this book to see if you can start the ball rolling. Remember, make sure that you are using the correct template or editing it appropriately otherwise, you may end up in a more difficult position with a simple typo or erroneous choice of words.

Legal representation is not a necessity unless you are destined to go to court. You may be better off not engaging an attorney in some cases especially at the beginning as a show of good faith. The following may be factors that can help you determine whether you should go directly to an experienced labour attorney.

1. Understand What You Want.

If you have been terminated, you should think about what you are looking for out of these negotiations. Are you looking for retraining costs or a career coaching service to be added to your severance package? Are you looking for more money or extended benefits? Are you looking for revenge? If it is the latter, you should stop where you are and start the thinking process over once your emotions have subsided.

If you are still employed, what outcomes are you seeking that will rebuild the relationship with your employer? Are these reasonable for both you and your employer?

You can't effectively proceed on the following points until you complete this task. You want to ensure that whatever you do come up with, that it is business focused (not emotional or personal) and feasible for the employer. Now is not the time to "prove a point" or "show them". It is about finding a reasonable and workable solution so that everyone can move forward with dignity and respect.

2. Open Discussions With Your Employer.

Don't doubt the effectiveness of direct discussions about your termination/severance with your employer. An employer will most likely take a less defensive approach if you start talking to them directly versus immediately sending them a letter from a lawyer. Once you engage a lawyer, the employer will need to engage their lawyer which will cost them money. Plus it may become combative once lawyers are involved which leave less room for negotiation.

3. Your Knowledge of Employment Law In Your Province.

If you are not knowledgeable in employment law (and unless you are a lawyer or have been through this before, you won't be), feel free to hire a lawyer to evaluate your case. S/he does not need to take anymore action than that. Don't just ask the lawyer if you have a good case; ask him/her if your employer has a good case against you. Make sure you reveal all the facts regardless of your indiscretions on the job. You will need an honest evaluation of what position you are actually in. Not being upfront about everything (even your misconduct) only ends up harming your case and costing you financially and emotionally.

4. Your Comfort Level With Negotiations.

If you are someone who is very uncomfortable with negotiations and how to make them work, then you may want to consider having an attorney by your side. S/he would be very experienced with these meetings and may bring a better resolution sooner.

5. Cost.

Lawyers, even for an initial consultation, are not cheap. Be sure that the outcome you are looking for is worth the cost. If you are looking for an attorney because you want revenge or a few extra dollars, then you may want to start negotiations yourself to begin with. You may want to hire a lawyer just to oversee or consult with you while you handle the direct employer communications.

How Do I Find The Right Lawyer?

If you know someone who has successfully sued his/her employer, then ask them for the attorney's name and phone number.

If you have another lawyer (real estate or will, etc.), then ask them for a referral to a labour lawyer. If s/he offers to take the case himself, be wary. You need someone who focuses on labour law. Ask them if they have handled similar cases and the outcome if those cases. If they have not handled several similar cases successfully, then they are not the lawyer you need. Tell them that you appreciate the offer but you simply need someone who specializes in employment and labour law. If possible, get a few names from your lawyer and ask him what order he recommends that you call them in.

You can also contact your local Bar association by going to this following link. http://www.cba.org/CBA/Info/main/Contact.aspx

Contact your provincial Legal Aid or Employment Insurance office to inquire about their recommendations.

Another recommendation for finding an appropriate lawyer is to go online to www.lancasterhouse.com. You can search labour lawyers by jurisdiction and read their professional biographies, listing their experience and other information, helping you determine which to follow up further with.

When Should I See An Attorney?

Sooner rather than later! The time to see a lawyer is when you start to see your relationship with your employer deteriorating (if you are still employed). It doesn't mean that you will automatically sue. But you will have more opportunity to diffuse the situation through legal advice even if it means reconciling with your employer.

If you have just been terminated or served with a termination notice, then check out the termination pay regulations for your province. If it does not fall into these guidelines and you have tried to rectify the situation with your company to no avail, then contact a lawyer as soon as possible. Most provinces have strict time limitations in which you can contest a termination package.

What Happens on The Initial Consultation?

Just like interviewing for a job or someone to perform renovations to your home or hiring a babysitter, it is essential that you are finding the best person for your case. As well, you need to understand if this case is worth pursuing. The cost, the stress, the time, among many other variables are all factors in whether you should pursue legal action or just move on.

Different lawyers have different fees for the initial consultation. Some will charge a special initial consultation fee in order to evaluate your case. Some will provide a free consultation fee. Regardless of the fee, make sure that you are consulting with an experienced, successful labour lawyer who will be honest with you about the probabilities of your case.

Just as important, you should bring all documentation that you have with you that relates to your case/situation in anyway. Don't waste your initial consultation because you are ill prepared. The more info you can provide your lawyer, the easier it will be for your lawyer to assess your situation and less expensive for you.

What does the office look like? Is it professionally run and organized? Or is it disorganized and messy?

Is the lawyer confident in his/her field? Does s/he ask the right questions? Does s/he explain clearly? Does s/he outline options, benefits and consequences clearly? Does s/he discuss whether your case is worthwhile or is s/he promising big money?

Questions to Ask During This Session:

1. What are the fees?

2. Who will handle the case? If a partner will handle it, you should meet that partner. Or, if a junior lawyer is handling it, are you paying a senior lawyer's fees and how experienced is this junior? It may sound great to have a junior who charges a lower rate to take on all or part of your case, but keep in mind that some juniors require more time to do the same work as a senior. And at an hourly rate, this has the potential to cost more than a senior.

3. How often will contact be and through what method(s)?

4. Will you be able to discuss with them any actions prior to them proceeding?

5. Will you get copies of all letters and documents?

6. How realistic are my expectations?

7. What is the expected timeline(s) for my issue to conclude?

8. What further information/documentation is required from me for this to succeed?

9. What would be the next step?

Checklist of Info for Your Initial Meeting with Your Lawyer

It is advisable that you have all this typed out to hand to your lawyer to save time during your first meeting. (Time is money!) By providing all your information upfront, the lawyer will have a clearer picture of your current situation.

Your Personal Information:

Name:

_____

Address:

_____

_____

_____

Telephone

Home: _____

Cell: _____

Work: _____

Email:

_____

Date of Birth:

_____

Social Insurance Number:

_____

Current Employer Information:

Employer: _____

Employer's Address: _____
_____
_____

Employer's Telephone ____ _____

Number of Employees: _____

Date Hired: _____

Compensation:
Salary/Wage:_____

Bonus:_____

Awards:_____

Annual Vacation in weeks:_____

Title(s):

(Include every role you have had at this company)
_____
_____

Level (Circle your current level):

Executive   Manager   Supervisor   Full-time Employee

Part-Time Employee   Contractor   Intern/Apprentice

Other: _____

Current Responsibilities: _____
_____
_____
_____

Supervisor: _____

HR Manager: _____

REASON FOR YOUR VISIT:

Terminated

Date of termination:_____

Date of notification:_____

Offered severance agreement

Deadline to sign:_____

Denied a promotion

Date I learned I would not be promoted:_____

Reasons given: _____

Harassment victim

Racial

Sexual

Other

Denied benefits

Date denial of benefits took place:_____

Denied commission or bonus or vacation pay

Date denied:_____

Reasons given:_____

Employer violated terms of his own policies/handbook or employment contract

Violation: _____

Date violation occurred:_____

Discrimination victim due to my:

Race   Gender   Age   Disability

Religion   Sexual Orientation   National origin/ancestry

Marital Status   Pregnancy   WSIB Claim   Illness/Injury

Other: _____

Victim of retaliation because I complained about/reported employers illegal conduct

Date of complaint/report:_____

Date of retaliation:_____

TERMS & CONDITIONS OF EMPLOYMENT

Union Member: Yes/No   Union Name:

Received employment letter when hired stating terms of employment. Yes/No (attach copy)

Company violated terms of this agreement as follows:

_____

_____

Received employee handbook when I was hired (copy attached) Yes/No

Company violated terms of this handbook as follows:

_____

_____

Company has specific policies that it goes by in making employment decisions but employees do not get a copy. I believe company violated terms of this handbook as follows:

_____

_____

Received periodic performance evaluations (copies attached). Yes/No

BASIS OF CLAIMS:

Treated unfairly. Yes/No   Description:

_____

_____

The following is my employer's explanation to me as to why I was treated as such:

_____

_____

The following is what I think is the REAL reason for this treatment:

_____

_____

I believe I was discriminated against. Evidence of this treatment:

_____

_____

I brought this discrimination to the attention of my employer:

    I reported discrimination of these dates: _____

    I reported discrimination to the following personnel: _____

    The following action was taken as a result of my complaint:

_____

_____

When I was terminated, I signed a resignation letter/waiver/release (copy attached)

Here are the circumstances in which I signed the document:

_____

_____

INJURIES OR DAMAGES

I suffered the following physical and/or emotional damage as a result of my employer's actions:

_____

_____

I sought medical and/or psychiatric attention as a result:

    Doctor's name and address: _____

    Telephone: _____

    Diagnosis: _____

I have lost wages as a result of my employer's actions

    Amount of wages lost to date: _____

I have suffered other financial losses as a direct result of my employer's actions.

Amount: $_____

Description of loss: _____

I have not received all of the direct payments I have earned and that are due to me from my employer.

Salary due:

Bonuses due:

Vacation pay:

Commissions:

Other (specify)

PREVIOUS LAWSUITS

I have filed complaints or sued an employer before (present or past employer)

Date of complaint/lawsuit_____

Reason for complaint/lawsuit_____

Result: _____

While you don't have to include everything listed above, you should try to include everything you can that does relate to your case or situation.

Costs

So, how much can it cost to go the lawyer route? Well, it depends on several factors:

Lawyers Fees

Hourly rates on average is $300 per hour. Contingency fees, where a lawyer doesn't charge you an hourly fee but takes their fee as a percentage of your winnings, are on average 33.3% plus expenses (court costs, photocopying, travel, long-distance calls, etc.). You will most likely be paying the hourly rate. Ideally, you should ensure that your lawyer is willing to reassess the situation after each communication with your employer. This way you can limit your costs depending on whether you want to continue to pursue the case any further.

Settlement

How willing are you or your company willing to settle? If not, then the case can drag on for a long time and increase costs.

How Effective Is The Counsel For The Employer?

If they are not particularly competent, they may be more willing to settle sooner which is advantageous to you.

Court

If you decide to have your case heard in court, there are filing fees, deposition costs, attorney's travel fees, etc.

Costs, of wrongful dismissal cases can escalate quickly, especially if you end up in court. Make sure it is worth it and that your lawyer is interested in providing the best arrangement for you, not him/her. The following is an example of a case that outlines the issue of cost and their risks when pursuing a case in court.

When an employer wins a case, they usually ask for the plaintiff (i.e. losing employee) to reimburse them for legal costs (not uncommon in any court case for the loser to pay the winner's legal fees). In this example, the judge notes that the employer's lawyers billed the employer close to $250,000 to defend the lawsuit. If the judge feels that the case brought by the employee was frivolous, the judge may grant the employer's request for total reimbursement. So not only did the employee not win his claim for damages, he is also responsible for paying both the employer's legal fees as well as his own. This result was far more costly to the employee than a private negotiation could have produced. If the employee cannot pay the employer's legal fees and needs to declare bankruptcy, the cost of not settling this case through negotiation is now considerable to both parties.

In the same example, after a review of the employer's request for reimbursement, the judge rules that some of the costs on the lawyer's bill were excessive, including 75 hours of legal research by three articling students at $70 per hour. The judge believes that the legal issues were basic and an experienced employment law firm should not have needed that much research done. In the end, the judge orders the plaintiff (the losing employee) to pay $37,000 (instead of $250,000) towards the employer's legal bill. Again, that would be on top of the money he had already paid his own lawyer. The employer has to pay the difference between the legal bill (around $250,000) and the $37,000 the employee was ordered to pay. So the lawsuit cost both the employer and employee a sizeable financial expense.

If the judge had decided that the employer was responsible for all the employer's legal expenses ($250,000) and the employee was suing for $230,000, then the lawsuit cost both parties far more than negotiating a settlement in private.

Litigating a wrongful dismissal case can be a costly, risky, and an economically unsound thing to do for both the employer and the employee. The only difference is that a large corporation can absorb the cost.

It is strongly recommended that you ensure that you have attempted all avenues to settle your complaint out of court before incurring the potentially high costs of the court system. You may end up settling for less money that you originally hoped, but your legal expenses may end up being less which may even out the financial outcome. However, be sure that you are not settling for less than what you are entitled to in the Employment Standards Act of your province or territory.

The Court Process

The court process is divided into two distinct categories: cases involving potential claims of $25,000 or less and those claims above $25,000. In regards to the former, there are different "simplified rules" that may expedite the process. For cases which exceed $25,000, the rules are more complicated and thus tend to draw out the process over a longer period of time. For example, a case in Toronto courts will take roughly 12 to 18 months to get to trial for larger claims. In addition to the time to get to trial, each party has a right to appeal which could easily take another 18 months. Therefore, it could take years to resolve your lawsuit if you are seeking a large settlement so be prepared.

Pre-Trial Discovery

Each case requires the opposing parties to produce all relevant documents. Then each party has the right to question the other party under oath to understand what the evidence will be to defend the position. Unlike the United States, where any person in the world may be deposed before trial, in Canada, one representative of the company is produced for pre-trial discovery.

After discoveries have been completed, the case is set for trial and assigned a court date for hearing.

Mediation

Typically mediation occurs at the early stages of a lawsuit when costs are much lower and the case will have lesser obstacles to settlement. The parties appoint an experienced lawyer or a retired judge to hear what is in dispute. The clients are encouraged to speak about why they feel they are right and also what other motivations have brought about the conflict. The mediator has no power to order anything. His/her influence is strictly persuasive. When entered into voluntarily, it has proven to be very successful.

One essential aspect has been that both parties have a desire to settle. In addition particularly in cases of wrongful dismissal, the company representative should be empowered to make decisions. Quite often the company may send someone as a figure head with no real decision making power or only up to a specific dollar figure.

In cases of mandatory mediation, both parties are dragged to the meeting as opposed to wanting to be there to settle. It is likely that it will not be as successful as the voluntary variety, but nonetheless will no doubt settle cases that would have required a trial otherwise.

Arbitration

This is an alternative to the court process. Sometimes the parties complete pre-trial discoveries and instead of going to trial, agree to use an arbitrator. The result is an agreement which is binding with no right of appeal. The advantages that drive the arbitration decision are usually the ability to litigate in privacy, the right to know who the decision maker will be, and a certainty of the date. The disadvantages are the costs involved. One party no doubt will lament the loss of appeal rights.

Negotiating a Package

Upon termination, employers usually anticipate that most employees will accept whatever package is given (provided it is within legal guidelines) to them. They tend to hope that the vulnerable state of the terminated employee will get them to agree to the first offer immediately. However, depending on the situation, there may be room for negotiation even if you do not have a legal case.

Step 1: Understand Your Losses

Call a local recruiter and tell them who you are, what you do, how much you make and how long it would take for your to get a similar job. They should tell you that it would take x months. Take that information to your employer and let them know that you cannot afford to be without income and benefits that long. Ask if the company is willing to help out.

You aren't threatening a lawsuit; you're appealing to the employer's fairness to assist you. Even if you do have a legal case, it is not a bad idea to use this as an initial tactic in order to get a better severance package in lieu of litigation.

You should also track what your benefit costs are (i.e. health, dental, life insurance) and what it will take to continue them while you are unemployed. Don't forget to include professional membership fees, training expenses, occupational certification costs, health memberships and business discounts that you were afforded as an employee. You may be able to recoup some of these losses during negotiation.

Take note of any other compensation that was due to you including bonuses, commissions, overtime pay, unused vacation and stock options. You want to ensure that you still receive what you earned or what you had been promised prior to termination. In addition, if you have been provided equipment or services such as a computer for your home, smartphone, home internet service, etc. document these items and source the costs if you were to pay for them yourself. Many companies allow some terminated employees to keep some of these items as part of their package.

You have a decent chance to open negotiation with your employer. If they are unwilling to cover you until you find another job, then feel free to counter propose. Just don't propose too low otherwise you will limit your lawyer's ability to negotiate if you go the litigation route. Further, don't propose an amount that is ridiculously high otherwise no one will take you seriously. A good rule of thumb here is, if your proposal denotes what is fair and reasonable, then your chances at succeeding with your negotiations will improve when you're at this stage.

Step 2: Evaluate the Contents of Your Package

In some cases, you can negotiate other aspects of the package aside from the financial aspect. Don't forget that severance can include extension of health benefits, extension of employee discounts, training allowance, career transition service, résumé service, outplacement services, computer equipment, company car purchase, etc. Be certain to use any of these items in your negotiation. For example, if your employer is offering a résumé service as part of your package and you already have a current effective résumé, then you may request to trade that benefit for an equitable training allowance.

Other items that may be negotiable: a letter of recommendation or ability to resign instead of termination to protect your employment record.

If you receive stock options, ensure that you understand how long they are valid for. While it is standard that you have the right to exercise the stock options until the end of your notice period, some employers insist that they become invalid at the date of termination. If the latter is the case, track the stock during your notice period. If there is a positive difference, then you may be entitled to that difference if the employer insisted that they expire on the date of termination.

If you were enrolled in a program that allowed you to purchase shares in the employer's company at a reduced rate through your payroll, find out what happens to those shares upon termination. Most companies will force you to sell them at the market rate shortly after your date of termination. If this is the case, be prepared for any possible capital gains taxes and include this added expense if you choose to renegotiate your package.

You may also be able to negotiate the pay out of your severance package if you were a long time employee of the company. If you have been with the company a long time and your severance payment equals 2 months' salary or more, many companies will pay you out as an employee on a regular pay period. Some people prefer to have a lump sum payment. Some things to consider in this case:

1. Make sure that the benefits extension lasts the full term of the original severance (e.g. if you are getting a lump sum payment for 3 months salary, your health insurance should still last 3 months past your termination).
2. It is possible that the lump sum option will be slightly less than the full term or you may be required to return some of the money if you find a job in less time than expected. Severance is meant to bridge some of the time until you secure another job.
3. Be mindful of your tax situation if your choose lump sum. If you choose a lump sum payment, you may increase your tax bracket for that year if you get another job quickly. The employer will only retain taxes at the level you were employed at and are not obligated to calculate your new rate.

For example, if you received a lump sum payment of three months' salary in July and you get a new job at your previous salary in August, you are increasing your annual salary by 2 months. If you are in a higher tax bracket, and you are being taxed for all your annual income at the lower tax bracket, you will get a nasty surprise in April from Canada Revenue.

Another example would be if you are entitled to a termination package due to an employee of 20 years, then you may be entitled to as much as 20 weeks' severance pay. If you receive this lump sum in November or December, you just added 5 months of salary in a year that you already worked most of the year. Unless you are already at the highest tax bracket, your tax rate (and taxed owed in April) will skyrocket. If you had the option of spreading this payment out for 5 months, then you have a better chance of keeping more in your bank account as the payments will spread out over the next calendar year. Therefore, sometimes a long term payroll may be more beneficial for taxes if it extends into the next calendar year or put a portion of your lump sum into an RRSP.

4. If you choose a lump sum payment, it will not shorten the time period in which you are eligible for Employment Insurance. If you get 3 months' salary in a lump sum payment, the government will still see 3 months' severance on your Record of Employment.

5. There may be a provision in your agreement that stipulates that if you get a job before the severance payments are completed, you will need to return a certain portion of the severance ("Clawback"). If you agree to it, it is legal.

Step 3: Understand What is Negotiable

The key to negotiation is to understand what motivates your employer to negotiate and what motivates you to stop negotiating.

Usually there are three common motivators that may open negotiations:

1. **Fear of negative publicity** – Some companies rely on having a positive image in the public. Therefore, if your company has a history of terminating a particular protected group (i.e. women, disabled, visible minority, etc.), you may be able to leverage this information.

2. **Fear of losing a lawsuit** – When terminations are conducted under "fishy" conditions, companies are more willing to open the door to negotiations to avoid a lawsuit. For example, if you had a record of positive performance evaluations and suddenly you are terminated and replaced with a friend of your supervisor, then there may be something suspicious about your termination. As well, if proper procedure was not followed, then you have facts that should motivate your employer.

3. **Deadlines** – Sometimes terminations occur on a certain schedule (i.e. before a shareholder's meeting, prior to new fiscal year, etc.) to appease upper management. If

this is the case, then you can motivate your employer by alluding that you don't think you can sign your current package by that time period.

Many times, you have motivators that will force you to accept an offer. Employers will try to reveal what these drivers are and exploit them. Be careful not to show your weaknesses.

1. **Fear of losing income** – Many people take the company's first severance offer out of their perceived desperation for the money. Sometimes two months' salary looks great in a lump sum when you have a stack of bills to pay and no knowledge of the current job market. However, if you have worked for the company for 8 years, this is unlikely to be a sufficient settlement. Take the necessary time to think about the offer and its complete implications and consult with a professional before settling.

2. **Fear of being seen negatively** – Too many people are worried about being seen as "greedy" or "not nice" if they demand more compensation. Firstly, you are fighting for what you deserve. Secondly, if you accept the first offer just to be likable, you will not be respected. Respect should be more important to you than being liked. After all, if "liking" meant anything to your employer, you would not be terminated to begin with. Thirdly, who cares what you perceive people think about you?

3. **Fear of retribution** – Don't be afraid that because you want to re-negotiate that the company will blackball you in the industry. This practice is illegal and they can be sued for large sums of money if they are proven to do so.

4. **Fear of the offer being rescinded** – Don't be afraid that the employer will rescind its offer if you don't accept it immediately. Especially if the offer isn't that great to begin with or only gives you a little above the required amount by law. Many employers will be eager to resolve this situation and if they take back the offer, this will only prolong it.

5. **Lack of knowledge of your legal rights** – Many employers assume that employees have limited knowledge of what is legal and equitable. Don't let them know this is your situation if this is the case. Tell them that you reserve your rights to consult with a lawyer and would need some time before you sign anything.

6. **Employer's hands are tied** – If you are part of a mass layoff, many employees think (or are told) that if they give you more, then they have to do that for everyone. This is malarkey and a common tactic used for severance negotiations by employers. All severance agreements are held to a confidentiality agreement that you will sign, therefore, other employees will not be privy to your settlement. Remember, other employees are probably settling for a bigger severance package too. Besides, even if it were true that the employer would have to match your settlement to other terminated employees, then that is not your problem.

Therefore, it is essential that you are well prepared before opening negotiations. Be prepared to give up points where you see fit if it moves negotiations further. Don't think that you will get everything you want – it is a negotiation, not a robbery.

Bear in mind that this is a mutual game of pushing buttons so don't fall for some of the tactics from your employer such as threats, anger and condescending attitudes. The employers' negotiator is most likely very experienced at this process and thinks s/he knows how to rattle your cage. The goal for the both of you is to get a resolution that both of you can live with, so stay on track and don't allow yourself to get distracted or deterred from your goals.

Step Four: Remember What You Are Negotiating For.

1. Family: People tend to negotiate better when they negotiate on behalf of their family instead of just themselves. Some people keep a picture of their family in their jacket pocket and touch it unobtrusively during discussions as a reminder and incentive.
2. Stress, wrongful treatment, needs, and fairness: These four things can be very persuasive in negotiations. Be prepared to discuss your claims, your basis for them, and your willingness to address the company's point of view as well.
3. Goals: Remind yourself of your true goals which you have determined beforehand. Don't be distracted by extraneous matters such as your emotions, your company's financial issues, or your counterpart's sympathy. These are all techniques to throw you off your game and break your focus.

Step Five: Prepare for Alternatives

Prepare a second list of settlement requests in case your initial request is turned down. If there is a stalemate, one of you will need to break it and it may be in your best interest to do so to progress the discussion. Your negotiation goals and substitute goals should be very clear in your mind and you should be prepared to express them clearly and confidently.

Understand all the options available. For example:

- Intellectual property – will you be able to retain samples to use in your portfolio?
- Positive reference.
- Departure statement or public announcement – will you be able to review or contribute to ensure a positive spin?
- Will outplacement or education assistance be provided?
- Technology - Can you retain computer equipment, cell phone, etc.?
- Car - Can you retain the company car until the lease expires?
- New business – if you decide to open a new business, will the employer agree to be a client?
- Non-competition clause – will the employer be willing to forgo or limit a non-competition clause if it exists?
- Solicitation of customers – Companies do not want you pilfering their customers. If this becomes a negotiation point, then get specifications – current customers only? Include

employees? Does it include working for a company that would be doing the solicitation?

- Reimbursement for legal expenses.
- Message and mail forwarding
- Payments upon death – it is hard to think about this point but you should consider it if your severance payments are over a long period of time, you may want to establish a continuance of payments in case of your death.
- Bankruptcy protection – in case of the company's bankruptcy prior to completing the payout of severance, the outstanding sum shall become an obligation of the shareholders.
- Mergers/acquisitions – in the case of a merger, acquisition, reorganization or sell-off of assets, the company is obligated to continue your outstanding payments.
- Bonus – Present Year – if you are terminated without cause, you should still be entitled to the anticipated bonus for the year of termination.
- Royalties, copyrights, or patent rights. – If you have participated in written works or inventions while employed, then you may be entitled to proceeds or royalties the employer may later collect. Make sure that this is outlined in the severance package.
- Credit for creative works – if you contributed creatively to your employer's projects, ensure that the appropriate creative credits are maintained. If royalties are due to you, ensure that they continue to come to you.
- Deferral – To avoid moving into a higher tax bracket, you may request for part or all severance payment to be deferred to January 2nd of the next calendar year.
- First Rehire Right – if you are part of a mass layoff or downsizing, you may request a "right of first rehire" when circumstances improve.
- Payback Inapplicable – Many severance agreements contain a stipulation that if you are rehired by the employer or another company before the severance period ends, you need to report it and reimburse severance moneys owed. Although common, you should be wary of such a clause.
- Voicemail and email continuation – In order to transition to unemployment, request continuation through reemployment or for a period of three to six months.

Step Six: Be Positive

Keep a positive attitude and don't take negotiations personally. This is just business. Your goal is to get what you need. Don't see results in terms of winners and losers. Experienced negotiators will try to intimidate, overpower, or even scare you. They may try to make you feel guilty or greedy. Always display a positive, friendly and happy demeanor regardless of your feelings churning inside you. Sarcasm, scowling and eye rolling will get you nowhere and will indicate to your counterpart that their technique is working.

Step Seven: Get It In Writing

As you come to an agreement, write the details down. Don't depend on your memory and definitely don't depend on the memory of your employer. At the conclusion of each meeting, review with your counterpart to the items agreed to for their confirmation. Once you have an agreement, ask them if they want a photocopy.

When the final agreement is documented, review your notes to ensure it is thorough and correct. Do not leave anything open to interpretation or assumption. If something is not completely clear or is omitted, then do not sign the document. Make your counterpart aware and ask for revisions to ensure that you are both on the same page.

Preparing For Severance Negotiation

Here is a checklist of items that you should gather prior to starting negotiations.

1. Gather any documentation that outlines your job responsibilities from when you were hired until now. Include as much of the following as possible:

    a) Employment contracts or letter of offer and any written modifications since then.
    b) Any performance evaluations that may describe your job duties and written modifications since then.
    c) Any HR-type job descriptions that outline your duties, responsibilities and terms. This could be any recent job postings within your company that have the same title as yours. For example, if there is more than one Accounts Payable Clerk in the company, the most recent job posting may be very similar to your job description.
    d) Any evidence of common knowledge that you and your employer have always worked under. (i.e. your title, your wage, your job grade, your pension program and/or benefits, your vacation entitlement, etc.)
    e) Any paperwork that outlines a termination agreement (or known for executives as a "golden parachute clause") or any reprimands that you received that you did not agree with.

2. Collect all other papers that may suggest or outline your terms of employment.

    a) Offer letter or onboarding material (documents given to you when you are first hired).
    b) New Hire memo that went out to co-workers when you started.
    c) "Welcome Aboard" letter.

d) Original posting for the position.

e) Pay stubs.

f) Personnel policy manuals or policy statements.

3. Organize a list of records and amounts reflecting your current compensation including all employment related benefits that you are entitled to receive.

a) Salary.

b) Bonus/Cost of living allowances.

c) Pension or RRSP contribution.

d) Stock options.

e) Vacation entitlement.

f) On-call or overtime pay.

g) Discounted house/car insurance, travel accommodations or other perks.

h) Salary grade.

i) Any inclusion in company succession planning or promotional expectations.

j) Business partnership discounts (home use software, discounted tickets, etc.).

k) Parking allowance or reserved spot.

l) Free public transit passes.

m) Health and/or life insurance.

n) Disability insurance.

o) Educational allowance or assistance.

p) Car or mileage allowance.

q) Company computer or cellphone or service to run them.

r) Discounted public transit passes.

s) Employee discounts (e.g.purchasing or lowered bank fees).

t) Club memberships.

u) Matching gift programs.

v) RRSP contribution programs.

w) Travel allowances.

4. Prepare any evidence of satisfactory employment performance.

a) Performance evaluations and annual reviews.

b) Awards and/or honours.

c) Promotions.

d) New titles.

e) New responsibilities.

f) Raises.

g) Emails/cards from supervisor or co-workers thanking you or crediting your efforts.

h) Bonuses.

i) Company newsletter articles.

j) Succession planning or promotional plans discussed between you and your manager.

5. Determine any benefit of any type that is scheduled to accrue in the upcoming months or years.

   a) Stock options.

   b) RRSP or Pension adjustments.

   c) Deferred compensation on deferred benefit programs.

   d) Bridging program to retirement or retirement program eligibility.

   e) Special programs (e.g. free lifetime health coverage for those with 25 years employment).

   f) Bonus or gift for defined number of years of employment.

   g) Performance bonus or cost of living allowance.

   h) Deferred commissions or earned bonuses based on performance or company performance.

6. Design a timetable of all matters pertaining to stock options.

   a) Number of shares optioned.

   b) Dates offered.

   c) Granted or to be granted.

   d) All exercise dates and methods.

   e) All strike prices.

   f) Current market prices.

7. Verify your insurance coverage and upcoming needs.

   a) Coverage for your or family members medical condition, disability, physical ailment or impairment.

   b) Upcoming treatment, surgery, procedure, tests or rehabilitation for you or your family.

   c) Upcoming follow up care or expenses related to above conditions.

   d) Special accommodations, dispensations or arrangements.

   e) Upcoming maternal/paternal leave or parental care leave.

8. Devise a schedule of available liquid assets (cash or short-term investments).

   a) List bank accounts, short term investment accounts, stocks, GICs, etc.

b) Lines of credits or loans available.
c) List financial obligations – child care expenses, education expenses, parent-care expenses, debts coming due, etc.

9. Prepare a written account of misconduct by your employer relative to your complaint.

    a) Discrimination/harassment/mistreatment claims.
    b) How they took place.
    c) Witnesses.
    d) Other victims.
    e) Complaints made by you or others.
    f) Was senior management made aware.
    g) Documentation involved (emails, memos, instant messages, etc.).
    h) Any journal that you may have to track these events.

10. Specific requests for your severance package that relates to your particular field.

    a) Upgrading technical skills for IT people.
    b) Registered Representatives in Securities field termination designation with their governing body.
    c) Executive MBA enrollment.
    d) Memberships in professional associations.
    e) Training to maintain your certifications.

11. Request a copy of your personnel file from HR.

12. Company's policies in negotiating severance packages.

    a) Ask around on the policy especially among former employees. If any of them were successful in re-negotiating, then they probably won't talk about it as they are usually bound to a confidentiality agreement. If they were not successful, they will blab and blab.

13. Strategic developments at the company that would make them concerned about litigation.

    a) Mergers.
    b) Acquisitions.
    c) Public offering or refinancing.
    d) Employee Stock Option Plans.
    e) Bankruptcy.

f) CEO retirement.

g) Partnerships with ethical programs or partners.

h) New business planning.

i) Negative image or process of re-building image.

14. Skeletons in your closet should be shared with your attorney.

a) Dating a subordinate.

b) Overextending an expense account.

c) Borrowed funds without authority.

d) Use company resources for personal use.

e) Complaints filed against you.

f) Unsatisfactory performance reviews or PIPs (Performance Improvement Plans).

g) Warnings or reprimands that you have received.

15. Outline a realistic career plan to understand your future needs.

a) Career plan over the next 5-10 years.

b) Job progression plan.

c) Salary and compensation plan needed to sustain your lifestyle needs.

d) Training needed.

e) Resources needed to find your next job.

f) Update your résumé and cover letter.

g) Costs associated to find a new job – wardrobe, travel, printing, etc.

h) Look into a career counselor for assistance.

i) Networking plan.

j) Professional associations you need to join.

Tips For Lawyer-Assisted Negotiations

If you choose to use a lawyer, you should ensure that you understand the most effective way to utilize him/her during negotiations. Ensure that both you and your lawyer are in sync prior to meeting with your employer.

1. Be Firm About Your Goals Before You Meet Your Lawyer.

You should be able to recite your negotiation goals without notes. You must also be knowledgeable what your minimal acceptable terms are. Your lawyer should be well aware of these as well and be able to advise you how realistic they are. Remember, if your employer was not willing to negotiate with you, they would not participate in a negotiation session.

2. Be Clear About Your Strategy.

Are you asking for $5,000 more but are willing to take $3,500? Is one aspect of your package a "deal breaker" but another part not of much value to you? You should prepare separate lists of items that you want but you are willing to sacrifice. Keep this list alongside the one that has your non-negotiable items.

3. Your Lawyer Needs To Set The Agenda Before Negotiations Commence.

The agenda should be outlined and distributed to the employer's team. Agenda items typically include:

- The purpose of the meeting.
- The anticipated outcome.
- The current state due to initial offer proposed.
- The specific topics to be discussed.
- The parties who will actively participate in negotiation.
- The understanding that neither plaintiff nor defendant will be deposed by attorneys.
- Determining who will take notes or recording and distribute results.
- Determining if any discussion is to be "off the record".
- Determining time allotment or restrictions on the meeting.
- Determining who of the parties are authorized to enter into an agreement.

4. At The Meeting, Sit Back and Let Your Lawyer Run The Show.

As the client, you have the authority to approve the strategy, goals and direction your lawyer will take. But during the negotiation meetings, you must take a backseat to your lawyer. Never overtly disagree with your lawyer or give any indication of dissention through your body language during these sessions. Any questions or concerns you have with your attorney should be done only in private. If you need to consult with your lawyer, you can ask for a private discussion alone with your lawyer.

5. Inform Your Lawyer of Any Issue That You Don't Want Raised or Concerned Will Be Mentioned During The Session Beforehand.

The more sensitive the topic, the more important it is that your lawyer is aware of it. Your attorney is on your side so don't be afraid to tell him/her about it beforehand. If you don't, then you run the risk of your opponent raising it which will blindside your lawyer and your case.

6. **Avoid Nervous, Anxious or Self-Doubting Emotions.**

   Pretend you are playing poker. Do not express your anger, betrayal, frustration or any other negative emotion. Remember, this is only business.

7. **Don't Hasten The Negotiation or Settlement Process.**

   If you are anxious, you are more likely to make concessions and compromises. Once you reveal them, then it is almost impossible to withdraw them from the negotiation process. Your attitude should be one of good faith and willingness to compromise. Just don't openly initiate the compromise yourself. Ask the other side to suggest the compromise.

8. **Don't Be Aggressive or Menacing.**

   Don't try to play games by threatening to sue or go to the media. Don't try to intimidate your negotiation partners by yelling or being abusive. This will hinder the process. These stunts never act in your favour.

9. **Never Be Pressured Into Any Decision or Concession Unless Your Gut Is Comfortable With It.**

10. **Never Agree To Anything Unless Your Lawyer Agrees With The Decision.**

How Much Should I Ask For?

Your initial offer from your employer may not be what you expected. Sometimes you don't really know what to expect so how can you determine whether to agree to an offer. Here are some guidelines that you may find helpful. Remember, however that a severance package is just that – a package. When deciding how good or bad an offer is, you need to consider all the elements included. Some items may be more important to you than others (e.g. continuance of full health benefits if you are a single parent or educational assistance if you wish to get your MBA).

Salary Compensation

Firstly, be well versed on what the minimums are in your jurisdiction so that you are not asking for less than you deserve by law. This is the first place people review to evaluate a package. Where employment has been ongoing for a prolonged period of time, a simple multiplier can provide a gauge as to what to expect.

For example:

Level	Current Norm
Senior Management	One month per year of service
Middle Management	2-3 weeks per year of service
Support staff	1-2 weeks per year of service

The maximum severance provided is usually two years in the case of employees that have been at the company for 20+ years. There are cases of larger settlements (up to 5 years) for senior executives who have negotiated "golden parachutes" prior to starting employment.

A common clause recently is employers requiring "mitigation of severance", a claw-back of salary payments if and when the terminated employee secures new employment. However, its popularity is decreasing as it is increasingly viewed as discouraging reemployment efforts and is difficult to administer.

Bonuses

The norm is to provide an employee with a portion earned of their bonus, incentive bonus or profit sharing on a pro rata basis (the amount they had accrued until termination). In some cases, companies will establish a policy that an employee must be employed by the company on the date of the bonus distribution in order to receive their bonus. If your bonus makes up a large portion of your compensation, this may be a key negotiating point for you.

Pension and Retirement

For older workers, pension rights are significant. Many people have stayed with their employer for decades in order to ensure pension security in their retirement. To lose all of that especially when the employee is close to retirement can be devastating. This is because it is statistically proven to be harder for an older worker to gain employment.

Those who fear either long-term difficulty or complete inability to secure employment can request to accelerate commencement of their pension payout. Increasingly common, is a measure called "bridging to retirement" by which an employee's period of salary continuance during severance is not paid out on a full-time basis but is instead stretched out through smaller payments to reach a minimum retirement age or period of service. For example, if an employee is entitled to 6 months of full salary continuance as part of a settlement, the bridge to retirement could be payment of 1/3 of the salary over eighteen months. In this example, employment is "bridged" to the necessary attainment of service or age.

Outplacement Assistance

Basic outplacement services consist of career assessment and counseling, telephone answering, resume preparation as well as seminars on such topics as job search and stress management.

Three months' outplacement assistance is now common when it comes to the duration of this benefit. While rarely seen a decade ago, it has become almost a standard in severance packages.

For those that don't need outplacement services (i.e. if you are a career counselor), you can request a cash payment in lieu of this benefit. Depending on your level, the standard compensation is between $3,000 to $9,000.

Departure Statement

Some employees, especially those in a managerial or executive level, are concerned about how their termination will be announced to other employees or the media (for high ranking public-facing employees). Most employers are willing to work with the employee toward the preparation of a mutually agreeable departure statement (i.e. reason for leaving the company) because it poses a win-win resolution that doesn't cost a dime. It gives both parties to save face and protect their reputations.

Stock Option Extensions

More companies are offering stock options to all level of employees these days. Some stock options have restrictions including loss upon employment termination.

Because stock options are often seen as valuable to the employee and low in cost to the employer, more and more companies are viewing requests for stock option extensions in a positive light. This allows the stock option holder to have at least the duration of the termination notice period to exercise his/her stock options.

Appendix A: Notice of Individual Termination of Employment

This section is an overview of your rights in regard to termination in your province/territory.

Source: www.servicecanada.gc.ca

At A Glance:

Jurisdiction	Termination of Employment
Alberta	1 week after 3 months 2 wks after 2 yrs 4 wks after 4 yrs
British Columbia	week after 3 months 2 weeks after 1 year 3 weeks for 3 years up to 8 weeks for 8 years
Federal	2 weeks after 3 months and two days wages per year employed
Manitoba	1 pay period after 30 days of employment (pay periods must be at least twice per month)
New Brunswick	2 weeks after 6 months 4 weeks after 5 years
Newfoundland	1 week after 1 month 2 weeks after 2 years

Nova Scotia	1 week after 3 months 2 weeks after 2 years 4 weeks after 5 years 8 weeks after 10 years
Nunavut	2 weeks after 90 days additional week per year after 3 years to a maximum of 8 weeks
Northwest Territories	2 weeks after 90 days additional week per year after 3 years to a maximum of 8 weeks
Ontario	1 week after 3 months 2 weeks after 1 year 3 weeks after 3 years 4 weeks after 4 years etc. up to 8 wks after 8 yrs
Prince Edward Island	2 weeks after 6 months 4 weeks after 5 years
Québec	1 week after 3 months 2 weeks after 1 year 4 weeks after 5 years 8 weeks after 10 years
Saskatchewan	1 week after 3 months 2 weeks after 1 year 4 weeks after 3 years 6 weeks after 5 years 8 weeks after 10 years

Yukon	1 week after 6 months
	2 weeks after 1 year
	additional week per year up to 8

Detailed Termination Legislation:

Federal – *Canada Labour Code* (Code) and *Canada Labour Standards Regulations*

Employees under federal jurisdiction commonly work for federal government departments and agencies, airlines, banks, railways, radio, television and telephone companies, or transport companies that do business in more than one province. Usually one indicator if you work for a federally-regulated company is if you receive Remembrance Day (November 11th) as a statutory holiday. If you do, then your rights will most likely be regulated by the Federal government instead of the province in which you work.

All non-federal jobs are governed by the Employment Standards Act of the province in which they work. If you do not work for a federally-regulated company, then please refer to the section of the province in which you work.

Minimum Written Notice Required (from the Employer)

Two **weeks'** notice or two weeks' wages in lieu, at regular rate for regular hours

Minimum Written Notice Required (from the Employee)

None

Expiration of Notice

Notice expires when an employee continues to be employed more than two weeks after the date specified for termination, except if the employee agrees otherwise in writing. Employment may still be terminated for just cause.

Deadline for Payment of Amounts Owed

Any wages or other amounts to which the employee is entitled under the CLC must be paid within 30 days from the time entitlement arose. Any vacation pay owed to employee must be paid "forthwith" when employment ceases.

Eligibility Requirements / Exclusions

An employer is not required to give notice (or pay in lieu) to an employee who has:

- completed less than three consecutive months of continuous employment; or
- who is dismissed for just cause.

Severance Pay

An employee who has completed 12 consecutive months of employment is entitled, in addition to notice of termination or pay in lieu of notice, to either two days' wages for each completed year of employment or to a total of five days' wages (at the regular rate for regular hours), whichever is greater.

However, an employer is not required to provide severance pay to an employee who has been dismissed for just cause.

Unjust Dismissal

An employee who has completed twelve consecutive months of continuous employment with an employer may make a complaint in writing to an inspector if s/he has been dismissed and considers the dismissal to be unjust.

Subject to certain exceptions, the complaint must be made within 90 days of the date of dismissal. On receipt of a complaint, an inspector is assigned to assist the parties in trying to reach a settlement. Should a complaint not be settled within a reasonable period of time, the complainant may request in writing to have it referred to an adjudicator appointed by the Minister of Labour. However, no complaint may be considered by an adjudicator where a procedure for redress is provided elsewhere in any Act of Parliament, or where the cause of the complaint is a layoff because of lack of work or the discontinuance of a function.

An adjudicator who decides that a dismissal was unjust may order the payment of compensation (equivalent to no more than the amount of remuneration that would have been paid to the person, but for the dismissal), order a reinstatement, or order to "do any other like thing that it is equitable to require the employer to do in order to remedy or counteract any consequence of the dismissal". Any order is final and may not be questioned or reviewed in any court.

Illegal Termination

An employer may not dismiss, suspend, lay off, demote or discipline an employee who exercises his/her rights under the Code's reassignment, maternity leave, parental leave or sick leave provisions. Nor may an employee be dismissed or laid off because of pregnancy or on the ground that garnishment proceedings may be or have been taken.

Continuity of Employment (Transfer of Establishment)

Where any particular federal work, undertaking or business, or part thereof is transferred from one employer to another by sale, lease, merger or otherwise, the employment of the employee, before and after the transfer, is deemed to be continuous with one employer, notwithstanding the transfer.

Moreover, an employee's continuity of employment is deemed uninterrupted by a layoff that is not a termination or by an absence from employment permitted or condoned by the employer.

Other

A layoff is deemed to be a termination unless:

- it is for a term of three months or less;
- it is for more than three months but the employee is given notice at or before the time of layoff that s/he will be recalled within six months of the layoff's start;
- it is for a term of more than three months and the employee continues to receive payments from the employer, the employer continues to make payments regarding a registered pension benefits plan or a group or employee insurance plan.

Conditions of employment: an employer may not reduce the rate of wages or alter any other term or condition of employment of an employee to whom a notice of termination has been given, except with his/her written consent. Furthermore, the employer must, between the time when the notice is given and the date of termination, pay to the employee his/her regular rate of wages for his/her regular hours of work.

Alberta - *Employment Standards Code*

Minimum Written Notice Required (from the Employer)

Where an employee has been employed:

·	More than three months but less than two years:	one week;
·	Two years or more but less than four:	two weeks;
·	Four years or more but less than six:	four weeks;
·	Six years or more but less than eight:	five weeks;
·	Eight years or more but less than ten:	six weeks;
·	Ten years or more:	eight weeks

Periods of employment with the same employer are considered to be one period of employment if not more than three months have elapsed between them.

Instead of giving notice of termination, an employer may pay an employee an amount equivalent to the wages his employee would have earned if s/he had worked his/her regular hours during the applicable termination notice period. [1]

The employer can also offer a combination of termination pay and termination notice, in which case the termination pay must be at least equal to the wages the employee would have earned for the applicable termination notice period that is not covered by the notice.

Expiration of Notice

A termination notice is of no effect if the employee continues to be employed by the same employer after the date specified for termination of employment.

Deadline for Payment of Amounts Owed

Upon termination, an employee's earnings (wages, overtime pay, vacation pay, general holiday pay and termination pay) must normally be paid no later than three days after the last day of employment. The three-day limit also applies if the employee terminates his/her employment by giving notice.

However, if an employer or employee terminates employment and no termination notice or termination pay is required, earnings must be paid no later than ten days after the last day of employment.

Eligibility Requirements / Exclusions

Employers are not required to give termination notice (or pay in lieu) to employees who are:

- employed for a definite term or task for a period not exceeding 12 months;
- employed for three months or less;
- temporarily laid off;
- terminated for just cause;
- laid off after having refused reasonable alternate employment; or
- employed under an arrangement whereby they may elect to work or not when requested to do so.

Nor is termination notice or termination pay required to be given to employees:

- who have refused work made available through a seniority system;
- whose employment has been terminated for failing to return to work within seven consecutive days of a recall (unless provided otherwise in a collective agreement); or
- whose contract of employment has become impossible to perform because of unforeseeable or unpreventable causes beyond the control of their employer.

Employees are not required to give termination notice if:

- they have been employed for less than three months;
- there is a different established custom or practice in an industry;
- continuing to be employed by the employer would endanger their personal health or security;
- the contract of employment is impossible to perform due to unforeseeable or unpreventable causes beyond their control;
- they are temporarily laid off, laid off after having refused reasonable alternate employment or laid off as the result of a strike or lockout;
- they are employed under an arrangement whereby they may elect to work or not when requested to do so;
- they terminate their employment because of a reduction in wage rate, overtime rate, vacation pay, general holiday pay or termination pay.

School employees and school bus drivers are not entitled to termination pay if they work until the end of the school year and are given the opportunity to work at the beginning of the next school year.

Severance Pay

N/A

Illegal Termination

An employer may not terminate the employment of, or lay off an employee who has started maternity leave, or who is entitled to or has started parental leave, unless the employer suspends or discontinues in whole or in part the business, undertaking or other activity in which the employee is employed. Nonetheless, the employer has the obligation to reinstate the employee or provide the latter with alternative work, in accordance with an established seniority system or employer practice, if operations are subsequently resumed within 52 weeks following the end of the employee's maternity or parental leave.

An employer or other person may not suspend, layoff or terminate an employee for the sole reason that garnishment proceedings are being or may be taken against the employee.

An employer or other person may not terminate or restrict the employment of an individual, nor discriminate against him/her, for exercising a number of rights—or complying with certain obligations—under the *Employment Standards Code*, namely:

- making a complaint;
- giving or having the potential to give evidence at any inquiry or in any proceeding or prosecution;
- requesting or demanding anything to which s/he is entitled; or
- making or being about to make any statement or disclosure that may be required.

Continuity of Employment (Transfer of Establishment)

The employment of an employee is deemed to be continuous and uninterrupted when a business, undertaking or other activity or part of it is sold, leased, transferred or merged or if it continues to operate under a receiver or receiver-manager.

When calculating length of employment for termination notice purposes, an employee's periods of employment with the same employer are considered to be one period of employment if no more than three months has elapsed between them.

Other

__Maximum duration of a temporary layoff:__ an employee's employment is deemed to be terminated, and the employer must pay termination pay, on the 60th day of a temporary layoff. The period of temporary layoff can be extended beyond 60 days, however, as long as the employer, under a mutual agreement, pays the employee his/her wages or an amount in lieu during the layoff. It can also be extended if the employer continues to make payments for the benefit of the laid off employee in accordance with a pension, employee insurance or other similar plan, or if a collective agreement binding the employer and the employee provides for recall rights after a layoff. Termination pay must nevertheless be paid once payments cease or recall rights expire.

__Conditions of employment:__ After the employer or employee has given termination notice, the employer may not reduce the wages, wage rate or any term or condition of employment of the employee until the date employment terminates, whether or not work is required to be performed during that period. Furthermore, the employee must remain employed by the employer during that period, unless the employer gives the employee termination pay, or unless the employer terminates the employment of the employee for just cause, because the employee has refused an offer of reasonable alternative work, has refused work made available through a seniority system, has not been provided with work by reason of a strike or lockout at the employee's place of employment or, finally, because the employment contract is or has become impossible for the employer to perform as a result of unforeseeable or unpreventable causes beyond its control.

British Columbia - *Employment Standards Act* (ESA) and *Employment Standards Regulations*

Minimum Written Notice Required (from the Employer)

Where an employee has been employed:

·	Three consecutive months or more but less than twelve:	one week;
·	Twelve months or more but less than three years:	two weeks;
·	Three years or more but less than four:	three weeks;
·	Four years or more but less than five:	four weeks;
·	Five years or more but less than six:	five weeks;
·	Six years or more but less than seven:	six weeks;
·	Seven years or more but less than eight:	seven weeks;
·	Eight years or more:	eight weeks

An employer may pay an employee an amount of money in lieu of the written notice. This amount is calculated by totaling the employee's weekly wages, at the regular rate, earned in the last eight weeks in which the employee worked normal or average hours of work, divided by eight, and multiplied by the number of prescribed weeks of notice. An employer may give an employee a combination of written notice and money in lieu.

When the employment of an employee is terminated at the end of a temporary layoff, the termination date is deemed to have occurred at the beginning of the layoff period.

Minimum Written Notice Required (from the Employee)

None

Expiration of Notice

A notice of termination given to an employee has no effect if his/her employment continues after the period of notice ends. A notice is also of no effect if it coincides with a period during which the employee is on annual vacation, leave, temporary layoff, strike or lockout or is unavailable for work due to a strike or lockout or medical reasons.

Deadline for Payment of Amounts Owed

An employer must pay all wages owing to an employee, including vacation pay, within 48 hours after the effective date of termination, if the employer terminates the employment, and within six days if employment is terminated by the employee.

Eligibility Requirements / Exclusions

The following are excluded from coverage under the ESA:

- practicing members of designated professions;
- students in certain approved work experience programs;
- students employed at the secondary school where they are enrolled;
- sitters (i.e., a person employed in a private residence to provide the service of attending to a child, or to a disabled, inform or other person); and
- persons receiving income assistance while participating in government training or work experience programs.

Moreover, the following are excluded from the ESA's notice of termination provisions:

- Employees employed at one or more construction sites by an employer whose principal business is construction;
- auxiliary or volunteer fire fighters;
- student nurses;
- teachers; and
- fishers.

No notice (or pay in lieu) is required where an employee:

- is discharged for just cause;
- terminates the employment;
- retires from employment;
- has refused reasonable alternative employment by the employer.

Severance Pay
N/A

Illegal Termination

An employer may not, because of pregnancy or because of a leave allowed under the ESA (i.e., pregnancy, parental, family responsibility or bereavement leave, or jury duty), terminate an employee's employment or change a condition of employment without the employee's written consent.

Continuity of Employment (Transfer of Establishment)

If all or part of a business or a substantial part of the entire assets of a business is disposed of, the employment of an employee of the business is deemed to be continuous and uninterrupted by the disposition.

Other

A layoff is deemed to be temporary if:

- it does not exceed 13 weeks in a period of 20 consecutive weeks or,
- in the case of an employee who has a right of recall, it does not exceed the specified period within which the employee is entitled to be recalled to employment.

A **week of layoff** means a week in which an employee earns less than 50 percent of his/her regular weekly wages, averaged over the previous eight weeks.

Conditions of employment: once notice has been given, the employer may not alter any condition of employment of the employee concerned, including the wage rate, without the written consent of the employee or the trade union representing him/her.

Constructive dismissal: the Director of Employment Standards may determine that the employment of an employee has been terminated if a condition of employment is substantially altered.

Minimum Written Notice Required (from the Employer)

Notice must be equivalent to the duration of **one pay period** (a "pay period" is defined as a period of employment of no more than 16 consecutive days).

Where the term of employment is not fixed and wages are paid less often than once in each month, the notice of termination must be for a period of not less than 30 days.

Instead of giving notice of termination, an employer may pay an employee the wages that the employee would have received had s/he worked his/her regular hours of work at the regular wage rate for the required period of notice, in addition to any other wages owed.

An employer may establish a practice regarding termination of employment that provides for greater or lesser periods of notice. To do so, an employer must give written notice to each employee and post a notice for at least 30 days in conspicuous places at the workplace. The notice must be kept posted as long as the employer continues the practice; moreover, all new employees must be given written notice of the practice at the time their employment begins.

Where an employer or an employee gives notice of termination, no part of the employee's annual vacation may be used to calculate the required notice period unless, in the case of an employee giving notice, the employer agrees otherwise. Moreover, the payment of a vacation allowance to an employee does not affect any other amount payable in respect of a termination.

Expiration of Notice

N/A

Deadline for Payment of Amounts Owed

The employer must pay all wages due to the employee within 10 working days after the termination.

Eligibility Requirements / Exclusions

The following are excluded from coverage under the ESC:

- volunteers for religious, philanthropic, political or patriotic institutions;
- employees working as beneficiaries under a rehabilitation or therapeutic plan or project;
- employees who are given training or work experience for a limited period of time through a program implemented or approved by a provincial or federal government authority, or a school board, and who are not paid a wage.

Moreover, the following are excluded from most of the Code's minimum standards, including notice of individual termination provisions:

- employees employed in agriculture, fishing, fur or dairy farming;
- in the growing of horticultural or market garden products for sale;
- employees employed in a private family home, paid by a member of the family, and whose employment in the home consists of working:
- as a domestic worker for not more than 24 hours in a week for the same employer;
- as a sitter attending primarily to the needs of a member of the household who is a child; or
- as a companion attending primarily to the needs of a member of the household who is aged, infirm or ill.

No notice (or pay in lieu) is required where an employee:

- is a construction worker;
- has not completed more than 30 days of employment, unless otherwise agreed in writing by the employer and the employee before employment begins;
- is laid off temporarily;
- is employed for a specified work or undertaking and for a period not exceeding twelve months, at the end of which employment is terminated;
- reaches the retirement age as established by custom or practice in the employer's business;
- is employed under an arrangement whereby s/he may elect to work or not when requested to do so by the employer;
- is employed under an arrangement or contract of employment that is impossible to perform or is frustrated by a fortuitous or unforeseeable circumstance;
- acts in a manner that constitutes willful misconduct or disobedience or willful neglect of duty that is not condoned by the employer;

- acts in a manner that is insubordinate toward the employer or dishonest in the course of the employment;
- fails to return to work within a reasonable time after being recalled from a layoff;
- is laid off after refusing an offer of reasonable alternate work made available by the employer or through a seniority system.

An employee is not required to give notice of termination to an employer that acts in a violent or improper manner towards him/her.

Severance Pay

N/A

Illegal Termination

No employer or other person acting on its behalf may suspend, terminate or restrict or threaten to suspend, terminate or restrict the employment of an employee, lay off or threaten to lay off an employee, or otherwise discriminate against an employee because:

- garnishment proceedings are taken or might be taken against the employee;
- the employee files or might file a complaint under the ESC or assists in the initiation of a complaint, prosecution or other proceeding under the ESC;
- the employee requests or receives information or advice from an employment standards officer or requests or demands anything to which s/he is entitled under the ESC;
- the employee gives or might give information or evidence in respect of an investigation, prosecution or other proceeding under the ESC;
- the employee makes or might make a statement or disclosure that may be required of the employee under the ESC, or because the employee refuses to work or attempts to refuse to work on a Sunday, if s/he is permitted to do so.

Nor may an employer lay off or terminate the employment of an employee who has completed seven consecutive months of employment with the employer solely because she is pregnant, gives notice of her intention to take maternity leave or s/he takes parental leave or gives notice of his/her intention to do so.

Continuity of Employment (Transfer of Establishment)

For the purpose of the ESC's provisions regarding annual vacations, statutory holidays, maternity and parental leave, when the business or part of the business of an employer is sold, leased, transferred, merged or otherwise disposed of whereby the control, direction of management of the business is given to another person, or the business continues to operate under a receiver, the employment of an employee is deemed to be continuous and uninterrupted.

Other

A layoff is not deemed to be a termination when:

- it is customary, during that period of year, to lay off employees because of the seasonal nature of the industry and the employee has been advised, upon being hired, that s/he will be laid off during that period;
- the layoff is for a term of eight weeks or less in any period of 16 consecutive weeks;
- the layoff is for more than eight weeks and the employer recalls the employee within the time specified by the Minister of Labour and Immigration; or
- the layoff is for more than eight weeks but the employer continues to pay wages or to make payments to the employee of an agreed amount, or the employer continues to make payments for the benefit of the employee to a pension plan and/or insurance plan

When a layoff becomes a termination, the employment of the employee is deemed to have been terminated without notice on the first day of the layoff and the employer must pay to the employee the wages to which the latter is entitled, under the ESC, in lieu of termination notice.

Conditions of employment

An employer that gives notice of termination may not change the working conditions or wage rate of an employee to whom the notice is given or of an affected employee, except in accordance with a collective agreement or with the written consent of the bargaining agent for the affected employee, or with the written consent of the affected employee, where the latter does not have a bargaining agent.

New Brunswick - *Employment Standards Act* (ESA) and *Employment Standards General Regulation*

Minimum Written Notice Required (from the Employer)

Where an employee has been employed by the employer for a continuous period of:

Six months or more but less than five years:	two weeks;
Five years or more:	four weeks.

Instead of giving notice of termination, an employer may pay an employee an amount equal to the pay the employee would have earned during the notice period.

Expiration of Notice

If an employee continues to work for the employer for one month or more beyond the end of the notice period, the notice of termination or layoff becomes extinguished and a new notice must be given if the employee is to be laid off or terminated.

Deadline for Payment of Amounts Owed

Not specified

Eligibility Requirements / Exclusions

The following are excluded from coverage under the ESA:

- Persons working in or about the private home of the individual who employs them;
- Agricultural workers employed by small employers (i.e., employers that employ three or less employees, who are not in a close family relationship, over a substantial period of the year).

No notice (or pay in lieu) is required where an employee:

- is dismissed for cause and the employer sets out the reasons in writing;
- is laid off due to an unforeseen lack of work;
- is laid off for a period of six days or less;
- has completed a definite assignment that s/he was hired to perform over a period not exceeding 12 months;
- is doing construction work in the construction industry;
- retires under a *bona fide* retirement plan; or
- refuses reasonable alternate employment offered as an alternative to a layoff or termination.

Severance Pay

N/A

Illegal Termination

An employer may not dismiss, suspend, lay off, penalize, discipline or discriminate against an employee because:

- The employee has applied for leave to which s/he is entitled under the ESA;
- The employee, if permitted to do so under the ESA, refused or attempted to refuse to work on a Sunday or sought to enforce his/her rights to a weekly rest period;
- The employee made a complaint or gave information or evidence against the employer with respect to any matter covered by the ESA or concerning an alleged violation of any provincial or federal Act or regulation;
- The employer attempts to evade any responsibility imposed under any provincial or federal Act or regulation; or
- The employer attempts to prevent or inhibit an employee from taking advantage of any right or benefit granted under the ESA.

Nor may an employer dismiss, suspend or lay off:

- an employee who has been granted a leave of absence under the ESA during the leave of absence or for reasons arising from the leave alone; or
- a pregnant employee for reasons arising from her pregnancy alone.

Continuity of Employment (Transfer of Establishment)

Where an activity, business, trade or undertaking is disposed of, transferred or sold in any manner or amalgamated, whether by agreement, will, instrument, transfer, including transfer of shares, or by operation of law, the period of employment of an employee of the activity, business, trade or undertaking at the time of such disposition, transfer, sale or amalgamation, is deemed to have been a period of employment with the disposee, transferee, purchaser or amalgamation and the continuity of employment is deemed to be unbroken.

Other

N/A

Newfoundland and Labrador - *Labour Standards Act* (LSA) and *Labour Standard Regulations*

Minimum Written Notice Required (from the Employer)

Where an employee has been continuously employed [3] by the employer:

·	Three months or more but less than two years:	one week;
·	Two years or more but less than five:	two weeks;
·	Five years or more but less than ten:	three weeks;
·	Ten years or more but less than fifteen:	four weeks;
·	Fifteen years or more:	six weeks.

Instead of giving notice, an employer may pay to an employee wages equal to the normal wages that the employee would have earned during the required period of notice, including overtime wages (based on overtime worked in the one-month period preceding the termination of employment).

Minimum Written Notice Required (from the Employee) [2]

Same notice as employer.

Instead of giving notice, an employee may pay to his/her employer an amount equal to what the employee would normally earn under the contract of service during the required period of notice, including overtime wages (based on overtime worked in the one-month period preceding the termination of employment).

Expiration of Notice

A notice of termination or temporary layoff has no effect if the contract of service continues beyond the period of expiry specified in the notice.

Deadline for Payment of Amounts Owed

The employer must pay all wages due to an employee within one week from the date of termination of the employee's contract of service.

In addition, the employer must, upon termination of the contract of service, pay to the employee the vacation pay to which s/he is entitled in addition to the wages properly earned by the employee for the period following the notice of termination.

Eligibility Requirements / Exclusions

The LSA's notice of individual termination provisions do not apply to persons employed in the construction industry.

Employers are not required to give notice (or pay in lieu) to an employee when:

- the employee is laid off for a period not exceeding one week;
- the employee is employed for a firm non-renewable term or specific task not exceeding 12 months and his/her employment is not terminated before the completion of the term or task;
- the contract of service between the employer and the employee has existed for less than 30 days;
- the employee has refused an offer by the employer of reasonable alternative employment of a similar nature requiring similar skill, effort and ability, and that would enable the employee to earn during a similar number of working hours a total wage comparable to what was provided in the contract of service being terminated;
- the employee has reached the age of retirement according to the established practice of the undertaking where s/he is employed;
- the employee has willfully refused to obey a lawful instruction of the employer or has committed misconduct or been so neglectful of duty that the interest of the employer is adversely affected, or the employee has otherwise been in breach of a material condition of the contract of service that warrants summary dismissal according to the director of the Labour Relations Board;
- the employer is required to terminate the contract of service on account of destruction of or major breakdown to plant machinery or equipment, or climatic or economic conditions that are beyond the foreseeable control of the employer and that necessitate declaration of redundancy.

Employees are not required to give notice (or pay in lieu) to their employer when:

- the contract of service between the employer and the employee has existed for less than one month;
- the employer has mistreated the employee or acted in a manner that has or might endanger the health or well-being of the employee;
- the employer has otherwise been in breach of a material condition of the contract of service that warrants no notice being given according to the director or the Labour Relations Board; or

Severance Pay

N/A

Illegal Termination

An employer may not dismiss or give notice of dismissal to an employee for the sole reason that the employee informs the employer that she is pregnant or that s/he intends to take or takes pregnancy, adoption or parental leave, in accordance with the LSA.

An employer may not discharge or threaten to discharge an employee contrary to the LSA or discriminate against an employee because the latter:

- has testified or is about to testify in a proceeding or help in an investigation made or taken under the LSA;
- has given information to the board or to the director or an officer or inspector appointed under the LSA to acquire information regarding the wages payable to that employee or other employees of the employer or the terms of the contract of service of that employee or other employees;
- has initiated or taken part in a proceeding, investigation or complaint initiated or made under the LSA; or
- has been dismissed by a former employer.

In addition, it is illegal for a person to seek to have an employer dismiss an employee because that employee has previously been dismissed by that person.

Continuity of Employment (Transfer of Establishment)

Where an employer transfers, assigns or conveys its undertaking to another person or firm, the continued and uninterrupted employment of the employee by the person having so acquired the undertaking is considered to be continuous with the period of employment with the 1st named employer and counts as against the new employer for the regulation of the rights, benefits and privileges of the employee under the LSA.

Other

Travel costs from remote site: an employee employed at a remote site must be provided free transportation to the nearest point at which regularly scheduled transport services are available if his/her employment is terminated or s/he is laid off by the employer.

A layoff is deemed to be temporary if: it does not exceed 13 weeks in a period of 20 consecutive weeks. However, a day during the 20-week period in which the employee receives pay, including pay received for a public holiday occurring during that period, is not counted in the calculation of the 13-week layoff period.

When a layoff becomes a termination, the employment of the employee is deemed to have been terminated at the beginning of the temporary layoff.

Northwest Territories and Nunavut - *Labour Standards Act* (LSA) and *Notice of Termination Exemption Regulations*

Minimum Written Notice Required (from the Employer)

Where an employee has been employed for:

·	90 days or more, but less than three years:	two weeks;
·	Three years or more but less than four:	three weeks;
·	Four years or more but less than five:	four weeks;
·	Five years or more but less than six:	five weeks;
·	Six years or more but less than seven	six weeks;
·	Seven years or more but less than eight:	seven weeks;
·	Eight years or more	eight weeks.

Instead of giving notice, an employer may pay termination pay to the employee. The amount of termination pay must be equal to the wages and benefits to which the employee would have been entitled had s/he worked his/her usual hours of work for each week of the required notice period.

The period of notice may not coincide with the annual leave of the employee whose employment is being terminated.

Expiration of Notice

Notice of termination is void and of no effect if an employee continues to be employed by his/her employer after the date of termination specified in the notice of termination.

Deadline for Payment of Amounts Owed

The employer must, within ten days after termination of employment, pay to the employee all wages owed. Any vacation pay must be paid to the employee without delay.

Eligibility Requirements / Exclusions

The following are excluded from coverage under the LSA:

- trappers;
- persons engaged in commercial fisheries;
- members or students of designated professions.

Furthermore, the LSA's notice of individual termination provisions do not apply to employees employed:

- in the construction industry;
- for less than 180 days in a year, seasonally or intermittently;
- for less than 25 hours a week; or

No notice of termination (or pay in lieu) is required where an employee:

- has been employed by his/her employer for a period of less than 90 days;
- is temporarily laid off;
- is terminated for just cause;
- has refused an offer by the employer of reasonable alternative work;
- following a temporary layoff, does not return to work within seven days after being requested in writing to do so by the employer.

Severance Pay

N/A

Illegal Termination

An employer may not terminate or unilaterally change a condition of employment of the employee because of the employee's pregnancy or because the employee has requested, is on or has taken pregnancy or parental leave in accordance with the LSA.

An employer or any other person may not terminate, threaten to terminate or restrict the employment of a person or discriminate in any way against a person because the person, either on his or her own behalf or on behalf of another employee, has made a complaint under the LSA, has given evidence or may give evidence at any inquiry or any proceedings or prosecution under the LSA, requests anything to which s/he or another employee is entitled under the LSA, or has made or is about to make any statement or disclosure that may be required of the employee under the LSA.

Continuity of Employment (Transfer of Establishment)

For the purpose of the LSA's annual vacation provisions, where any industrial establishment in which an employee is employed is sold, leased, merged or otherwise transferred to another employer, the employment of the employee is deemed to be continuous with one employer, despite the transfer.

For the purpose of the LSA's termination of employment provisions, where an employee has been employed by the same employer more than once, those periods of employment are deemed to be one period of employment if not more than 90 days have elapsed between each period of employment.

Other

Constructive termination: a Labour Standards Officer may declare that an employer has terminated the employment of an employee if satisfied that the employer has substantially altered a condition of employment to discourage the employee from continuing his/her employment.

A layoff is deemed to be temporary if: it does not exceed 45 days in a period of 60 consecutive days; it exceeds 45 days, but the employer recalls the employee to employment within a time fixed by the Labour Standards Officer.

A layoff is deemed to be a termination if: the employer has not given a written notice of temporary layoff, indicating the expected date of return to work, to the laid off employee; or the layoff exceeds the maximum duration for a temporary layoff. In the latter case, the employee's employment is deemed to have been terminated on the *last* day of temporary layoff and termination pay must be paid by the employer.

Conditions of employment: once notice of termination is given, the employer may not reduce the wages or rate of wages or alter any term or condition of employment of the employee concerned. The employer must also pay the wages and benefits to which the employee is entitled, between the date notice is given and the date of termination.

Nova Scotia- *Labour Standards Code* (LSC) and *Labour Standards Code Regulations*

Minimum Written Notice Required (from the Employer)

Where an employee has been employed continuously:

·	Three months or more but less than two years:	one week;
·	Two years or more but less than five years:	two weeks;
·	Five years or more but less than ten years:	four weeks;
·	Ten years or more:	eight weeks.

Instead of giving notice of termination, an employer may pay an employee an amount equal to all pay to which the employee would have been entitled, at the regular rate for a non-overtime work week, had s/he performed work during the required period of notice. The period of notice of termination may not include any week of vacation unless the employee, after receiving the notice, agrees to take a vacation during the period of notice.

Minimum Written Notice Required (from an Employee)

Where an employee has been employed continuously:

·	At least three months but less than two years:	one week;
·	Two years or more:	two weeks.

Expiration of Notice

Where an employee continues to be employed, after the expiry of the notice of termination, for a period exceeding the length of the notice, his/her employer may not terminate his/her employment without giving a new notice of termination or pay in lieu of notice.

Deadline for Payment of Amounts Owed

At the expiry of a notice of termination, the employer must pay to the employee all pay to which the latter is entitled, including any amount owed for a replacement holiday that had not yet been taken at the time employment was terminated. In addition, the employer must pay the employee, within 10 days after the date of termination, all accumulated vacation pay earned.

Eligibility Requirements / Exclusions

The following are excluded from coverage under the LSC:

- employees employed in a private home by the householder to provide domestic service for a member of the employee's immediate family, or for no more than 24 hours per week.

Moreover, the following are excluded from most of the Code's minimum standards, including individual notice of termination provisions:

- employees engaged in work as real estate salespersons, automobile salespersons, or salespersons—other than route salespersons—who are entitled to receive all or part of their remuneration as commissions for purchase offers or sales which are normally made outside the employer's establishment; and
- employees who work on fishing vessels or in the operation of fishing vessels on water.

Although notice of termination provisions apply to duly qualified practitioners or students of designated professions and to certain senior civil servants of the province, these persons are not covered by the LSC's provisions regarding protection against dismissals without just cause.

Employers are not required to give notice (or pay in lieu) to an employee who:

- has been employed less than three months;
- is employed for a definite term or task for a period not exceeding 12 months and does not continue to be employed for a period of three months or more after completion of the term or task;
- is laid off or suspended for no longer than six consecutive days;
- is discharged or laid off for any reason beyond the control of the employer (e.g., complete or partial destruction of plant, destruction or breakdown of machinery or equipment, unavailability of supplies, lack of orders for products, accident, labour disputes, weather conditions, government actions) if the employer has exercised due diligence to foresee and avoid the cause of discharge or layoff;
- has been offered reasonable alternate employment by his employer;
- has reached the age of retirement according to the established practice of the employer;
- is guilty of willful misconduct or disobedience or neglect of duty that has not been condoned by the employer;
- is employed is the construction industry.

Employees are not required to give notice to their employer if:

- they are employed in the construction industry;
- they have been employed continuously for less than three months; or
- the employer is guilty of a breach of the terms and conditions of employment.

Severance Pay

N/A

Dismissal Without Just Cause

Where the period of employment of an employee with an employer is 10 years or more, the employee may not be suspended or discharged without just cause. However, this does not apply to a person: who is discharged or laid off for any reason beyond the control of the employer if the latter has exercised due diligence; who has been offered reasonable alternative employment by his/her employer; whose employment is terminated after having reached the age of retirement, in accordance with the employer's established practice; who is employed in the construction industry; or who is not covered by the LSC or its termination provisions. An employee who is discharged or suspended without just cause may make a complaint to the Director of Labour Standards. A six-month time limit applies to complaints under the Code.

If the Director concludes that the Code has been contravened after inquiring into the complaint, s/he may order in writing the employer to comply with the Code, rectify the injury or make compensation, and/or reinstate the employee. Appeals may be filed with the Labour Standards Tribunal, which may also make an order for compensation and/or reinstatement.

Illegal Termination

An employer may not discharge, lay off or discriminate in any other manner against an employee because garnishment proceedings have been or may be taken against that employee.

Nor may an employer discharge, lay off or discriminate against any person because that person:

- has made a complaint pursuant to the LSC;
- has testified or is about to testify, or the employer believes that person may testify, in any proceeding pursuant to an enactment;
- has made or is about to make any disclosure required or permitted to be made under the LSC; or

- has taken or has evidenced an intention to take, or the employer believes that that person may take, a leave of absence to which the person is entitled under the LSC.
- In the latter case, an employer may not discharge, lay off or suspend an employee within three months of that person taking, evidencing an intention to take, or the employer believing that the employee may take, a leave of absence to which the employee is entitled, unless:
- the employee is guilty of willful misconduct, disobedience or neglect of duty that has not been condoned by the employer;
- the employer has just cause to discharge or suspend the employee;
- the reason for the discharge or layoff is beyond the control of the employer and the employer has exercised due diligence to foresee and avoid its cause; or
- the employer, in good faith and for legitimate business reasons, ceases operation or eliminates the employee's position and is unable to provide him/her reasonable alternative employment.

Continuity of Employment (Transfer of Establishment)

If an activity, business, trade or undertaking is disposed of, transferred or sold in any manner or amalgamated, whether by agreement, will, instrument, transfer, including transfer of shares, or by operation of law, the period of employment of an employee at the time of such disposition, transfer, sale or amalgamation, is deemed to have been employment with the disposee, transferee, purchaser or amalgamation and the continuity of employment is not broken.

For termination purposes, successive periods of employment with the same employer that are less than 13 weeks apart constitute one period of employment.

Other

Conditional notice of termination: a notice of termination may be made conditional upon the happening of a future event if the length of notice complies with the LSC.

Conditions of employment: an employer may not alter the rates of wages or any other term or condition of employment of a person to whom or by whom notice has been given.

Where a layoff becomes a termination: a laid off employee who was not entitled to notice of termination, due to the duration of the layoff, and whose employment is terminated must receive payment in lieu of notice from his/her employer. In such a case, employment is deemed to have been terminated on the day the employee was laid off.

Ontario- *Employment Standards Act, 2000* (ESA 2000) and *Termination and Severance of Employment Regulation*

Minimum Written Notice Required (from an Employer)
Where employee has been employed:

·	Three months or more but less than one year	one week;
·	One year or more but less than three:	two weeks;
·	Three years or more but less than four:	three weeks;
·	Four years or more but less than five:	four weeks;
·	Five years or more but less than six:	five weeks;
·	Six years or more but less than seven:	six weeks;
·	Seven years or more but less than eight:	seven weeks;
·	Eight years or more:	eight weeks.

An employer may terminate the employment of an employee without notice or with less notice than required if the employer pays the employee a lump sum equal to the amount the latter would have earned during the prescribed period of notice.[4] The employer must also continue to make all benefit plan contributions required to maintain the benefits to which the employee would have been entitled to receive had his/her employment continued during the period of notice.

The period of a notice of termination given to an employee may not include any vacation time unless the employee, after receiving the notice, agrees otherwise.

Minimum Written Notice Required (from an Employee)

An employee to whom notice has been given as part of a group termination of employment may not terminate his/her employment without first giving the employer at least **one week's** written notice if his/her period of employment is less than two years or at least **two weeks** if his/her period of employment is two years or more. Such notice is not necessary if the employer constructively dismisses the employee or breaches a term of the employment contract, whether or not such a breach would constitute a constructive dismissal.

An employee who takes pregnancy or parental leave may not terminate her/his employment before the leave expires or when it expires without giving the employer at least four weeks' written notice of termination.

Expiration of Notice

An employer may provide temporary work to an employee who has been given notice of termination, for up to 13 weeks after the termination date specified in the notice, without being required to provide a further notice of termination.

Deadline for Payment of Amounts Owed

The employer must pay any wages to which the employee is entitled, including any accrued vacation pay, within seven days of termination or on the day that would have been the employer's next pay day, whichever occurs later.

Eligibility Requirements / Exclusions

The following are excluded from coverage under the ESA 2000:

- certain persons receiving training;
- employees of an embassy or consulate of a foreign nation and their employer;
- students performing work under an authorized work experience program;
- participants in community participation under the *Ontario Works Act, 1997*;
- inmates, including those in custody under the *Young Offenders Act* , participating in a work project or rehabilitation program;
- offenders performing work under a court order or sentence, or as part of an alternative measure under the *Young Offenders Act* (Canada);
- individuals performing work in a simulated job or working environment for rehabilitation purposes;
- holders of political, religious or judicial office;
- members of quasi-judicial tribunals;
- holders of elected office in organizations, including a trade union;
- police officers;
- directors of a corporation.

The following are not covered by the Act's notice of termination provisions:

- an employee employed for less than three months;
- an employee who has been guilty of willful misconduct, disobedience or willful neglect of duty that is not trivial and has not been condoned by the employer;
- subject to the *Human Rights Code*, an employee whose contract of employment has become impossible to perform or has been frustrated by a fortuitous or unforeseeable event or circumstance;
- an employee whose employment is terminated after refusing an offer of reasonable alternative employment with the employer
- an employee whose employment is terminated after refusing alternative employment made available through a seniority system;
- an employee who is on temporary lay-off and does not return to work within a reasonable time after having been requested by his or her employer to do so;
- an employee whose employment is terminated during or as a result of a strike or lock-out at the place of employment;
- construction employees;
- an employee who is employed under an arrangement whereby s/he may elect to work or not to work when requested to do so;
- an employee who having reached the age of retirement according to the employer's established practice, has his or her employment terminated in accordance with that practice;
- an employee on temporary lay-off;
- employees whose employer is engaged in building, alteration or repair of a ship or vessel with a gross tonnage of over ten tons designed for commercial navigation and who have agreed, personally or through a bargaining agent, to be exempted from statutory notice of termination provisions in return for a supplementary unemployment benefit plan.

Moreover, an employer is not required to give notice of individual termination to an employee who has been provided notice (or pay in lieu) as part of a *group* termination of employment.

Severance Pay

In addition to notice of termination or pay in lieu of notice, an employee with five years of service or more (whether or not continuous or active) who is dismissed, constructively dismissed, laid off[5] for 35 weeks or more in a period of 52 consecutive weeks, laid off because of a permanent discontinuance of the employer's business at an establishment, or whose employer refuses or is unable to continue employing him/her, may be entitled to severance pay.

To be eligible, the employee's employment must be severed by an employer who has an annual payroll of $2.5 million or more, or the employee must be part of a group of 50 or more employees whose employment is severed in a six-month period as a result of a permanent discontinuance of all or part of the employer's business at an establishment.

Employees who resign after receiving notice of termination retain their right to severance pay, provided they give at least two weeks' notice to their employer. For the purpose of determining eligibility to severance pay, their employment is deemed to have been severed on the day the employer's notice of termination would have taken effect. When calculating the amount of severance pay, however, their employment is deemed to have been severed on their effective date of resignation.

The minimum amount of severance pay due to an employee is calculated by:

- adding the number of years of employment completed by the employee (whether or not continuous or active), including any partial year of employment (i.e., the number of additional months of employment divided by 12); and
- multiplying this sum by the employee's regular wages for a regular work week,[6] for a total of up to 26 weeks of wages.

An employee's length of employment is deemed to include any period of notice of termination that should have been given by the employer under the ESA 2000.

When calculating severance pay, if the employee does not have a regular work week or if the employee is paid on a basis other than time, the employee's regular wages for a regular work week is deemed to be the average amount of regular wages earned by the employee for the weeks in which the employee worked in the period of 12 weeks preceding the date on which the employee's employment was severed or on the date on which the lay-off began.

Severance pay may be paid in installments over a period of up to three years with the agreement of the employee or the approval of the Director of employment standards.

Employers are not required to provide severance pay to an employee:

- employed in construction;
- engaged in the on-site maintenance of buildings, structures, roads, sewers, pipelines, mains, tunnels or other works;
- whose employment is severed as a result of the permanent discontinuance of business caused by the economic consequences of a strike;
- who retires at the time his/her employment is severed and who receives an actuarially unreduced pension benefit reflecting any service credits the employee would normally have earned had employment not been severed;

- whose employment is severed after refusing reasonable alternative employment with the employer or made available through a seniority system;
- who has been guilty of willful misconduct, disobedience or willful neglect of duty that is not trivial and has not been condoned by the employer;
- who is employed under an arrangement whereby s/he can elect to work or not when requested to do so; or
- whose contract of employment has become impossible to perform or has been frustrated (unless the impossibility or frustration is the result of a permanent discontinuance of business because of a fortuitous or unforeseen event, the employer's death, the employee's death if notice of termination had been received before the death, or is the result of an illness or injury suffered by the employee, and the *Human Rights Code* prohibits severing the employment).

Illegal Termination

An employer or any person acting on its behalf may not intimidate, dismiss or otherwise penalize an employee or threaten to do so because the employee:

- asks the employer to comply with the ESA 2000 and regulations;
- makes inquiries about his/her rights under the ESA 2000;
- has filed a complaint with the Ministry under the ESA 2000;
- exercises or attempts to exercise a right under the ESA 2000;
- gives information to an employment standards officer;
- testifies or is required to testify or otherwise participates or is going to participate in a proceeding under the ESA 2000;
- participates in proceedings respecting a by-law or proposed by-law under section 4 of the Retail Business Holidays Act;
- is or will become eligible to take a leave, intends to take or takes a pregnancy, parental or emergency leave under the ESA 2000; or
- because the employer is or may be required, because of a court order or garnishment, to pay to a third party an amount owing by the employer to the employee.

Continuity of Employment (Transfer of Establishment)

If an employer sells, leases, transfers or disposes of a business or a part of a business and the purchaser employs an employee of the seller, the employment of the employee is deemed not to have been terminated or severed for the purpose of the ESA 2000 and his/her employment with the seller is deemed to have been employment with the purchaser for the purpose of any subsequent calculation of the employee's length or period of employment. However, this provision does not apply if the purchaser hires the employee more than 13 weeks after the earlier of either the employee's last day of employment with the seller, or the day of the sale. The provision applies if the building services provider for a building is replaced by a new provider and an employee of the replaced provider is employed by the new provider.

For termination of employment purposes, two successive periods of employment that are not more than 13 weeks apart must be added together and treated as one period of employment.

Other

A layoff is deemed to be temporary[7] and an employer is not required to provide notice of termination if:

- it is for no more than 13 weeks in any period of 20 consecutive weeks;
- it is for more than 13 weeks in 20 consecutive weeks but for less than 35 weeks in any period of 52 consecutive weeks and
- the employee continues to receive substantial payments from the employer;
- the employer continues to make payments for the benefit of the employee under a legitimate retirement or pension plan or a legitimate group or employee insurance plan;
- the employee receives supplementary unemployment benefits;
- the employee would be entitled to receive supplementary unemployment benefits but is employed elsewhere during the layoff;
- the employer recalls the employee within the time approved by the Director of employment standards; or
- when the employee is not represented by a union, the employer recalls the employee within the time set out by mutual agreement;
- it is for more than 35 weeks in any period of 52 weeks and the laid off employee is represented by a trade union and recalled by the employer within the time set out in an agreement between the employer and the union. [8]

Lay-off of an employee who has a regular work week: for the purpose of the previous paragraph, an employee is laid off for a week if:

- in that week, the employee receives less than one-half the amount s/he would earn at his/her regular rate in a regular work week; and
- the week is not an excluded week

Lay-off of an employee who does not have a regular work week:

- occurs when an employee is laid off for a period longer than the period of a temporary lay-off if for more than 13 weeks in any period of 20 consecutive weeks he or she earns less than one-half the average amount s/he earned per week in the period of 12 consecutive weeks that preceded the 20-week period. [9]

· can also occur when the employee is laid off for a period longer than the period of a temporary lay-off if for 35 or more weeks in any period of 52 consecutive weeks he or she earns less than one-half the average amount s/he earned per week in a period of 12 consecutive weeks that preceded the 52-week period. [10]

An excluded week means a week during which the employee, for one or more days is not able to work, unavailable for work, subject to a disciplinary suspension or not provided with work because of a strike or lock-out occurring at his/her place of employment or elsewhere.

Conditions of employment: during a notice period, the employer may not reduce the employee's wage rate or alter any other term or conditions of employment (unless the employee displaces another employee in accordance with applicable seniority provisions—see below). The employer must in each week pay the employee the wages s/he is entitled to receive, which in no case may be less than his/her wages for a regular work week[11] and must continue to make whatever benefit plan contributions are required in order to maintain the employee's benefits until the end of the notice period.

Notice of termination where seniority rights apply: where employees' contracts of employment provide seniority rights allowing for the bumping[12] of less senior employees in case of layoff or termination of employment, the employer may post a notice in a conspicuous part of the workplace setting out the name, seniority, job classification and proposed lay-off or termination date of the employee; this notice is deemed to constitute notice of termination, as of the day of posting, to any employee displaced by the employee named in the notice. The employer is not required to maintain the wage rate or other conditions of employment of an employee who displaces another employee in such a circumstance.

Prince Edward Island - *Employment Standards Act* (ESA)

Minimum Written Notice Required (from the Employer)

Where an employee has been employed continuously for a period of:

- Six months or more, but less than five years: two weeks;
- Five years or more, but less than ten years: four weeks;
- Ten years or more, but less than fifteen years: six weeks;
- Fifteen years or more: eight weeks.

This notice applies to a termination of employment or layoff.

Instead of giving notice of termination, an employer may pay an employee a sum equivalent to the employee's normal wages, excluding overtime, for the number of weeks in the prescribed notice period.

Minimum Written Notice Required (from the Employee)

Where an employee has been employed continuously for a period of:

- Six months or more, but less than five years: one week;
- Five years or more: two weeks.

Expiration of Notice

N/A

Deadline for Payment of Amounts Owed

Any pay to which an employee is entitled on termination of employment must be paid by the employer no later than the last day of the next pay period after termination of employment.

Where an employee's employment ceases after having worked for the employer for less than a continuous 12-month period, the employer must, no later than the next regular pay period after employment ceases, pay the employee an amount equal to four percent of his/her wages during the period of employment.

Eligibility Requirements / Exclusions

The following are excluded from coverage under most provisions of the ESA, including those regarding termination of employment: farm labourers (except those employed in commercial undertakings); salespersons whose income is derived primarily from commissions on sales; employees covered by a collective agreement.

Employers are not required to give notice (or pay in lieu) to an employee if:

- the employee has been employed continuously for less than six months;
- the employee is discharged or laid off for just cause;
- the discharge or layoff is due to complete or partial destruction of the plant, destruction or breakdown of machinery, inability to obtain supplies and materials, or cancellation, suspension or inability to obtain orders for products, where the employer has exercised due diligence to foresee and avoid these problems; or
- the discharge or layoff is due to labour disputes, weather conditions, or actions of any governmental authority directly affecting the operations of the employer.

Severance Pay

N/A

Illegal Termination

An employer may not dismiss, lay off or suspend an employee on the sole basis that she is pregnant, temporarily disabled because of pregnancy or because the employee has applied for maternity, parental or adoption leave in accordance with the ESA.

Continuity of Employment (Transfer of Establishment)

Not specified

Other

Conditions of employment: where notice of termination is given, the employer must pay the employee at least a sum equivalent to the employee's normal wages, exclusive of overtime, for the required period of notice.

Québec- *An Act respecting labour standards* and *Civil Code of Québec* (C.C.Q.)

Minimum Written Notice Required (from the Employer)

Where the employee has at least three months of employment but:

- · Less than one year of uninterrupted service: one week;

- · One year or more, but less than five years: two weeks;

- · Five years or more, but less than ten years: four weeks;

- · Ten years or more: eight weeks.

An employer that does not give notice of termination, or gives insufficient notice, must pay to the employee a compensatory indemnity equal to his/her regular wage,[13] excluding overtime, for the remaining period of notice to which s/he is entitled.

This indemnity must be paid:

- · at the time the employment is terminated,
- · at the time the employee is laid off (if the layoff is expected to last more than six months), or
- · at the end of a period of six months after a layoff of indeterminate length, or a layoff expected to last less than six months but which exceeds that period.

Where an employee is entitled to ***recall privileges*** for more than six months under a collective agreement, the employer must pay the compensatory indemnity on the date recall privileges expire, or one year after the layoff, whichever is earlier; however, an employee is not entitled to such a compensatory indemnity if s/he is recalled before an indemnity is due and subsequently works for a period at least equal to the required notice period, or if s/he is not recalled owing to a fortuitous event.

A notice of termination of employment given to an employee during a period when s/he is laid off is absolutely null, except in the case of seasonal employment that usually lasts no more than six months each year.

Under the Civil Code of Québec, either party to a contract of employment with an indeterminate term must, barring a serious reason, provide notice to the other party before terminating the contract. The notice of termination must be given in reasonable time, taking into account the nature of the work, the special circumstances in which it is carried on and the duration of the period of work.

Minimum Written Notice Required (from the Employee)

See last paragraph above.

Expiration of Notice

Not specified

Deadline for Payment of Amounts Owed

Not specified. Generally, wages must be paid on regular pay days, at intervals of not more than 16 days. In addition, any annual leave indemnity owed must be paid to the employee when his/her contract of employment is cancelled.

Eligibility Requirements / Exclusions

The following are excluded from coverage under the Act respecting labour standards:

- employees whose exclusive duty is to provide care to a child or to a sick, handicapped or aged person, in the dwelling of that person, including the performance of domestic duties directly related to the immediate needs of the person, if that work does not serve to procure profit to the employer;
- employees in the construction industry governed by the Act respecting labour relations, vocational training and manpower management in the construction industry (except with respect to provisions regarding certain family-related absences);
- students enrolled in approved job induction programs during the school year;
- senior managerial personnel (except with respect to provisions regarding certain family-related absences).

Notwithstanding these exceptions, the Act's provisions prohibiting compulsory retirement apply to all employees and employers.

No notice of termination (or pay in lieu) needs to be given to an employee:

- who has less than three months of uninterrupted service;
- who has committed a serious fault;

Under the Civil Code of Québec, one of the parties may, for a serious reason, unilaterally terminate the contract of employment without prior notice.

Severance Pay

N/A

Dismissal Not Made for Good and Sufficient Cause

An employee credited with two years of uninterrupted service in the same enterprise who believes that s/he has not been dismissed for a good and sufficient cause may submit a complaint in writing to the Commission des normes du travail (Labour Standards Commission) (CNT) within 45 days of his/her dismissal, except where a remedial procedure, other than a recourse in damages, is provided elsewhere in a statute or in an agreement.

Upon receiving the complaint, the CNT may, with the agreement of the parties, appoint a mediator to attempt to reach a mutually satisfactory settlement. If no settlement is reached following the receipt of the complaint, the CNT must, without delay, have the complaint deferred to the Commission des relations du travail (Labour Relations Board) (CRT) for arbitration. Except in the case of domestics and sitters (who may be entitled to compensation but not to reinstatement), the CRT may order a reinstatement, order the payment of an indemnity,[14] or render any other decision that it "believes fair and reasonable, taking into account all the circumstances of the matter". The decision of the CRT, which must be rendered in writing, is without appeal and binding on both the employer and the employee.

Illegal Termination

An employer or its agent may not dismiss, suspend or transfer, practice discrimination or take reprisals against, or impose any other sanction on an employee on the grounds that:

- an inquiry is being conducted by the CNT in an establishment of the employer;
- the employee has exercised one of his/her rights under the Act or a regulation;
- the employee has given information to the CNT or one of its representatives or has given evidence in a proceeding related to the application of labour standards;
- the employee is pregnant;
- the employee is a debtor of support subject to the *Act to facilitate the payment of support*;
- the employee is subject to a seizure by garnishment;[15]
- the employee has refused to work beyond his/her regular hours of work because his/her presence was required to fulfill obligations related to the care, health or education of a minor child, or because of the state of health of the employee's spouse, father, mother, brother, sister or one of the employee's grandparents, after having taken all reasonable steps to assume those obligations otherwise.

In addition, an employer or its agent may not dismiss, suspend or retire an employee, practice discrimination or take reprisals against him/her on the ground that s/he has reached or passed the age or the number of years of service at which s/he should retire according to a general law or special Act, retirement plan, collective agreement, arbitration award, decree, or common practice of the employer.

Continuity of Employment (Transfer of Establishment)

Labour standards continue to apply, notwithstanding the alienation or concession in whole or in part of an undertaking or the modification of its juridical structure, namely by amalgamation, division or otherwise.

A contract of employment is not terminated by alienation of the enterprise or any change in its legal structure by way of amalgamation or otherwise. The contract is binding on the representative or successor of the employer.

"Uninterrupted service" is defined as "the uninterrupted period during which the employee is bound to the employer by a contract of employment, even if the performance of work has been interrupted without cancellation of the contract, and the period during which fixed term contracts succeed one another without an interruption that would, in the circumstances, give cause to conclude that the contract was not renewed."

Other

Work certificate: at the expiry of the contract of employment, an employee may require his/her employer to issue to him/her a work certificate providing only the following information: the nature and duration of the employment, the dates on which employment began and terminated, and the name and address of the employer. Such a certificate may not mention the quality of the work or the conduct of the employee.

Renewal of contract of employment: a contract of employment is tacitly renewed for an indeterminate term if the employee continues to carry on his work for five days after the expiry of the term, without objection from the employer.

Right to compensation may not be renounced: an employee may not renounce his/her right to obtain compensation for any prejudice s/he suffers where insufficient notice of termination is given or where the manner in which this was done is abusive.

Saskatchewan - *Labour Standards Act* (LSA) and *Labour Standards Regulations*

Minimum Written Notice Required (from the Employer)

Where an employee has been employed:

- Three continuous months or more, but less than one year: one week;

- One year or more, but less than three: two weeks ;

- Three years or more, but less than five: four weeks;

- Five years or more, but less than ten: six weeks;

- Ten years or more: eight weeks.

An employer who discharges or lays off an employee without having given notice must pay to the employee a sum equivalent to the normal wages, excluding overtime that s/he would have earned during the prescribed period of notice.

An employer may not lay off or discharge an employee because of a shortage of work where the employee has been in the employer's service for at least 13 continuous weeks, without giving the employee at least one week's written notice for each year of employment or portion of a year of employment with the employer, to a maximum of 10 weeks' notice.

A period of notice may not form part of any annual holiday, nor may payment of annual holiday pay to the employee be considered as pay in lieu of notice.

Minimum Written Notice Required (from the Employee)

None

Expiration of Notice

Not specified

Deadline for Payment of Amounts Owed

Where the employment of an employee terminates for any reason, the employer must pay to the employee all wages due, including any annual holiday pay to which the employee is entitled, within 14 days after the effective date of termination.

Eligibility Requirements / Exclusions

The following are excluded from coverage under the LSA: employees employed primarily in farming, ranching or market gardening, except in the case of egg hatcheries, greenhouses and nurseries, bush clearing operations and commercial hog operations; employees in undertakings in which only members of the employer's immediate family are employed; sitters

No notice of termination (or pay in lieu) is required if:

- the employee is discharged or laid off for just cause other than shortage of work;
- the employee has completed less than three continuous months of service;
- the layoff does not exceed six consecutive days.

Severance Pay

N/A

Illegal Termination

An employer must not dismiss, lay off, suspend or otherwise discriminate against an employee because she is pregnant, she is temporarily disabled because of pregnancy, or she has applied for maternity leave in accordance with the LSA.

An employee may not be dismissed or disciplined for taking bereavement leave or for an absence due to illness or injury to which s/he is entitled.

An employee may not be discharged or laid off only because a garnishee summons issued pursuant to *The Attachment of Debts Act* was served on the employer with respect to the employee. Finally, an employer may not discharge, threaten to discharge or discriminate in any manner against an employee because the latter has reported or proposed to report to a lawful authority any activity that is or is likely to contravene provincial or federal legislation, or has testified or may be called on to testify in an investigation or proceeding under provincial or federal legislation; however, this protection does not apply where the actions of an employee are vexatious.

Continuity of Employment (Transfer of Establishment)

Where a business or part thereof is sold, leased, transferred or otherwise disposed of, the service of the employees affected is deemed to be continuous and uninterrupted by the sale, lease, transfer or other disposition.

Other

Conditions of employment: when giving notice of termination, the employer must pay to the employee the sum s/he earned during that period or, at a minimum, a sum equivalent to the employee's normal wages, excluding overtime, for the period.

Yukon - *Employment Standards Act* (ESA) and *Employment Standards General Exemption Regulation*

Minimum Written Notice Required (from the Employer)

Where an employee has been employed for:

· Six consecutive months or more, but less than one year	one week;
· One year or more, but less than three:	two weeks;
· Three years or more, but less than four:	three weeks;
· Four years or more, but less than five:	four weeks;
· Five years or more, but less than six:	five weeks;
· Six years or more, but less than seven:	six weeks;
· Seven years or more, but less than eight:	seven weeks;
· Eight years or more:	eight weeks.

A period of notice may not coincide with an employee's annual vacation.

Where an employer terminates the employment of an employee without having given the prescribed notice, the employer must pay termination pay in an amount equal to the employee's regular wages for his/her normal hours of work to which s/he would have been entitled during the notice period.

Minimum Written Notice Required (from the Employee)

Where an employee has been employed for:

· Six consecutive months or more, but less than two years:	one week;
· Two years or more, but less than four	two weeks;
· Four years or more, but less than six:	three weeks; and
· Six years or more:	four weeks.

Where an employee terminates his/her employment without having given the prescribed notice, the employer may deduct from the employee's wages, with the consent of the employee, an amount equal to one week's wages at his/her regular rate of pay for his/her normal hours of work. Where the employee does not consent to the deduction, the employer must pay the amount to the Director of employment standards. The director must then determine whether the employee was required to give notice under the Act and whether or not it would be inequitable in the circumstances to deprive the employee of his/her wages, before deciding who, of the employer or employee, is entitled to that amount.

Expiration of Notice

A notice of termination is without effect if an employee continues to be employed after the period of notice expires.

Deadline for Payment of Amounts Owed

When the employment of an employee is terminated before the completion of the employee's year of employment, the employer must pay to the employee all wages owing, including vacation pay,[16] within seven days from the date of termination.

When the employment of an employee is terminated at any time, the employer must pay to the employee within seven days from the date of termination all wages other than termination pay in lieu of a termination notice, which must be paid within 10 days of the expiration of the pay period.

However, any termination pay owing to an employee under the ESA may be paid in installments equal to the amount that would have been paid for a regular pay period on the employee's regular pay days, as long as all termination pay is paid within the prescribed period of notice to which the employee would have been entitled.

Eligibility Requirements / Exclusions

The following are excluded from coverage under the ESA: sitters, the Government of the Yukon and its employees.

The requirement to provide notice of individual termination (or termination pay) do not apply to:

- the construction industry;
- seasonal or intermittent undertakings that operate for less than six months in a year;
- an employee discharged for just cause;
- an employee employed for less than six consecutive months;
- an employee whose employer has failed to abide by the terms of the employment contract;
- an employee on temporary layoff;
- an employee employed under a contract of employment that is impossible to perform due to an unforeseeable event or circumstance;
- an employee who has refused reasonable alternative employment by his/her employer;
- an employee who has completed a project or assignment that s/he was hired to perform over a period not exceeding 12 months;
- an employee who has completed his/her term of employment, unless s/he is still employed for more than one month after completion of the term;

Severance Pay

N/A

Illegal Termination

An employer may not terminate an employee or change one of his/her conditions of employment without his/her written consent because of a maternity or parental leave authorized under the ESA or because of the employee's pregnancy, unless the employee has been absent for a period exceeding that permitted under the ESA. In addition, an employer may not dismiss or lay off an employee who takes sick leave or bereavement leave to which s/he is entitled

Continuity of Employment (Transfer of Establishment)

Where an employer employs an employee in connection with a business, and the employer transfers the business to another employer, the employment of the employee by the two employers before and after the transfer of the business is deemed to be continuous with the employer to whom the business is transferred.

Other

A layoff is deemed to be a termination unless: it is for a period not exceeding 13 weeks in a period of 20 consecutive weeks; or it is for more than 13 weeks, but the employer recalls the employee to work within a time fixed by the Director of employment standards.

Conditions of employment: where notice of termination has been given, the employer may not, without the consent of the employee, alter his/her rate of wages or any other term or condition of employment.

Constructive dismissal: the Director of employment standards may declare that an employer has terminated the employment of an employee when satisfied that the employer has substantially altered a condition of employment to discourage the employee from continuing his/her employment.

Travel costs from remote site: an employer who terminates or lays off an employee employed at a remote site must provide free transportation for the employee to the nearest point at which regularly scheduled transportation services are available.

Notes:

[1] For example: if an employee who has worked for the same employer for five years, gives three weeks of notice, and the employer wants to terminate the employment immediately, it will have to pay the employee the equivalent of the wages s/he would have earned during four weeks (the notice the employer would have had to give the employee) at their regular wage rate.

[2] According to the "Employment Standards Guide" published by Manitoba Labour and Immigration, "if an employee fails to provide proper notice, the employer may be entitled to retain or recover an amount equivalent to the employee's wages for 1 pay period."

[3] "Continuously employed" includes the employment of seasonal workers engaged under a contract of service of two or more consecutive seasons of at least five months in each season during which the employee is occupationally engaged.

[4] Where the employee does not have a regular work week or is paid on a basis other than time, the employer must pay the employee an amount equal to the weekly average amount of regular wages earned by the employee for the weeks s/he worked in the 12-week period immediately preceding the day of termination.

[5] For severance pay purposes, a week of layoff is defined as a week in which the employee receives less than one-quarter the amount s/he would earn at his/her regular rate for a regular work week, and that is not an "excluded week" (i.e., a week during which the employee, for one or more days, was not able to work, was subject to a disciplinary suspension or was not provided with work due to a strike or lock-out at the place of employment or elsewhere). In the case of an employee who does not have a regular work week, the amount of "earnings" used to determine layoff status is deemed to be the average amount earned per non excluded week in a specified 12-week period.

[6]Where the employee does not have a regular work week or is paid on a basis other than time, severance pay is based on the average amount of regular wages received by the employee for the weeks in which s/he worked in the 12-week period preceding the date employment was severed or the date on which began the layoff that resulted in severance of employment.

[7]An employer who lays an employee off without specifying a recall date is not considered to have terminated the employment of the employee, unless the period of the lay-off exceeds that of a temporary lay-off.

[8]For the purpose of a temporary lay-off, an excluded week must be counted as part of the periods of 20 and 52 weeks.

[9]For the purposes of this paragraph: (1) an **excluded week** is not counted as part of the 13 or more weeks but must be counted as part of the 20-week period; and (2) if the 12-week period contains an excluded week, the average amount earned must be calculated based on the earnings in weeks that were not excluded weeks and the number of weeks that were not excluded.

[10]For the purposes of this paragraph: (1) an excluded week is not counted as part of the 35 or more weeks but must be counted as part of the 52-week period; and (2) if the 12-week period contains an excluded week, the average amount earned shall be calculated based on the earnings in weeks that were not excluded weeks and the number of weeks that were not excluded.

[11]Where the employee does not have a regular work week or is paid on a basis other than time, the employer must pay the employee an amount equal to the weekly average amount of regular wages earned by the employee for the weeks s/he worked in the 12-week period immediately preceding the day on which notice was given.

[12]i.e., a procedure whereby an employee who is to be laid off or whose employment is to be terminated may displace another employee who has less seniority.

[13] An employee fully or partly remunerated by commission is entitled to an indemnity based on his/her average weekly wage, calculated from the complete periods of pay in the three months preceding the termination of employment or layoff.

[14]In such a case, the maximum amount of an indemnity may not exceed the amount of wages that the employee would normally have earned had s/he not been dismissed.

[15]The *Code of Civil Procedure* also prohibits the dismissal or suspension of an employee because his/her salary or wages have been seized by garnishment.

[16]However, an employer is not required to pay an employee any vacation pay unless the employee has been continuously employed by the employer for a period of 14 days or more. Where an employee works irregular hours or does not work at least five days a week, it is sufficient if the employee has worked his/her usual work days and usual hours in a two week period.

Appendix B: Complaint Process

Alberta

http://www.employment.alberta.ca/SFW/1697.html

How long do I have to file a complaint with Employment Standards?

You must file a complaint with Employment Standards within six months of your last day of employment.

If more than six months has passed, the Director of Employment Standards may grant an extension if the Director considers there were extenuating circumstances. For example, the Director has extended time limits when:

- through illness or incapacity an employee was unable to file a claim.
- an arbitration award held that no remedy was provided for an employee under a collective agreement.

To request an extension to file a complaint, write a letter outlining your extenuating circumstances to:

Alberta Employment and Immigration
Employment Standards Branch
Main floor, 9940 – 106th St.
Edmonton, AB T5K 2N2

OR

Alberta Employment and Immigration
Employment Standards Branch
Suite 150, 717 – 7 Ave. SW
Calgary, AB T2P 0Z3

Is there any action I can take to resolve my concerns without direct government intervention?

Yes. Employees can attempt recovery of unpaid earnings directly with their employer. In order to assist you, Employment Standards has designed an Employee Self-Help Kit.

Do not use the Self-Help Kit if:

- your employment ended more than five months ago.
- your employer has stopped operating the business.
- you have received an NSF cheque from your employer.

Self Help Kit:

http://www.employment.alberta.ca/documents/WRR/WRR-ES_es0799.pdf

British Columbia

http://www.labour.gov.bc.ca/esb/self-help/sh-start.htm

A complaint must be in writing and must be delivered to an office of the Employment Standards Branch within six (6) months of the last date of employment.

If you and your employer don't solve the problem, or if your employer does not respond to your request within 15 days, you may file a complaint with the Employment Standards Branch. Complaint forms are available at our offices and on our website.

Complaint form:

http://www.labour.gov.bc.ca/esb/forms/esb_comp.htm

Once a determination has been issued by the Branch regarding your complaint, no further action should be taken by you to enforce your claim, without written consent of the Director of Employment Standards.

Manitoba

http://www.gov.mb.ca/labour/standards/forms.html

Employees who believe their employers did not pay them correctly, can file a claim with the Employment Standards Branch. Claims must be filed within six months of the last day of work or when the incident happened. Employment standards staff can only investigate and collect up to six months of unpaid and overtime wages and up to 22 months for vacations and general holiday pay.

If the employer and employee cannot settle an employment standards problem, either person can file a complaint. The complaint must be filed within six months.

What happens after you file a complaint?

Staff in the Customer Service Centre will speak with both the employer and employee to gather information, review the facts and the applicable legislation, and work towards resolving the complaint.

Complaints that cannot be resolved in our Customer Service Centre are referred to a field officer. The field officer investigates all the relevant information and advises the employer and employee about their mutual employment standards rights and obligations. If the complaint is resolved voluntarily, the file is closed.

Staff in the Customer Service Centre will speak with both the employer and employee to gather information, review the facts and the applicable legislation, and work towards resolving the complaint.

Complaints that cannot be resolved in our Customer Service Centre are referred to a field officer. The field officer investigates all the relevant information and advises the employer and employee about their mutual employment standards rights and obligations. If the complaint is resolved voluntarily, the file is closed.

If the employer and employee cannot resolve the complaint, an Order requiring the payment of wages may be issued. A minimum $100.00 administration fee is applied to each order issued. Either the employer or employee may appeal an Order by making a written request to have the matter heard by the Manitoba Labour Board. There are strict time limits on filing an appeal.

If the matter goes to a hearing, the employers and employees must testify and present evidence in support of their case to the Manitoba Labour Board.

Complaint form:

http://www.gov.mb.ca/labour/standards/asset_library/forms/Claim_Form.pdf

New Brunswick

http://www.gnb.ca/0308/02-e.asp

Employees who believe that their employer may be in violation of the Employment Standards Act are encouraged to contact our office for assistance and to discuss the circumstances surrounding their complaint. You can file a complaint in one of several ways:

1) You can contact us by phone, toll-free at 1-888-452-2687

2) You can visit the Employment Standards Branch nearest you and speak with an officer.

3) You can write to us at Department of Post-Secondary Education, Training and Labour, Employment Standards Branch, P.O. Box 6000, Fredericton NB E3B 5H1.

4) You can print and complete the complaint form and send it to us either by fax at 1-(506) 453-3806 or by mail at the above-noted address.

An Employment Standards Officer will work with both the employer and the employee to determine whether a violation of the Act has occurred. In the event either party is unsatisfied with the results of the investigation, they have the right to refer the matter to the Labour and Employment Board for adjudication. This is the final step in the complaint process, where employers and employees are able to present their arguments before the Labour and Employment Board by members, or with representation. The Board, after hearing and considering the evidence, makes a final and binding determination of the case either upholding, overturning, or altering an order, or dismissing the complaint.

Complaint Form:

https://www.pxw1.snb.ca/snb7001/e/1000/CSS-FOL-61-6264-04E.pdf

Newfoundland & Labrador

http://www.hrle.gov.nl.ca/lra/labourstandards/default.htm

When employees believe they have received less than minimum employment standards and are unable to resolve the matter with their employer, Labour Standards staff will investigate the matter upon receipt of a written complaint. Employees who wish to file a complaint must do so within 6 months of their employment termination date.

Labour Standards staff are available to provide interpretation and service advising parties of their rights and responsibilities related to a broad range of employment standards issues, by calling the province-wide information line at 1-877-563-1063, the St. John's line at (709) 729-2742, the Corner Brook line at (709) 637-2364, or via e-mail at LabourStandards@gov.nl.ca.

 If you believe that you have been discriminated against and wish to file a complaint with the Human Rights Commission, you must contact the Commission within twelve months of the date that the alleged discrimination occurred. The following process will then be followed:

Investigation Phase

STEP ONE: The complaint will be given to one of the Commission's Investigators. The Respondent (the person or organization against whom the complaint has been filed) will be notified that there has been a complaint filed and that it is being investigated. The Investigator may interview the individuals involved, inspect records or documents, and has certain powers to enter buildings and obtain warrants during investigations.

STEP TWO: The Commission will attempt to help the parties involved in the complaint come to a settlement (a solution to the problem that both parties agree to). Where a settlement is agreed to, there is no further action taken by the parties or the Commission unless the terms of the settlement are not complied with. If no settlement is reached, or if the terms of a settlement are not complied with, the complaint proceeds to STEP THREE.

STEP THREE: The Executive Director reports the complaint to the Commissioners, and they decide whether to refer the complaint to the Board of Inquiry. If the complaint is not referred to the Board of Inquiry, the matter is closed, subject to an appeal (see STEP SIX). If the complaint is referred to the Board of Inquiry, dates are set for a hearing.

Board Of Inquiry Phase

STEP FOUR: The Board of Inquiry is made up of a number of Adjudicators. Each complaint that reaches this stage is heard before one Adjudicator in a formal public hearing. The Complainant and Respondent each have a chance to present their arguments. The Commission takes the lead in presenting the complaint, but all parties can choose to be represented by legal counsel if they wish.

STEP FIVE: After hearing all of the evidence the Adjudicator will decide if there has been a violation of the Code. If there has been a violation of the Code, the Adjudicator will order the Respondent to stop the violation, and can also order the Respondent to provide opportunities or privileges that have been denied, or to pay compensation to the Complainant. The Adjudicator's decision is legally binding on the parties.

Appeal Phase

STEP SIX: Both the Complainant and the Respondent have the right to appeal the decision of the Board of Inquiry to the Supreme Court of Newfoundland and Labrador. **An appeal must be filed within thirty days of the date on which the prospective Appellant received the order of the Board of Inquiry..** The Supreme Court can either confirm, reverse, or vary the decision and orders of the Board of Inquiry. A Complainant can also appeal to the Supreme Court if the Commissioners choose not to refer a complaint to the Board of Inquiry (see STEP THREE). In this case, the Complainant can ask the Supreme Court to order the Board of Inquiry to hear the complaint despite the refusal of the Commission to refer the matter. The Supreme Court can either affirm or deny this request.

If you think that you may have a complaint, or have questions about the complaint process, please contact the commission.

Nova Scotia

http://www.gov.ns.ca/lwd/employmentrights/

You can make a complaint by filling out our Complaint Form. We can send you a copy of the form, or you can pick one up from our offices.

Once you get the form, complete all information, including the following:

Describe your complaint. Include what happened, when it happened, why it happened, and who was involved. Give the names of any others who can support your claim.

State the amount claimed, if you are claiming money. Give the dollar amount that you are claiming and the dates that are involved.

Example: 2 weeks' pay instead of notice:

October 6, 2003-October 10, 2003 $300.00

October 13, 2003-October 17, 2003 + $300.00

Total $600.00

Sign the form. You must sign the form, certifying that the information is correct.

Initial the form to show you understand that the information will be shared. Our officers will need to talk to both parties. We will share information we collect with both parties.

We must receive your Complaint Form within 6 months of the incident happening.

Always keep documents such as pay stubs, cheques, work schedules, letters of termination, employment contracts, and other records.

Give us as much information as you can. This helps our officers when they look into your complaint.

When you attach documents, give us copies only. Do not give us originals.

File your complaint in plenty of time. Remember, we must receive your complaint no later than 6 months after the incident happened.

In some cases you can make an anonymous complaint. If you think you have a reason for keeping your identity unknown, talk to us about it. We can explain what we can and cannot do without your name.

After we receive your complaint, we will assign one of our Labour Standards officers to look into it. Labour Standards officers are impartial and do not represent either party in a case. The officer will review your situation and contact both sides to try to reach an agreement. Many complaints are settled using this method. If the complaint is not settled, an officer will investigate. During an investigation, the officer will contact you and the other party. The officer may ask you to provide information such as witnesses or employment records to support your claim. Based on the information collected, the officer will make a decision about your case. At any time during this process, you may employ a lawyer to assist in your case.

After an investigation, if you and the other party have not settled, a Director's Order may be issued. A Director's Order is a legal document which may:

- order a party to comply with the *Labour Standards Code* by, for example, paying money that is owed
- order that a complaint be dismissed if the evidence does not support it

If you get a Director's Order you can either accept the decision and comply with it, or you can appeal the decision.

http://www.gov.ns.ca/lwd/employmentrights/complaintfiling.asp

Ontario

http://www.labour.gov.on.ca/english/es/forms/claim.php#claim_form

If you believe your rights have been violated you may use the Employee Self Help Kit from the Ministry of Labour to resolve the matter with your employer. The Employee Self Help Kit has a letter that you can send to your employer.

You may also file a claim with the Ministry of Labour. Claim forms are available online as well as at ServiceOntario Centres.

Filing a claim is free.

It is against the law for your employer to punish you for filing a claim.

If you file a claim, Ministry of Labour staff will investigate your claim. Claims are investigated as quickly as possible. The time it takes to complete the process varies.

There are some situations where an employee is not entitled for file a claim. Learn more.

Making it Easier

Follow these four steps:

1. Read the Important Employment Standards Claim Information located at the beginning of the claim form
2. Fill out the claim form
3. Send your claim form to the Ministry of Labour and receive your claim number:
4. It is recommended that you file your claim online below. You will receive your claim number immediately.

5. You may also file your claim:

    o   In person at a Service Ontario Centre (1-800-267-8097). Use PDF version below. You will receive a letter, with your claim number, in the mail.

    o   By mail to the Provincial Claims Centre, Ministry of Labour, 70 Foster Drive, Suite 410, Roberta Bondar Place, Sault Ste. Marie, ON, P6A 6V4. Use PDF version below. You will receive a letter, with your claim number, in the mail.

    o   By fax: 1-888-252-4684. Use PDF version below. You will receive a letter, with your claim number, in the mail.

6. **Please only file your claim once.** For example, if you have filed your claim online, please do not send another copy of your claim form to the Ministry of Labour.

7. Send copies of your documents to the Ministry of Labour

The investigation of your claim will take time.

During an investigation:

·   The officer must first collect and review all of the evidence before deciding if the employer has violated the ESA.

·   If the officer finds that there was a violation, the employer can resolve the issue by voluntarily complying with the officer's decision.

·   If the employer does not comply with the officer's decision, the officer can issue an order which the employer can appeal to the Ontario Labour Relations Board.

·   If the Ministry of Labour is unable to collect money that is owed to you, the Ministry may then authorize a collection agency to try to collect the money.

·   The Ministry of Labour may also choose to prosecute the employer. The Court may impose a fine or term of imprisonment, or both.

It is important for you to file a claim within a certain time

There are three different time limits:

Six-Months

In most cases, the Ministry of Labour can only recover wages that became due within the six months before the date you file the claim.

Generally, wages become due (owed to you) on your regular payday. However, if the employer terminated your employment, all wages the employer owes you are due either **within seven days, or on your next regular payday, whichever is later.**

One Year

If the officer finds the employer has committed the same violation of the ESA in respect of wages owed to you more than once, including at least once in the previous six months, the officer can issue an order for wages owed to you as a result of the violation in the 12 months before the date you file the claim. Also, the Ministry of Labour can issue an order to recover vacation pay that came due in the 12 months before the date you file the claim.

Two Years

In some cases, an employee can file a claim up to two years after the violation of certain rights, including:

If there has been a reprisal:

Employers cannot punish an employee or threaten an employee because s/he asked his/her employer to follow the **ESA**, filed an **Employment Standards Claim**, exercised or tried to exercise his/her rights under the **ESA** or because an employee's wages are subject to a garnishment order.

Clients of a temporary help agency cannot intimidate an assignment employee, refuse to have an assignment employee perform work, terminate an assignment employee's assignment, or otherwise penalize him/her because s/he asked his/her employer to follow the **ESA**, filed an **Employment Standards Claim**, exercised or tried to exercise his/her rights under the **ESA** or because an employee's wages are subject to a garnishment order.

- If a temporary help agency has a) charged prohibited fees or b) restricted the temporary help assignment employee's ability to secure direct work with a client of the agency.
- If the employer has violated other non-monetary standards such as not providing proper meal breaks or failing to provide wage statements.

Complaint Form:

https://www.empstdsclaims.labour.gov.on.ca/EClaim/welcome.do?action=language&language=en

Prince Edward Island

http://www.gov.pe.ca/cca/index.php3?number=1025374

You may feel that your employer/employee has acted in a manner that violates the Employment Standards Act.

The complainant is expected to file all documentation and information in their possession relevant to the complaint. The complainant is expected to have attempted to resolve the matter with their employer/employee prior to filing a complaint.

When an inspector begins to investigate a complaint, they will talk to the person who made the complaint to clarify all issues in dispute. If the inspector finds the respondent has violated the Act, the inspector will talk to the respondent about the problem and how to correct it. Correcting it may mean: keeping better payroll records, compliance with specific sections of the act or paying money that the inspector has determined the respondent owes.

If the respondent does not agree with the inspector, the inspector may issue an order that states what the respondent must do to ensure that the *Act* is followed and how long the respondent has to make that happen. The order also gives the respondent a chance to appeal the decision to the Employment Standards Board. The respondent has 10 working days from the day they received notice of the decision to file an appeal. Failure to respond within the 10-day time limit will result in a judgment for any monies deemed owing being filed with the Supreme Court of Prince Edward Island.

The inspector, after investigation of the complaint, also has the option of referring the matter to the Employment Standards Board for final determination.

Complaint form:

http://www.gov.pe.ca/forms/pdf/1425.pdf

Québec

http://www.cnt.gouv.qc.ca/en/in-case-of/dismissal-not-made-for-good-and-sufficient-cause/index.html

Do you believe that you were dismissed without good and sufficient cause?

Remember

- You have to have been working for at least 2 years for the same employer to be entitled to file a complaint for a dismissal not made for good and sufficient cause

- You have 45 days to file a complaint from the time of dismissal

The complainant's collaboration is essential for the processing of his complaint. He will have to:

- support the claims he makes with verifiable facts
- collaborate with the various representatives of the Commission des normes du travail.

The complainant will have to provide:

- his name, address and telephone number
- the name, address and telephone number of his former employer
- the date when his employment began
- the date when his employment ended
- a short text mentioning the circumstances that led to his dismissal
- his signature
- a copy of his record of employment and a pay sheet if possible.

He should know that:

- his former employer will be informed of his complaint
- only the Commission des relations du travail can determine if he was indeed dismissed without good and sufficient cause.

It will be up to the employer to show that he had good and sufficient cause to dismiss his former employee.

Here are the different steps in the complaint processing.

Reception of the complaint

Can the complaint be accepted?

The Commission des normes du travail makes sure that the complaint is admissible. A representative gets in touch with the complainant and checks:

- that he worked for the same employer for at least 2 years
- that he was an employee within the meaning of the Act respecting labour standards
- that he does not benefit from an equivalent recourse under another law or a collective agreement
- that the enterprise for which he worked is under provincial jurisdiction
- that he filed his complaint in the 45 days following his dismissal.

When the complaint cannot be accepted

If the Commission des normes du travail considers the complaint inadmissible, it writes to the complainant to notify him that it is putting an end to the process and it explains why. The complainant has the right to apply in writing to the Director General of Legal Affairs at the Commission for a review of this decision within 30 days of receiving it. The Director General of Legal Affairs in turn has 30 days after receiving the application for review to make his decision. If the Commission does not receive an application for review, it closes the file.

When the complaint is admissible

If the claim is deemed admissible, the Commission des normes du travail:

- notifies the complainant that it will follow up on the complaint as soon as possible

- informs the former employer that a complaint for a dismissal not made for good and sufficient cause has been filed against him

- designates a mediator who contacts the complainant and the former employer.

Mediation is accepted in more than 85% of the cases and a satisfactory settlement is reached 7 out of 10 times. When there is an agreement following mediation, the Commission des normes du travail puts an end to its intervention.

If there is no agreement following mediation, the complaint is sent to the Direction générale des affaires juridiques of the Commission des normes du travail in preparation for a hearing before the Commission des relations du travail.

Mediation offer

If the complaint is admissible, it is entrusted to a mediator who contacts the complainant and his former employer to offer them his services.

With the help of the mediator, they endeavour together to find solutions that are satisfactory to both parties. They may call on the mediation service during every stage of the complaint process. This service, which is very efficient, makes it possible to settle close to 40% of the complaints.

A service geared to communication

In a climate that is conducive to discussions, the mediator helps the parties to establish a dialogue. In the presence of one another, they can express their respective points of view, examine possible solutions and negotiate the terms of an agreement to which they freely consent.

An advantageous service

Mediation makes it possible to:

- actively participate in the search for satisfactory solutions

- retain control over the decisions to be made

- save time and money, while limiting worries

- arrive at an agreement freely consented to.

A professional service

The mediators with the Commission des normes du travail are subject to rules of ethics. Their role, their duties and their responsibilities, notably concerning impartiality, fairness and confidentiality, are specified in this pamphlet.

The mediator is a neutral person, who does not take sides with the former employer or the complainant. He must:

- explain to them the rules of mediation

- inform them of their rights and obligations

- provide them with his support throughout the initiative, without ever taking their place

- create a climate that is conducive to dialogue

- help the complainant and the former employer to explain the facts related to the conflict

- help them to find settlement avenues

- help them to clearly evaluate the situation and the proposed solutions

- make sure that the complainant and the former employer are satisfied with the draft agreement.

To be fully objective, the mediator cannot already have been active in other capacities in the case. He must act in complete confidentiality. No one may compel him to disclose the information entrusted to him during his mandate.

Sending of the complaint to the Commission des relations du travail

Hearing

Mediation may be refused by the complainant or the former employer. Moreover, it may not necessarily produce an agreement. The complaint is then sent to the <u>Commission des relations du travail</u> for a hearing before a commissioner. Only the commissioner can determine if the employee was dismissed without good and sufficient cause.

Preparation

When the complaint is sent to the Commission des relations du travail, the case is submitted to a lawyer at the Direction générale des affaires juridiques of the Commission des normes du travail. He will contact the complainant to offer to represent him free of charge and to invite him to prepare.

The complainant may wait from 6 to 8 months before obtaining a hearing date. Before the planned date of the hearing, the lawyer from the Commission des normes du travail can accompany the complainant to a conciliation session offered by the Commission des relations du travail. If an agreement is reached on that occasion, the hearing will no longer be necessary.

If the complainant prefers, he can be represented by the lawyer of his choice at his expense.

A few tips for the day of the hearing

- Dress appropriately: avoid attracting attention or offending others
- Make sure that you are present in the hearing room before the set time
- Avoid discussing your case outside the hearing room
- When testifying, speak clearly, in a loud voice and with assurance
- Pay attention to each question asked
- Remain calm

Powers of the Commission des relations du travail

If the complaint is accepted, the labour commissioner can make the following decisions:

A. order that the employer reinstate the complainant in the position that he occupied prior to his dismissal
B. order that the employer pay the complainant an indemnity equal to the wages lost since his dismissal
C. make any other decision that he deems reasonable.

You can file a complaint in two ways:

1. <u>On-line</u>

2. By telephone at 1 800 265-1414 or 514 873-7061

Complaint form:

<u>http://www.cnt.gouv.qc.ca/en/on-line-services/plaintes-en-ligne/demande-de-plaintes-en-ligne/index.html</u>

Saskatchewan

<u>http://www.publications.gov.sk.ca/prdtermlist.cfm?t=1596&cl=2</u>

Once an Application is filed

Once an application has been filed with the Board, a copy of it is forwarded by the Board to the parties affected by the application together with instructions about how to reply to the application. If the respondent intends to contest the application, it must file a reply in the appropriate form. In the case of an application for certification, the employer must also file a statement of employment. Replies and statements of employment must be sworn before a Commissioner for Oaths or Notary Public. Once the respondent files a reply, a copy of it is forwarded to the applicant.

Scheduling a Pre-hearing and/or Hearing

After both parties have filed the required forms with the Board, the Board Registrar contacts the parties to advise of the next step in the proceedings. Usually, this next step involves the Board Registrar sending out scheduling information forms to the parties to determine when they are both available for a pre-hearing and/or hearing of the case. Once the scheduling information forms have been completed and returned to the Board Registrar, dates are set for a pre-hearing and/or hearing of the case and the parties are advised of those dates.

Pre-hearings

Pre-hearings are conducted by either the Chairperson, a Vice-Chairperson, the Board Registrar or the Board Investigating Officer. Pre-hearings are "off-the-record" and are less formal than hearings. They are used to try to settle cases which can be settled and to manage those cases which cannot be settled by narrowing the issues and hopefully shortening the hearing.

Hearings

Hearings are formal and resemble a court trial with sworn witnesses giving evidence before a three person panel of the Board. The applicant must lead evidence, through witnesses, to establish its position and the respondent must lead evidence in response. The respondent is able to cross-examine the applicant's witnesses and vice versa. The Board is neutral and does not take sides in the hearing.

The Use of Legal Counsel

A party before the Board does not have to be represented by a lawyer. The issue of whether a lawyer's assistance is necessary is one which must be decided by each party in each case before the Board. The Board is accustomed to hearing from unrepresented parties and does its best to ensure that the hearing process is "user-friendly."

Adjournments

Once a hearing date has been set by the Board Registrar, it may only be changed by consent of both parties or by Order of the Board or the Executive Officer of the Board. A party seeking an adjournment should first contact the other party to see if consent can be obtained. If a consent adjournment is possible, the parties should advise the Board Registrar of this fact. If a consent adjournment is not possible and one party still seeks an adjournment, that party should contact the Board Registrar to arrange for a hearing on the issue of an adjournment either before a panel of the Board or before the Executive Officer of the Board.

The Board's Decision

In some cases, the Board gives its decision "from the bench" at the close of the hearing. In most cases, however, the Board reserves its decision. If the Board reserves its decision, the parties will receive that decision by mail once it is written. It can take the Board from several days to many months to make a decision, depending upon its complexity and the Board's hearing schedule.

Most of the Board's decisions are unanimous. However, there are occasions where one panel member disagrees with the majority decision of the Board. On those occasions, the dissenting panel member is encouraged to write a formal dissent which is forwarded to the parties together with the majority's decision.

Parties are not permitted to speak to members of the Board panel which heard the case about when the Board's decision might be rendered. Board staff do not know and cannot speculate on when decisions will be released by the Board. All inquiries about Board decisions should be directed to the Board Registrar.

The Board's decisions are final and binding upon the parties before the Board. There is no appeal from a decision of the Board and review of a Board decision by the courts is strictly limited.

Questions about Board process may be directed to Board staff or the Board Registrar at:

1600-1920 Broad Street
Regina, Saskatchewan
S4P 3V2(telephone) (306) 787-2406
(fax) (306) 787-2664

(e-mail) fred.bayer@gov.sk.ca

Complaint Form:

http://www.sasklabourrelationsboard.com/forms/index.htm

Northwest Territories

An employee may make a written complaint to the Employment Standards Officer on the grounds that

a) the employee was not paid an amount to which he or she is entitled;

b) the employer, without the written consent of the employee, changed a condition of employment or terminated the employment of an employee contrary to section 37; or

c) the employment of the employee was suspended or terminated or the employee was laid off because the employee

     i.   was subject to garnishment proceedings,

     ii.   gave evidence or may give evidence at any inquiry or in any proceeding or prosecution under this Act,

     iii.   requested or demanded anything to which the employee is entitled under this Act, or

     iv.   made or is about to make any statement or disclosure that may be required of the employee under this Act.

A complaint may be made at any time within 12 months after the date on which the subject matter of the complaint occurred.

An employee may not be charged a fee for making a complaint or for the investigation of a complaint.

The Employment Standards Officer may refuse to accept or investigate a complaint, in whole or in part, if the officer is satisfied that

a) the complaint is frivolous or vexatious;

b) there is insufficient evidence to substantiate the complaint;

c) there are other means available to the employee to deal with the subject-matter of the complaint that the Employment Standards Officer considers should be pursued before the complaint is accepted or investigated; or

d) the employee is proceeding with another legal proceeding in respect of the subject-matter of the complaint or has obtained recourse in respect of the subject-matter of the complaint before a court, tribunal or arbitrator or by some other form of adjudication.

The Employment Standards Officer or an inspector may mediate between an employer and an employee for the purpose of settling the differences between them. In mediating, the Employment Standards Officer or inspector may

a) receive from an employer, on the employee's behalf, the money agreed on by the parties in settlement of their differences;

b) pay to an employee money received on the employee's behalf; and

c) do any other things that he or she considers necessary to assist an employer and employee to settle their differences.

If the Employment Standards Officer determines that wages are due to an employee and is unable to mediate or settle the difference between the employer and employee, the Employment Standards Officer shall, by order, require the employer to pay to the employee, or to pay to the Employment Standards Officer on behalf of the employee, the wages to which the employee is entitled. Subject to the regulations, an order made may require payment of compensation for a period not exceeding 12 months after the date that

a) the employment of the employee was suspended or terminated;

b) the employee was laid off; or

c) the employer failed to reinstate the employee or to provide the employee with reasonable alternative work with the employer, in accordance with the provisions of this Act respecting pregnancy leave, parental leave or compassionate leave.

Complaint form:

http://www.ece.gov.nt.ca/PDF_File/Employment%20Standards/ComplaintEnglish.pdf

Yukon

http://www.community.gov.yk.ca/labour/comp.html

A complaint must be filed at Labour Services within 6 months of the day the wages should have been paid or the day the issue arose.

Any employee who believes they have not been treated in accordance with the *Employment Standards Act* can file a complaint. The Director of Employment Standards can also initiate a complaint if there is reason to believe there are violations of the *Act*. The Director will not accept a complaint based on rumour or innuendo. Reasonable and probable cause must be established. Cause can be established through, for instance, a payroll statement showing an employee worked overtime but was not paid at the time and one-half rate. In some cases, the complainant will be required to swear an affidavit attesting to the truth of their statement regarding the complaint.

Anyone who knowingly files a false third party complaint commits an offense and is liable on summary conviction to a fine not exceeding $10,000.

A complaint may be filed in person, by letter, or by telephone. If the complainant is unable to come to the Labour Services offices, a complaint form will be mailed out. An employee filing a complaint by telephone will be asked to send a letter of confirmation. The employee should be prepared to supply details of their employment such as date of hire and termination, hours of work, wage rate, location, etc. If the employee kept an independent record of the hours of work, those should be supplied as well as copies of their pay slips and Record of Employment. Additional information about the employer such as the business name, owner or manager, and the employer's financial status, is also useful.

The Employment Standards Officer will investigate the complaint and determine the proper course of action. During the investigation, the officer will discuss the complaint with the employer, the employee, and any other person who has relevant information and will also attempt to find a solution acceptable to both parties. If the officer is unable to resolve the complaint, a certificate may be issued or court proceedings may be initiated.

The employee should not expect an immediate resolution. The time it takes to resolve a complaint is affected by the timeliness of the complaint, the validity of the complainant's information, the availability of the employer and the employer's records, the financial position of the employer, the employer's and the complainant's right to dispute or to appeal results of the investigation, and the need for court action to resolve the complaint. An employee can request that their name be kept confidential when filing a complaint. In that case, the complainant's name will not be released unless absolutely necessary.

Complaint Form:

http://www.community.gov.yk.ca/pdf/complaint_infoform_2009.pdf

Nunavut

http://www.workrights.ca/content.php?sec=6

A Complainant Alleging Harassment must inform the harasser of the unwelcome conduct and request that it stop. Witnesses and details of events should be documented. The Complainant must establish that the alleged harassing behaviour did occur.

How do I file a complaint?

If you feel your employer is violating your rights under Labour Standards law, find out how to file a complaint and the details of the complaints procedure by contacting:

Labour Standards Compliance Office
Building 224
PO Box 1000, Station 590
Iqaluit, NU X0A 0H0
Phone: (867) 975-7293
Toll Free: 1-877-806-8402
Fax: (867) 975-7294

Federal

How do I file a complaint?

If you feel your employer has violated your employment rights and you want to file a complaint, contact the Labour Program Office nearest you.

Unjust Firings

Can I file a complaint if I'm unjustly fired?

Yes. All non-union workers with at least 12 consecutive months of continuous employment with the same employer can file a complaint for an unjust firing.

You must file your complaint at a Human Resources Development Canada (Labour Program) office **within 90 days** from the date you were dismissed. You can make the complaint yourself, or it can be made by your representative, such as a lawyer. The complaint must identify you, say you were fired, include the date of dismissal, and say the firing was unjust.

What happens after I file the complaint?

A Labour Affairs Officer will try to negotiate a settlement acceptable to you and your boss. This could include a monetary settlement, changes to your employment record, or a return to your job.

If the problem isn't solved at this stage, you can request that your complaint go to an adjudicator. Then the Minister of Labour will decide whether or not to appoint one.

If an adjudicator is appointed, there will be a hearing. Both you and your boss can present evidence at the hearing. With few exceptions, the burden of proof is on the employer to prove the firing was warranted.

The adjudicator can make a decision which is binding on you and your boss. If it's found that your firing was unjust, your employer may be ordered to give you your job back, with or without lost wages; pay you lost wages; or do anything else that is fair to remedy the effects of the firing.

These provisions also apply to "constructive dismissals."

The adjudicator's decision is final and can't be appealed.

Getting Money That's Owed To You

How do I file a complaint about wages?

To find out how to file a complaint, contact the Labour Program Office nearest you.

What happens once the complaint is filed?

A Labour Affairs Officer (federal inspector) will investigate your complaint. If the complaint is valid, the inspector will try to get your employer to pay up voluntarily.

If the inspector decides the complaint is unfounded, you will be notified of this in writing. You can appeal this notice to the Minister of Labour within 15 days of the notice being served. If the inspector decides the complaint is founded, he or she can issue an order to pay. Your employer can appeal this order within 15 days.

A referee will hear the appeal launched by you or your employer. The referee's order is final.

Harassment

Informal Complaint Process (Early Mediation)

The Informal Complaint Process is intended to provide a mechanism through which an employee is able to discuss a claim of harassment in an open, honest and non threatening manner with the person who is offending him/her. The hope is that through early mediation both parties will understand the point of view of the other, and that the behaviour causing the problem will cease. This approach provides an opportunity for the problem to be eliminated expeditiously, and hopefully before the parties become entrenched and adversarial.

An employee who feels that he or she has been subjected to harassment should, where possible, immediately make his or her disapproval clearly known to the individual(s) concerned and ask that the behaviour stop. The employee should also make notes of both the incident and the discussion. These notes should be specific, and include the dates, times, locations and the names of any other people or witnesses involved. If the employee is uncomfortable to approach the individual(s) concerned alone, s/he should seek the assistance of the supervisor, Human Resource Advisor or Senior Staff Relations Advisor (Harassment Caseworker). Should the parties decide that the services of an additional mediator would be helpful; the Harassment Caseworker will coordinate the acquisition of a mediator who is satisfactory to all.

Should the employee decide not to proceed with the matter, his/her wishes will be respected. However, if the situation which caused the complaint is considered serious, management will be informed because of their need to know. Because of the managers' responsibility to ensure that the workplace is harassment free, action may be taken to address the situation, in a confidential manner as an organizational matter without reference to the complaint itself.

Formal Complaint Process

When the complainant wishes, s/he should forward the complaint in writing to the department Coordinator of Harassment Complaints, Staff Relations and Compensation Division, 140 Promenade du Portage, Phase IV, Gatineau, Québec K1A 0J9 (Fax: (819) 953-1271).

When the department Coordinator of Harassment Complaints receives a complaint, it will normally be assigned to the Harassment Caseworker (Senior Staff Relations Advisor) for the Sector involved. The Harassment Caseworker will review the complaint and will meet with the complainant to establish and confirm all of the basic facts.

The employee/person against whom a harassment complaint has been lodged and the complainant will be notified in writing, as soon as possible, that the complaint has been received. This notice will include a statement of the nature of the complaint and the assertions made, the names of any witnesses, and any relevant documents. It will also include a statement of the steps that the Harassment Caseworker will follow to have the complaint mediated and/or investigated, and the proposed time frames. Both parties will be provided with a copy of the department

Harassment Policy, so that they understand the broader context of the process. They will also be advised of their right to be accompanied by a person of their choice (including a representative of their union/bargaining agent) during any interviews related to the complaint.

At the same time, the Assistant Deputy Minister of the Sector concerned will be made aware of the complaint and a proposed action plan for its resolution. The Assistant Deputy Minister may decide at that time to involve the applicable Director General or Director. If necessary, the Assistant Deputy Minister will be advised to take immediate action and direct the line manager to physically or hierarchically separate the employee against whom the complaint has been lodged and the complainant. Such action may include the identification of alternate work for one of the employees; consideration of telework for one or both of the employees; or consideration of an application for leave for one or both of the employees.

Step 1: Informal Mediation/Resolution

In all cases of a complaint made to the department Coordinator of Harassment Complaints an attempt will be made, subject to the agreement of the parties, to resolve the matter informally, prior to beginning a formal investigation. Such resolution would require the agreement of the complainant and the respondent(s). The Harassment Caseworker will contact the parties, inform them of their right to representation and interview them separately concerning the reported incident(s) of harassment.

If the Harassment Caseworker then determines that the issue can be resolved informally at the complaint stage, an attempt will be made to reconcile the parties. This would normally be coordinated by the Harassment Caseworker although a neutral mediator may be acquired, either from within the department or from the private sector, when the case warrants. Both the respondent and complainant will be consulted during the selection of a mediator, and must approve of the choice. When early mediation resolves the complaint, the basis for the final confidential report will be limited to a description of the agreement between the parties.

Step 2: Formal Investigation

In those cases where a formal investigation is required the Assistant Deputy Minister will be advised immediately, and s/he will approve the acquisition of the services of an Investigator. Bargaining agents/unions will be consulted during the selection of the investigator, where appropriate.

The Investigator will be selected from one of four lists: (a) employees and managers selected and trained from among the department staff, (b) trained investigators from other parts of the Public Service, including the Public Service Commission, (c) investigators from the private sector who are approved by the Coordinator of Harassment Complaints/Harassment Caseworker, or (d) trained investigators from the department bargaining agents/unions. In cases where costs are incurred in order to investigate a complaint, those costs will be borne by the Sector in which the complaint has occurred.

The Investigator will proceed in accordance with terms of reference established for the investigation, in consultation with the Assistant Deputy Minister. The investigator will document the situation accurately and completely. The individuals who provide information during the investigation will be advised that the information they provide will form part of a confidential report, a copy of which will be provided to both the complainant and the person against whom the complaint has been lodged. They will also be advised that they may be called upon in the future to testify before a third party, should that become necessary. At the conclusion of each interview, the Investigator may wish to read his or her notes back to the witness.

Upon completion of the formal investigation, the written confidential report will be provided to the Harassment Caseworker. That report will include all relevant factual information, signed testimony of the parties, and appropriate analysis of the information.

Step 3: Report to Assistant Deputy Minister

Upon receipt of the Investigator's report, the Harassment Caseworker will:

1. contact both the complainant and the person against whom the complaint was lodged, provide each of them with a copy of the investigation report, and give them an opportunity to respond to the statements in the report and/or provide any additional information relevant to the complaint;

2. make any changes that either party believes are necessary, after verifying them with the Investigator;

3. bring the report to the attention of the Assistant Deputy Minister of the Sector concerned, provide him/her with a copy, and provide advice concerning any corrective action considered appropriate;

4. prepare a letter for the department Coordinator of Harassment Complaints, to advise the person against whom the complaint has been lodged and the complainant of the outcome of the investigation and of the ADM's decision.

Follow up on Complaints

Assistant Deputy Ministers are responsible for ensuring that corrective action is taken by management when warranted. Such action may include discipline in cases when an employee has unreasonably pursued a claim that is unfounded and determined to have been frivolous and/or vexatious. The Harassment Caseworker will liaise with local management to follow up on such action, and the Coordinator of Harassment Complaints will report the outcome to the Assistant Deputy Minister.

Once a complaint has been investigated, whether informally or formally, managers and supervisors will monitor the situation closely to ensure that all parties to the complaint make the transition back to their assigned work as smoothly and as quickly as possible. When warranted, that may include the acquisition of professional counseling to assist all parties to deal with the outcome of the process. Managers and supervisors will also monitor their work environment closely to ensure that there is no potential for repeating the unwelcome behavior.

List of Labour Program Offices:

http://www.hrsdc.gc.ca/eng/labour/contact_us/labour.shtml

Appendix C: Sample Letters

Writing an effective complaint letter is a skill that everyone needs to perfect in today's litigious society. In order to protect your legal rights and start the document process, you should always lodge your complaints in writing and send them via registered mail. Even if a registered letter is not required to present your complaint, it is still often a sound idea to spend the few dollars to send the letter. And we recommend that you send a copy in sealed envelope to yourself so that you have an authentic date stamp to verify what was sent in case your employer tries to deny the contents of your complaint.

The key to an effective letter is to:

- Include relevant business information. Don't get emotional or go on unrelated tangents.

- Send copies of documentation if you feel it is important to back up the contents of your letter. Do not send originals!

- Put thought into your letter. You want to sound professional. Don't use inappropriate language or slang and do not make accusations or threats. You don't want to hinder any possible legal case you may have.

- Don't be dramatic. If you use statements like:" I feel that I have been compromised in every regard and cannot function any longer in this climate." While you may be expressing your stress, the reader(s) of this line will assume that you have resigned.

- Do not be disrespectful or sarcastic. This will result in justifying cause for dismissal. You need to prove that you are a professional.

- Do not question the abilities or motives of the person you are filing the complaint against. For example, do not describe your manager as taking no action out of fear or weakness or surmising that your supervisor had it in for you. This mistake will highlight insolence on your part.

- Make sure there is a reasonable action statement assigned to the employer (i.e. send missed wages to you, contact you, etc.) and within a set period of time (e.g. 5 business days). Otherwise, it will be unlikely that the employer will respond and the ball will remain in your court, so to speak.

- Keep it brief. Try to keep it to one page.

- Start with a rough draft and keep editing it until you are comfortable with the contents. Have a trusted friend or family member read it over to get the perspective of a recipient.

- When you are satisfied with the above tasks, write the final draft. Remember, to be careful on tone and content as it will be used as evidence in any legal case or complaint to the Labour Board.

- Send it via registered mail so that you have a record of their receipt. At the same time, send an exact copy to yourself via mail and don't open it on receipt. Just file it with the registered mail receipts.

The following are some sample letters that we have included that should assist you in your composition. While your exact situation or information may not be listed, one of them should inspire you in how to compose a professional letter while getting your points across.

If you are uncomfortable to send a letter on your own, please consult an experienced labour lawyer.

Sample Demand Letter For Unpaid Wages

[*insert date*]

[*Insert Employer's Address*]

Dear [*EMPLOYER'S NAME*]:

My job ended on [*insert the day of your firing, lay-off or resignation here*]. More than 15 days have passed since then and you still owe me money for my work. You owe me at least [*insert the amount you believe you are owed here*]. I ask for immediate payment of the amount due. If you do not pay this in full, you may become liable for payment of all costs and attorney's fees if I have to hire a lawyer and file a lawsuit to get what you owe me. You may also be liable for payment of additional money as a penalty, as well as legal interest.

If you believe you do not owe me the full amount I have stated, but only a part of it, the law requires you to pay me immediately the amount you agree you owe me. You should also tell me the reason why you are not paying the full amount.

Please send the amount due me to my current address:

[*insert your address here*]

Sincerely,

[*Insert your name*]

Sample Letter To Retract Spontaneous Resignation

[Insert date]

[Insert Name of Supervisor]
[Insert Employer Company & Address]

Dear [Insert Supervisor's Name]:

I am sending this letter via registered mail in response to your letter received today.

For the record, I vehemently dispute the contents of your letter; in particular to the statement that "I quit [insert in the exact wording from situation]". My understanding from our discussion on Thursday, October 29th is that I was given some time (with pay) to recover from the stress of the events of the day's conflict. In that regard, I had planned to return to work [Insert date you plan to return] to resume my responsibilities.

As you are aware from my [insert number of years with the company] years of employment with your company, I am a dedicated and capable employee who would never abandon her position regardless of the mounting duress existing in the work environment. However, as a result of your letter with the inaccurate claim of my resignation, I feel that I have suffered great embarrassment and damage to my reputation.

[Insert Supervisor's Name], this issue needs resolution as soon as possible. I will expect to hear from you within five (5) business days from delivery of this letter to discuss this issue further.

Sincerely and without malice, ill-will, prejudice or vexation,

[Insert Your Name]
All Rights Reserved, Non-Assumpsit

Sample Discrimination Complaint Letter

[insert date]

[Insert Employer's Address]

Dear *[Insert name]*:

I am writing regarding your recent decision to *[insert details about the job action you are complaining about; for example, "your recent decision to fire me from my job" or "your recent decision to write me up for absences" or "your recent decision to put me on probation"]* at *[insert your employer's name]*. I have obtained information about my legal rights and I believe that your termination of me from my job was in violation of my rights under the Employment Standards Act in regards to Family and Medical Leave Act *(verify the provincial/federal labour act)*.

[Insert details regarding situation. An example follows.] As you know, I have been a loyal employee of *[insert your employer's name]* for the last two years. As your primary receptionist, I have received nothing but positive employment evaluations from you. Over the last six months, I have been forced to use my vacation and sick leave to attend to personal issues and injuries.

Most recently, I missed a week of work to heal from a bruised rib and other injuries. I called you the morning of April 4, 2005 before my shift to inform you of my need for leave and I faxed you a note from my doctor the same day indicating that I was unable to work for the week. Nonetheless, when I returned to work the following week, you informed me that I was fired and handed me my termination letter. This letter stated that you fired me for excess absences from work. I believe that your termination of me was in violation of my rights and I would like to be reinstated as soon as possible and to receive compensation for my lost wages.

The Employment Standards Act in regard to Family and Medical Leave covers employers like *[insert your employer's name]* that employee fifty or more employees. Eligible employees under the ESA are employees who have worked for the employer for at least a year and at least 1250 hours in the last 12 months *(verify for your jurisdiction as each one is slightly different)*, which I have. An employee may take job-guaranteed leave under the for a "serious health condition" that makes her unable to perform her job. In April, I went to the emergency room and saw my doctor to receive treatment for my bruised rib and other injuries. I was prescribed pain killers and other prescription medication and was directed by my doctor not to work for a week. This qualifies as a "serious health condition" under the act. It is illegal for an employer to punish or retaliate against an employee for taking ESA-qualifying leave. Because the leave that I took was ESA-qualifying, your decision to terminate me for taking this leave is in violation of my rights under the ESA.

This is a very private issue and it is very important to me that my situation be kept confidential. I understand that you may need to consult with a limited number of other managers about my specific situation, but I request that you let me know whom you speak with.

Additionally, I expect that, in compliance with the law, you will only discuss my request for time off with other managers who need to know about the situation, and that you will ensure that they too keep this information confidential.

As you might imagine, I would prefer to address this situation informally rather than by filing a claim with the [Province/Federal] Labour Board or pursuing a claim in court. I would like to be returned to my job and receive back pay as soon as possible.

Please contact me by [*insert date in one week*] at [*insert phone number*]. If I do not hear from you I will take further action to enforce my rights to the full extent of the law.

Sincerely,

[*Insert name and address*]

Sample Sexual Harassment Complaint

[Insert date]

[Insert Employer's Address]

Dear Ms. Jones:

Since *[month, year]*, I has been employed by *[Insert company name]* as a *[Insert title or position]*. Within two weeks of my start at *[Insert company name]* (mid-June 2003), I was approached by *[insert name of harasser and title]*. *[Insert name of harasser]* asked me if we be able to have sex now. During the time that he asked this question, he put his hands on my rear end and patted it. Later that day, he asked me about _____, a prospective client and person I had recently met, who worked for _____. *[Insert name of harasser]* instructed me to sleep with Mr. _____in order to acquire the new account for *[insert company name]*. I protested and said that I would do no such thing.

Immediately after being spoken to by *[Insert name of harasser]*, I went to my own supervisor, _____, and explained what had happened. To her knowledge and as the following facts indicate, no action was taken.

In [month, year], *[Insert name of harasser]* again confronted me and asked if I was interested in him. I told him no and walked away.

At the Christmas party, 2009, *[Insert name of harasser]* approached me and asked me if I wanted to go up to his suite and "do it," saying that they should take advantage of the room and make use of it. *[Insert name of harasser]* went so far as to reach into his coat pocket and produce the key to confirm the room number he had mentioned me. I declined the offer and again told him to refrain from dealing with her in this way.

After the Christmas party and on or before [date], I and *[Insert name of harasser]* had a telephone conversation where I informed him, again, unequivocally, that she did not want to have anything romantically or sexually to do with him. *[Insert name of harasser]* responded that he had more to lose than she did. In mid-January 2010, I approached my supervisor, *[Insert name of supervisor]*, for the second time and explained what had occurred between me and *[Insert name of harasser]*. *[Insert name of supervisor]* replied that this incident had happened before and that it would not be the last time it occurred.

On [date], *[Insert name of harasser]* stated to me that they should have "a nooner," inferring that they should go somewhere and have sex around the noon hour. *[Insert name of harasser]* mentioned that they should have a "nooner" because it was, in his words, convenient; I, who worked nights, could easily disappear during the day. I immediately told my supervisor, *[Insert name of supervisor]*, about this encounter and expressed to him my concerns about my job.

The next day, [date], *[Insert name of harasser]* again approached me and whispered to me, inquiring if he had a 50/50 or 60/40 chance of sleeping with me. I informed him, in no uncertain terms, that he had a zero chance of sleeping with me.

Ten days later, [date], *[Insert name of harasser]* again approached me and said that he would like to "fax" her. I took this to mean that he would like to have sex with her. This conversation happened within earshot and plain sight of my supervisor, [*Insert name of supervisor*]. [*Insert name of supervisor*], later that day, asked me if I was all right. I told him that I was not all right and explained what had occurred. [*Insert name of supervisor*] suggested that I contact Human Resources or set up an appointment with her harasser, [*Insert name of harasser*].

Four days later, on [date], [*Insert name of harasser*] approached me at work in an edit bay and proceeded to touch my rear end with his hand. I immediately went to my supervisor, [*Insert name of supervisor*], and told him everything that had just happened.

[*Insert company*] and [*Insert name of harasser*] were obligated to treat me in a manner which protected my civil rights. Instead, [*company*] and [*Insert name of harasser*] discriminated against and harassed me, physically and verbally assaulted and battered me, amongst other wrongs. Based on the above evidence, I can establish that [*Insert name of harasser*] and [*company*] are liable for sex discrimination and harassment, and failure to prevent discrimination and harassment, all in violation of the [*Provincial/Federal Employment Standards Act*].

[Discuss recent comparable jury verdict in your jurisdiction. You can find them online. For example: According to data compiled by Attorney, Attorney & Attorney, a management law firm law firm based in Medicine Hat, and the law firm's survey of jury verdicts from Provincial and Federal Courts in Alberta from 1999 to April 2009, the average jury award for employment cases in Alberta Court exceeded $100,000.].

In order to settle my claims and thereby prevent the necessity of turning to a more formal and costly means of resolution, I request the following for settlement of all claims against [*Insert name of harasser*] and [*company*]:

1. Compensate me for pain and suffering in the amount of $100,000;
2. Provide me with a positive letter of recommendation;
3. Reimburse me for her attorneys' fees and costs incurred as a result of the drastic and upsetting course of events [if you have retained a lawyer already]; and
4. Agree to put [*Insert name of harasser*] through one year of psychotherapy and/or anger management to avoid the abuse of other employees.

Please be advised that if I am forced to file a civil action in this matter, my claim will be substantially greater.

There are several ways in which this matter can be resolved, including the following:

1. <u>Civil Litigation</u>. Litigation will be time consuming, extremely expensive for both parties and could result in adverse publicity. Note, of course, that the complaint filed in this matter will be a public document, and the press could show great interest in the facts of this case, something neither party is really interested in.
2. <u>Discussion</u>. The least expensive way to resolve this dispute is if [company]'s counsel and/or you and this office discuss the case through an exchange of correspondence, telephone calls, meetings, etc. Our experience is that if both parties are reasonable and act in good faith, they can settle matters such as these.
3. <u>Mediation</u>: The parties can agree to a private mediation with someone skilled in the employment area. This option works only if both sides are motivated to resolve the case.

4. Government Complaint: While less expensive than civil litigation, you will still incur attorney's fees as well as be under investigation by a government board which may result in detailed scrutiny and public proceedings.

This letter is written solely for the purpose of furthering settlement discussions. Therefore, neither this letter nor any of the information contained in it may be used for any purpose in any subsequent litigation.

Your immediate review of this matter is requested. I look forward to your reply on or before [*date*].

Very truly yours,

[*Insert your name*]

Sample Racial Discrimination Letter

[insert date]

[Insert Employer's Address]

Re: Complaint of Discrimination
[Complainant] **v** *[Employer]*

Dear Ms. [*Recipient*]:

Please allow this letter to serve as my complaint of discrimination against the [*Employer*]. I have contacted your office both by phone and in person and have received no response. Most recently, on October 16, 2010, I came to your office to file a complaint of discrimination and filled out an Information Inquiry Summary. Since that date, I have received no further communication from your office. I have therefore sought timely counseling but no representative has contacted me. Thirty days have passed and this is a Formal Complaint of Discrimination.

My complaint of discrimination includes the following:

- I am a 51 year old Asian female and I began working for [*Employer*]. As of today, I am still in the same position.

- There are 6 [*Position*] with same series and title. Every one of them, including 4 Caucasian females, is a [*level*] except for me. We all have the exact same job title, and have at times performed similar work. Yet, I have remained as a [*your level*].

- I requested a desk audit at the same time as a Caucasian worker for the same work; she was promoted but I was not.

- I have requested, on a continuous basis, Flexiwork/work at home. I have been denied and a Caucasian co-worker was approved but it is not clear what, if any, work she does at home.

- Management has intentionally given the Caucasian employees better work assignments in order to promote them.

- I feel that I am being discriminated based on my race and age by management because I have been treated differently than other, Caucasian, [*Position*].

- Secondly, I have been treated differently than other employees in that I have received a lower rating than all of the other employees. My lowered ratings are also discriminatory in nature. This has meant that I do not receive any monetary awards.

- I have also been subject to harassment and a hostile work environment by my supervisors including [*Insert name of harasser*], [*Insert harasser's title*]. He told me on several occasions that I should not speak to other supervisors about any problems I am having. He told me that he put my name on a list of people who were going to retire without having received my permission.

- Mr. [*Insert name of other person you spoke to*], Chief of [*Department*], told me to go find a job somewhere else. His actions were discrimination based on my age and race. [*Insert name of another supervisor who would not help*] also said that I would be sitting here in 10 years complaining about the same thing. These discriminatory remarks and the constant and severe harassment by my supervisors have lead to a hostile work environment.

- Lastly, on October 6, 2010, I was given a memorandum of counseling by [*Insert name of harasser*], which was unfair and discriminatory in nature.

- When [*Insert name of harasser*] became my supervisor in September 2010, he interviewed me and cancelled my company credit card which I had used for purchasing. No other employee had their credit card taken from them.

- [*Insert name of harasser*] then asked me to work on supplies and repeatedly harassed me regarding status reports. No other employees were subject to this behavior. I was then unfairly accused of not working fast enough.

In short, I am being subjected to disparate treatment and a hostile work environment based upon illegal factors such as my race.

Please be aware that I am being represented by counsel in the above referenced matter.

After reviewing the Complaint of Discrimination, please contact my attorney so the appropriate actions can be taken.

Sincerely,

_____ _____
Complainant Date

ATTORNEY CONTACT INFORMATION

Sample Letter Notice of Default

[insert date]

[Insert Employer's Address]

Dear *[Insert Employer]*:

Re: [*EMPLOYER*] and [*YOUR NAME*]
Severance Agreement dated March 1, 2011
NOTICE OF DEFAULT

By this letter, you are advised that [*Employer*] is in default of its obligations to me under my Severance Agreement with that company dated March 1, 2011. To be more precise, Paragraph 19 of our Severance Agreement provides that [*Employer*] will pay to me, mailed to my home address written above, a cheque for $9,772.50 every month for twelve consecutive months, to arrive no later than the second day of each calendar month. Thought today is the ninth day of this month, I have not yet received my check for this month.

This obligation is a "material" obligation. The payment of monies under this agreement is a central obligation; it is not an insignificant one. This would make your default a material breach of the severance agreement, and entitle me to consider it null and void or to sue the company for the monies due me, as well as for other related "damages", including among others, interest on the monies owed and legal costs of enforcement and collection.

If I am mistaken in my belief that [*Employer*] has defaulted in its obligations to me, please let me know, in writing. If [*Employer*] has, indeed, defaulted, but the default is accidental and to be promptly corrected, or "cured", please also let me know in writing.

If you believe that [*Employer*] either has not defaulted or has not paid me with good reason, please also let me know, in writing.

If I do not hear from you within seven days of your receipt of this letter, I will have no choice but to initiate legal proceedings to protect all of my interests and rights. I sincerely hope that will not be necessary.

Very truly yours,

[Insert your name]

Sample Non-Acceptance Letter

[Insert date]

[Insert employer address]

Re: SEVERANCE DISCUSSIONS

Dear [*Name*]:

Following our recent talk about [*Company*]'s termination of my employment, I have carefully reviewed the details of the severance package presented. I have thought long and hard about my termination, discussed it extensively with my spouse, and have come to accept its inevitability. I have also consulted with my accountant as well as an attorney who specializes in severance packages. The latter suggests that I work out the basics with you, and that I reach him to finalize details after an agreement is reached.

Everyone I have talked with agrees that I have to be comfortable with the package, and that is why I am writing you. There are two aspects of my life that make this situation so very much more difficult; the needs created by my health, especially my heart condition, and the needs of my family. Both weight heavily on me; neither is very flexible.

I appreciate very sincerely the spirit of the overall package offered, but four certain elements are just not in keeping with my very real, urgent needs. As you can surely imagine, my utmost concern is how long I will remain unemployed, and what damage that delay and its stress may do to my finances, my health, and my insurance coverage. All of them are related.

A. Compensation

Severance: In the narrow sense of the term, the severance element of my package – two weeks for each year worked – seems short. Even middle-level management in the [*Company1*] /[*Company 2*] merger received, after their notice period, three weeks per year, while Managing Director level received four weeks per year, if not more. The just-announced four weeks per year from [*Other Company*] further recognizes the need for a material severance component in today's brutal employment market in financial services. This makes me question why I should deserve less than the increasingly standard four weeks per year of severance they and others are receiving, and I have real difficulty accepting less.

Notice/salary continuation: Each of these seems fair, at least at this time, though I'm certain that, as they come closer to being exhausted, the feeling of fairness will run thin. To address my very real concerns about the time it may take to achieve re-employment, I ask that [*Company*] permit combined notice, salary, and severance (with company benefits) to be paid to me as salary, and to run through December 2011 but to end as soon after June 30, 2011 if I am reemployed. This I would consider reasonable, and only, fair, under the circumstances of my termination.

Continuation of the combined compensation as salary through at least June 30, 2011, is absolutely critical to me: it gets me to the ten-year service level, and therefore allows for possible retirement at age fifty-five, an extremely important option considering my health; and it provides me for the approximate amount of time someone at my level could expect to need to find a comparable position.

B: Service Length and Calculations

In speaking to others who have gone through this before, I am told that the most common area of severance discussions these days is in pension "accommodations". Since I had planned to remain at [*Company*] and would have, except for this restructuring, I ask that, for pension calculation purposes, five years be added to my service length, especially in light of my very positive performance record and loyalty to the company. This would bring total service length to at least fifteen years, assuming I remain on the payroll until June 30, 2010.

C: Insurance Coverages

With my serious heart condition and, more recently, back problems, and my pressing financial needs – two kids fast approaching college age—these are crucial. I would hope and expect that all coverage be continued and paid through the period of my combined compensation, that is, through December 2011, but as early as June 2011, if I am reemployed. Expiration of any one or more of life insurance, disability insurance or health benefits could be disastrous, as replacement without my being reemployed may prove impossible because of requalification requirements. The prospect of no insurance is daunting, to say the least. The prospect of no insurance and no work, given my situation, is frightening.

The necessary minimum coverage would be achieved by continuation of compensation through June 2011, as I have requested above.

D. Outplacement

Along with the three basic concerns above, I would request as extension of coverage to eighteen months, that is, through June 2011, to cover the possible gap in employment. Of course, upon reemployment I would discontinue the service.

[*Insert Supervisor's name*], you have always been fair and straightforward with me, and I thank you for that. I've always been a team player at [*Company*] and am in position of need that requires that I ask the company to go the extra yard for me. These requests are surely not beyond the company's resources, nor precedent setting. As you know, I preferred to remain a contributing member of the Group rather than be in my current position, but that is no longer possible.

I would like you to know that your commitment to consider these requests for me is highly appreciated.

Sincerely

[*Insert your name*]

Sample Reprimand Protest Memo

[Insert date]

[Insert Employer's address]

Dear [*Name*]:

This letter serves as a formal protest to the letter of reprimand and case of corrective action unlawfully made against me, that I received regarding a formal yet unsubstantiated claim against me on January, 23rd, 2011.

Firstly, I whole-heartedly condemn the company's use of dishonourable methods of approaching me with unsubstantiated claims regarding the "supposed" formal complaint unjustly made against me by Genevieve Baxter. A proper "formal" complaint would firstly include a documented statement signed by the complainant and be submitted for review by management. Once management receives said complaint, they would then be accountable to substantiate whether the allegations have any merit. Once merit is determined through including the person the complaint is against (me in this case), through civilized discussion, a solution would be brokered for the two persons in conflict to agree to and the matter would then be dealt with, accordingly. What the complainant did, further bolstered by the corporation's management team's lacking in affording me my undeniable rights to confront my accuser and deciding my culpability in these false claims without my proper inclusion in the clearly defined process as mandated by law, was a clear and malicious departure from the description of "formal" process, above.

Genevieve Baxter claims that she was privy to hearing information over her private telephone that inspired her to be offended and make her not-so-formal-after-all complaint against me. The law, as it stands, may not be clearly understood by the present management team and if that is the case, allow me to reference some highly applicable law in this regard so that there may indeed be absolute clarity. Under the Criminal Code of Canada, particularly Part VI – the section titled "Invasion of Privacy"; in short, this portion of the Code addresses the issue of interception of private communications. In summary, the applicable Code makes it illegal for the interception of private communications unless either authorised by a legal warrant or consented to by the alternate party involved in the communication. I am in no way substantiating that anything Genevieve reports to have occurred happened but what I am stating for the record quite clearly is that I have never consented to any communication between Genevieve Baxter and myself being recorded nor has Genevieve ever asked me for my consent. This and I highly doubt there was any legal warrant issued for any communications between Genevieve and myself. Hearsay (or "he-said, she-said") is absolutely inadmissible in a court of law for very specific and highly logical reasons. Violating this law results in the undue harassment of those finding themselves, like me, on the dark-hearted intentions of the Genevieves of the world.

Further, management has approached me with the letter of reprimand and demanded that I sign it, further violating my undeniable rights. Management does not have the right to demand any signature form me, at any time and I will never consent to the brow-beating tactics displayed regarding this matter. Under the Canadian Charter of Rights and Freedoms, I reserve my right to live my life, free of harassment from any legal entity, let alone any corporation both privately and in the work-place. The actions that Genevieve and subsequently the management team took in dealing with this unsubstantiated and ludicrous matter constitutes harassment as it is defined by the Charter, mentioned above, and will not be tolerated.

Consider this letter my official and formal complaint against Genevieve Baxter for making false and unsubstantiated claims against me, tarnishing both my good-standing and respectable reputation, culpable as liable and slander against my name. This type of action will not be tolerated. I expect the management team to conduct themselves accordingly, sighting my concerns within the body of this letter's text as substantiated evidence to support my claim. I am available, in coordination with my lawyer's presence, to discuss the matter further and expect an invitation to do so at your convenience.

Further, consider this letter to serve as an official and formal complaint against Gary Smith for taking Genevieve Baxter's unsubstantiated claims, giving them merit without my inclusion in the rightful process to defend myself and show that Genevieve's intent is both dishonourable and without substance. Further, Gary Smith having played the role of judge, jury and executioner in the farce and façade called my due-process, has affected my ability to live "harassment free" and I intend to hold him accountable, to the fullest extent.

On the over-all matter at hand, it is unfortunate that this situation has spiraled out of control but it doing so is not within my range of accountability. It started with Genevieve lighting the fire and was fuelled by Gary pouring way too much gasoline all over it. I feel I have had no choice but to respond as I have.

Unless Genevieve's claims are substantiated and I believe they never will be, I will not tolerate any further undue harassment nor will I be addressing any further comments about this or any other matters unless my legal council is present. My distrust for management in these affairs, sighting the disgraceful methods applied to me so far, is warranted and is exercised out of self protection. If Genevieve and Gary realize that they have acted without honour and were out-of-order, in the interest of honour and peace, I will accept a written letter of apology from each of them and consider the matter closed. If not and they or the corporation for that matter continue to persist, I am fully capable and more than willing to protect my rights and will hold any offender fully accountable to the letter of the law.

Without ill-will, vexation or malice,

Your Name

Sample Probation Termination Letter

[Insert date]

[Insert Employee's Address]

Dear *[Name]*:

I am writing to you in regard to your letter of termination dated *[date of letter]* that I received during my meeting with *[supervisor/hr]* on *[meeting date]*. I understand that under the provincial Employment Standards Act that I may be dismissed while under probation with no notice due to "unsuitability". However, I feel strongly that my termination without notice violates the provisions for probationary employees under the Act.

[Please select the appropriate reason(s) and delete the others]

[Upon receipt of the formal offer of employment, the offer letter did not contain any reference to or definition of a probationary period. As per the Employment Standards Act, probation cannot be implied and must be agreed to in writing.]

[Upon receipt of the formal offer of employment, I acknowledge that the offer letter did contain a reference to a probationary period. However, in regard to the probationary term, the letter was ambiguous because it did not spell out that it is meant to be a period when I (the "employee") was under the obligation to demonstrate that I was suitable for regular employment as a permanent employee and that I was required to go through a period of assessment to determine such suitability for the job. As per the court case Easton v. Wilmslow Properties Corp., an employee was not subject to a probationary term because the offer did not clearly set out the probationary period and what would happen if the employment relationship terminated prior to the end of the probationary period. I feel strongly that my situation mirrors this case.]

[Upon receipt of the formal offer of employment, the offer letter did contain a reference to probationary period. However, I was not required to sign this document as a prerequisite to my employment period to commence. As a matter of fact, you will not find a signed copy of this letter in my personnel file acknowledging my receipt and understanding of the terms. Similar to the precedent set in the court case Dang v. North American Tea, Coffee & Herbs Trading Co., I had every reason to believe that this employment was long term as the probationary terms were never explicitly explained to me verbally or in writing. The omission of my signature is evidence of this lack of understanding.]

[During my discussions with _____ prior to my receipt of an offer for employment, I was promised specific training in order to assist me in executing the functions of my job effectively. This training was fundamental in providing me with the tools that I required to perform my responsibilities successfully. To date, I have not received the training that I was pledged. Therefore, I was not allowed the opportunity to prove that I have the ability to do the job that was I hired for.]

[As you are aware, your company and it representatives pursued me for this role. I did not initiate any contact when this role became available. I was a successful independent contractor [or long time employee at XXXXX company] when your representatives contacted me to encourage me to apply for this role. Your representatives insisted that, with my experience and qualifications, I would be an excellent fit for the responsibilities required and your company's culture and that I could build a career over the long term at your firm. Because I was being induced from a secure and successful role, I had every right to expect reasonable job security and career prospects.]

[As an employee under probationary terms, any opportunity to address concerns in regard to my performance was dismissed. At no time was I provided with any feedback of my performance during this period. Under the Act, I have a right to a reasonable and objective assessment of my performance and suitability for the position as a permanent employee. It is also reasonable that I should also expect that the relevant aspects of my employment to be evaluated regularly by my supervisor and discussed with me so as to give me an opportunity to correct any defective action.]

I am confident that you will agree that, in my case, the protections afforded me by law were breached and this issue needs to be rectified as soon as possible. I would prefer to address this situation informally rather than filing a claim with the Labour Board or pursuing a claim in court. I would like to receive the equitable compensation that is due to me in a timely manner in order to put this issue behind us.

Please contact me by [insert date in one week] at [insert phone number]. If I do not hear from you, I will be forced to pursue other remedies to address my concerns.

Sincerely and without malice, ill-will, prejudice or vexation,

[Insert Your Name]
All Right Reserved, Non-Assumpsit

Case Studies

The following case studies outline real world examples in order to highlight how the labour laws can be applied as well as mistakes that the employee or employer may make. While some situations seem simple when they start out, the application of the law is usually dependent on the actions of the parties involved.

Allegation: Racial Discrimination

Employee's Basis for Allegation: David, a minority, feels that neither he nor other minorities in the company are receiving promotions in comparison to non-minorities.

Background: David has been working for Widget Inc. for a few years. David feels discriminated against due to his race because he feels that new job assignments and promotions are going to non-minorities. He wants to address the topic but does not want to do it directly for fear that he would be seen as a troublemaker.

David goes to see his supervisor and during the conversation, he mentions how hard it is for people to move up the ladder at Widget. David makes sure that he doesn't mention the word "race". He also mentions how he knows he performs well while other co-workers do not but they seem to be receiving the better job assignments and promotions.

As a result of the conversation, David's supervisor assumes that the plant manager is holding a grudge against David and they discuss some minor incidents that have occurred that may have tainted the plant manager's view. David knows that the plant manager might have similar issues with non-minorities who still get promotions and good assignments, but he doesn't mention that in the conversation.

At no point does David clarify that his complaint is based on racial discrimination. He is afraid that by raising this issue using the words "race" and "discrimination", he will jeopardize his job.

Within six months, David is fired. Widget does not look fondly on instigators as they feared that he was setting them up for a discrimination lawsuit.

Justification: After the discussion with David, his supervisor started monitoring David's work more closely. He recorded every incident, no matter how small, that would call into question David's performance on the job. Eventually, David was placed on formal discipline for poor performance, rule violations and attendance/tardiness issues even though some of these items may have been overlooked in the past. After another short period, David is terminated for violating the terms of his discipline by committing additional poor performance or rule violations.

Action: David contacted a lawyer as he felt that he had been wrongfully terminated because he got disciplined for infractions that others don't get disciplined for. He feels that he has a case for racial discrimination and retaliation. David tells the lawyer about the conversation that he had with his supervisor.

Resolution: David's case does not get very far as his lawyer advises him that he made several errors in his complaint to his supervisor:

- David did ***not*** say he felt discriminated against because of his race. It would have been to his advantage to openly state the legal category that might apply to his complaint that he was making rather than be evasive. As a result, the employer will argue that he did not in fact make a race discrimination complaint and therefore did not gain protection against retaliation.

- David did ***not*** state any facts in his complaint which directly show that discrimination might be occurring. He could have talked about non-minorities getting treated better, but he did not. It's not necessarily enough even if he had mentioned "race". A solid complaint that will hold up in court will mention "race" and will use race-related examples.

- David said damaging things during the complaint process about how he agreed that the plant manager might hold a grudge towards him due to some incidents in the past. This makes it look like David did not believe he was being discriminated against due to race but rather because of ongoing problems resulting from old events including ongoing personality conflicts.

- David did not complain to Human Resources or to some designated high-level manager. It's best to get the problem into the hands of Human Resources or people with more power to fix it than front-line supervisors, especially if front-line supervisors are the source of the problem.

- David did not complain in writing. It's best to make a written complaint using relevant facts. Verbal complaints allow the employer to dispute what he claims he said in his complaint, even though he is still allowed to testify to his own recollection, however, a written complaint would end any speculation about what David said. With a verbal complaint, it is easy to jeopardize your credibility in court if you testify with even the slightest differential from your original statements.

Those problems could cause the case to get tossed out of court on the technicality that David didn't say enough of the right issues and he said too much of the wrong issues in his complaint. So what could have been a thriving retaliation and discrimination case is now a more questionable case that may not be worthwhile pursuing.

Allegation: Wrongful Dismissal during Probation

Employee's Basis for Allegations: While only six weeks into a three month probation, Alya's supervisor insisted that Alya hire a former employee for a subordinate role in the department that she manages. When Alya expressed her concern about the past behaviour of the former employee being imposed upon her, as well as her progress with finding a better replacement at lower salary, her supervisor refused any further meetings with her. Not many days afterwards, the supervisor directed Alya to follow him. He escorted Alya to the offices of Human Resources where she was immediately terminated. When asked for a reason, the supervisor told her that because she was on probation, he did not need to give her a reason. While she did receive two weeks termination pay, she felt that there were no grounds related to performance that would justify her termination. Later, she heard from insiders in the company that the former employee was immediately hired in her managerial role.

Background: While employed on a contract at ABC Industries, Alya received a call from a recruiter informing her about a permanent managerial role at CLI Insurance. While Alya told the recruiter that she was not interested in a permanent role, the recruiter insisted that she consider this role as she would be a perfect fit and it was an opportunity to run her own department.

After several more discussions, Alya agreed to apply for the job and soon received an offer of employment. Part of the immediate job responsibilities would be managing a department of 4 people as well as hiring for one of the vacancies. It was told to Alya that the role she was to hire for was vacant because Jimmy left the company disgruntled with no notice and no transfer of knowledge. Alya was further told that the decision as to who to hire was at her sole discretion. Ultimately, Alya agreed to accept the offer and gave notice to ABC Industries, informing them as to her intentions to end her contract early.

One facet in the offer letter given to Alya was a probationary period of three months. This was a standard clause at CLI and Alya had no concerns as she had always performed well on any job that she took on. As a matter of fact, Alya received verbal accolades from her supervisor and other co-workers during her short tenure at CLI.

Then one day, her supervisor told her that he had spoken to Jimmy and that he was interested in getting his old job back. When Alya expressed her concerns that Jimmy left CLI in an unprofessional manner, her supervisor asked her to interview him anyway. She did and was not impressed with what he had to offer as explanation for his unprofessionalism. In addition, she had already completed the first round of interviews with other candidates and had three in mind that would be a better fit and would also be willing to work for less than what Jimmy earned at

CLI. Alya's supervisor insisted that she hire Jimmy anyway. She insisted that upon hiring, he had told her that this decision was hers to make and that she needed to make a choice that was best for CLI.

The next few days, Alya was unable to find her supervisor in order to continue the discussions. On the following Monday, her supervisor did not show up for their weekly status meeting. He gave her no indication that it would be cancelled and she was unable to find him anywhere. At 4pm that afternoon, her supervisor interrupted a meeting that Alya was having with members of another department and requested that she come with him immediately. She followed him to another meeting room where a member of Human Resources was waiting. After closing the door, Alya's supervisor informed her that her employment with CLI has now been officially terminated. When she inquired as to the reason, her supervisor stated that because she was still on probation, he wasn't required to provide her a reason.

Justification: Under the Employment Standards Act, when it comes to terminating an employee on probation status, the burden of proof is lower. A probationary employee can be dismissed if s/he is simply found not to be suitable. If the employee does not meet the standards of conduct reasonably imposed by the employer, s/he can be terminated in the probationary period. Similarly, a probationary employee who proves not to be compatible with the workplace culture or with other employees can be terminated. This legality is dependent on the employer acting in a manner that is above-board.

Action: Alya contacted a lawyer and although the lawyer agreed that the employer, in particular the supervisor, acted questionably and inappropriately, there was no basis upon which to prove that the actions violated the Act. However, when it was discussed that Alya was approached by the recruiter and induced to leave her successful business as a contractor, the lawyer had evidence to prove that CLI acted in bad faith. Because Alya was actively pursued by CLI, she had a reasonable expectation to a long term commitment from CLI including any opportunity to discuss suitability or performance issues before termination.

Resolution: Alya's lawyer contacted the lawyer's for CLI to discuss the matter. While CLI's legal team contends that CLI was within their rights to terminate a probationary employee with no notice, Alya's lawyer raised the issue of inducement. After review of the facts around CLI's pursuit of Alya to join the company, CLI's lawyer agreed to provide one month's salary as compensation to resolve the issue.

In this case, an expensive court case was avoided by both parties and a settlement was reached. Reinstatement was not an option for either party. By reinstating Alya, CLI would be announcing that it made a mistake which would tarnish its image to its employees. Reinstatement was not in Alya's interest as her job was no longer available and she would not be comfortable working with the supervisor again.

Allegation: Sexual Harassment by a Superior

Employee's Basis for Allegation: Working in the Accounting department of XYZ Corp., Pam was a dedicated employee who got along with everyone in the department. After about one year on the job, Mark, who was the Controller and one of Pam's supervisors, started making inappropriate comments towards her and giving her "gifts" of a sexual nature. While there were currently no demands on Pam to get involved in a physical relationship with Mark, this ongoing unwanted attention impacted Pam's work performance as well as her comfort in the workplace. She also suffered from sleeplessness, headaches and chronic stomach pain from the stress.

Background: While the reporting structure of the Accounting department was relaxed in practice, the department had a hierarchy. It had one Manager (John) who ran the team, one Controller (Mark) who reported directly to the Manager. The staff reported to both the Manager and Controller. After about a year on the team, Pam noticed that Mark's behaviour towards her changed. He would make comments to her such as "Let's hear about Pam's wild weekend with her boyfriend. I'll bet I know what she did" in a team meeting or "Only Pam makes me hot and sweaty" when he came back from a lunchtime run. He also gave Pam a deck of cards with scantily clad people on them as a Christmas gift. In addition, he would put newspaper articles that related to sexual studies on her keyboard when she wasn't at her desk.

While disgusted with suggestive nature of Mark's behaviour, Pam collected the evidence by keeping the "gifts" and recording his inappropriate comments in a journal with dates and names of witnesses. It got to a point where Pam felt the need to put an end to the situation without jeopardizing her career at XYZ. She contemplated going to HR to file a complaint, however, she felt that in her best efforts to contain the situation, she would go to the team's Manager, John, to present her evidence. Besides, the HR Manager was usually travelling to conferences and it would be another week until she returned.

While meeting with John, she presented her evidence, detailed the circumstances and emphasized how this has impacted her emotionally, physically and professionally. When John asked Pam what she was anticipating the outcome to be, she said that she just wanted the harassment to stop. He agreed to speak to Mark and asked to keep the evidence to show Mark during their discussion. Pam reluctantly complied.

After John's discussion with Mark, the harassment ceased. However, when Pam requested the return of her evidence, John told her that he had destroyed it while stating that it was no longer necessary. While Pam was not pleased about this, she felt that there was nothing she could do at this point.

Months later, Pam decided that the atmosphere at XYZ was still uncomfortable for her and decided to take a job at another company. During her exit interview with HR, the HR Manager asked her questions about how well XYZ handled employee concerns. Pam told her the extent of her experience with Mark. Surprised, the HR Manager asked if she had any evidence available. Pam told her that she presented it to John who later destroyed it.

Justification: In hindsight, Pam should have gone directly to HR with her evidence but felt that the HR Manager was not accessible with her travelling schedule. However, Pam was still following company protocol by going to John as he was a department manager at a senior level and is in a position to deal with these matters. Pam did everything right by documenting the incidents and keeping any tangible proof. However, she could have strengthened her case by writing an email to John after their meeting outlining their discussion points and copying the HR Manager. She also could have offered John photocopies of her evidence instead of giving him the originals but Pam had every reason to trust John to not tamper with such important items.

Action: Under the Employment Standards Act, Pam had every right to pursue an alternative settlement rather than feeling that it was necessary for her to leave the company. She could have taken the company to court for damages or asked for Mark to be formally reprimanded or transferred. However, initially, Pam felt that getting the harassment to stop would be enough to go back to normal but soon after she realized that it was not enough. While she left XYZ on her own volition, she felt compelled to leave for her own emotional well-being.

Resolution: After the HR Manager spoke with Pam and then John, she realized that Mark has put the company at risk even though Pam had no intention to sue and even stated that to HR. However, this was not sufficient for XYZ regardless of Pam's departure from the company. Mark was formally reprimanded and was later terminated for additional performance issues. John's conduct was also questioned. He was warned about his inappropriate handling of this case and was sent on training to strengthen his people management skills. He left the company soon after.

Allegation: Attempted Dismissal Using Harassment

Employee's Basis for Allegation: Jane, a visible minority who had emigrated from Asia, felt harassed and intimidated by her employer and their attempts to bully her into signing their written justification to fire her for causes completely manufactured by both her counterpart and her manager.

Background: Jane had been working for 5 years as a manager of a consumer product distribution company with several outlets; one of which she had complete management control upon being hired. Jane was hired by another recently hired manager at the time by the name of Genevieve. Jane was hired to do the exact same job as Genevieve and that was to manage her own distribution outlet. Jane was trained by Genevieve at her respective location and she just so happened to be a very quick study and had completed her training in record time, impressing both Genevieve and Gary, the Regional Sales Manager. Upon Jane's completion of training, she was promptly assigned her own business location and began her managerial duties. In a short period of time, Jane began producing exceptional sales results, customer and employee satisfaction levels that her specific location had never seen before. In fact, Jane's numbers and over-all performance were on par with and trending towards surpassing Genevieve's.

Soon after Jane's performance exceeded Genevieve's, Genevieve started to exhibit behaviours that were indicative of her outright jealousy. She began speaking sarcastically and critically of Jane to both the Regional Manager and to Jane's own employees at every opportunity; nit-picking about mundane, irrelevant and trivial matters, at best. No matter how hard Genevieve tried to belittle Jane over the years, Jane's store continued to outperform Genevieve's as well as breaking its own previous sales and over-all performance records.

Throughout the company, it was generally understood that if an employee was "written up" for three violations of the company's rules, that the company was within its rights to immediately terminate the employee with just cause. Genevieve had approached Gary, the Regional Manager, and in a closed-door meeting accused Jane of violating three separate company rules. The first accusation related to Jane's alleged selling of merchandise at a heavily and unauthorized discount rate to her own employees. The second accusation was that Jane had allegedly returned said merchandise and provided a full refund on the item, well after 4 months from the time of the unauthorized sale. The third accusation was that Jane had allegedly spoken in an ill-intended and slanderous fashion about Genevieve to one of Jane's employees (Linda) in the workplace while that same employee was on the phone to Genevieve.

After having heard Genevieve's claims and accusations, Gary immediately wrote a letter of reprimand referencing the three accusations that Genevieve had put forth and that Jane should expect to receive "Corrective Action" in the very near future. The letter included an area at the bottom for Jane to sign, acknowledging the letter and its contents. Upon completing the letter, Gary began to fax it over to Jane's location and proceeded to call Jane on her personal cell phone. Jane answered to hear Gary yelling at her with disgust, informing her of the three separate complaints having been made against her and that her fax machine should be receiving her letter of reprimand for these infractions. Gary then proceeded to demand that Jane sign the document immediately upon receipt and fax it back over immediately and that he would deal with her accordingly shortly thereafter. Jane, on at least two occasions of Gary's tantrum, tried to interject and inform Gary that he had things rather unfairly mixed up and attempted to discuss her side of the story. Gary yelling louder told Jane that he was not interested in hearing anything more from her about this and that the matter was not up for any discussion. Gary, still yelling and rather rudely reminded Jane to sign the letter or else. Gary then hung up the phone abruptly.

Jane received the fax and read Gary's letter in shock. With Jane being emotionally upset by the treatment she just endured and by what she felt were unfair accusations, Linda approached Jane and asked her why she was so upset. Jane explained that, among the other accusations, she was accused of slandering Genevieve during a recent and obviously secret phone call that Linda had made to Genevieve. Linda told Jane that she knew that Jane had never spoken ill of Genevieve nor did her character in the past five years ever show a single reflection of the accusations she was facing. Linda told Jane that she had usual cell phone contact with Genevieve for work purposes but at no time did she intentionally try to trick Jane into speaking ill of Genevieve while in contact with Genevieve via Bluetooth cell phone. Linda looked into her cell phone records with Jane and it was found that she there was a phone call made from her phone at the time Jane was accused of slander. Linda could only offer Jane the explanation that she may have accidentally dialed Genevieve's number (it was on speed dial) as she wore her phone on her hip and had regularly bumped into things resulting in unintended calls out. The phone call was found to have taken place over 12 minutes, something Linda never does, as her communication requirements with Genevieve require only a minute or two at a time; no more. Further, she does not recall Genevieve ever saying "hello" upon the receipt of the call in question. Linda told Jane that she was willing to stand by her side and tell Gary that she never participated in any secret calls and that at no time did Jane say anything ill-willed about Genevieve or anyone else. Jane appreciated Linda's support and retired to her office for a few minutes to determine her next course of action.

While trying to settle down, Gary had phoned Jane back demanding to know if the fax had come through and what was detaining her from signing it and returning it. Jane told Gary that she felt absolutely sick to her stomach about all of this and that she was headed home right away. She further informed Gary that she would have an answer to his letter upon her imminent return. She told Gary that she had nothing more to say and wasn't going to be taking phone calls from anyone until her return and calmly ended the conversation and went straight home.

Action: After arriving home and taking some time to calm down, Jane spoke of her issues with her husband over dinner that night. Jane's husband mentioned a friend that happened to be a labour lawyer and that she should contact him first thing in the morning and let him know all of the details. Jane indeed called and the lawyer mentioned that she had one heck of a case. He asked Jane what she really wanted at the end of the day and Jane replied that she really liked her job and that she was hoping to put this behind her and go back to doing a really good job and enjoying her career. The lawyer commended Jane for her positive attitude and offered to help her write a few letters in attempt to salvage the situation as he was currently working an numerous cases and did not have sufficient time to represent her right away. Jane agreed and they started immediately. Jane returned to work after two days of absence and had multiple copies of her letter of response ready for distribution. Jane was approached by Gary and she handed him an envelope with a copy of her letter, citing that an official copy was on its way to him, the President, Human Resources and the Ontario Minister of Labour and that she was not going to engage in any discussions until all parties had a chance to read what she had to say.

The letter that Jane and her lawyer had crafted was sent to each recipient through registered mail prior to her return. Jane's letter began by condemning the company's dishonourable method of approach regarding the unsubstantiated claims made against her and their threats of unwarranted corrective action. Jane, rather professionally, then criticized the management team for not allowing her any opportunity to speak to any of the alleged infractions that she was being accused of. Jane went on to address Genevieve's slander allegations by informing the letter's addressees of Part VI of the Criminal Code of Canada that addresses the issue of invasion of privacy, specifying its applicability to her situation as it is illegal to intercept her private communications without her consent. As well, the letter accused the company of undue harassment for taking this route with her. Jane asserted further acts of harassment by referencing Gary's pressure that Jane sign his letter of reprimand; something Jane knew she had no legal obligation to do. Jane continued by claiming her response to serve as a formal complaint against both Genevieve and Gary for making false accusations and tarnishing her good reputation in the workplace. Jane insisted that speaking in person about these issues would not occur unless both she and her lawyer were present and that she looked forward to hearing back from the management team to make an appointment to do so and that for their offenses against her, she was prepared to hold all parties accountable to the fullest extent that the law allowed.

Jane closed out her letter citing the unfortunate and no longer tolerable choices that management had made through Gary's actions. Jane warned the company that she was more than willing to hold all parties accountable if the company insisted on pursuing their questionable and dubious claims any further. However, Jane did offer a resolution to all involved citing that if Gary and Genevieve agreed to provide her with a written letter of apology acknowledging their wrongdoings, she would forgive them and move forward with continued success at her business location, putting the entire matter behind her.

A few days went by and Jane was invited to meet with Gary and the Human Resources department to discuss the issue. Jane attended but when questioned about anything to do with the alleged accusations, she reported that everything she had to say was in her letter and would not speak to any issues until her concerns with the violation of her rights were addressed. The Director of Human Resources repeatedly tried to coax Jane to talk about the unfounded allegations but Jane stood her ground. She told the Director that if she was to endure the same repeated questions over and over again, she would conclude the meeting and go back to her work. The Director instructed Jane to return back to her duties and that she would be in touch with her about the matters at hand soon.

Justification: Through the help of her lawyer, Jane understood that the company she worked for had no right to treat her in the fashion that they did. She fully understood that they were highly accountable for gross violations of her rights as an employee, her rights as afforded by the Canadian Charter of Rights and Freedoms, as well as her rights as a human being. Her lawyer, knowing that all Jane wanted was to continue doing the great job she was known for, thought it appropriate for Jane to clearly communicate her knowledge of her rights and her willingness to defend them completely, if necessary. Jane left the matter in the company's hands and awaited their response.

Result: After some days of discussion amongst its representatives, the company including the President, the Director of HR and Gary, the Regional Manager, realized that their position was a very weak one and they requested a meeting with Jane to discuss their perspective and what they intended to do about the complaints at hand. At that meeting, the company's representatives informed Jane that they would like to consider the matter resolved and they expressed their hopes that they could all put this unfortunate incident behind them and move forward as per Jane's original desires. Being intimidated by Jane's inclusion of the Ontario Minister of Labour, the company requested Jane write a letter to all of the original addressees, including the Minister of Labour withdrawing her official complaint. Jane asked for a moment to call her lawyer and did so, explaining to him the proceedings and what the company was asking from her. Jane's lawyer was pleased to hear the news and advised her that he would draft the letter being requested of Jane and submit it to the Labour Board and the rest of the company representatives soon. Jane returned to the meeting after a few minutes and informed the group that her legal representative agreed and that a letter would be forthcoming. Under the instruction of management, Gary apologized verbally to Jane for his inappropriate behaviour. Jane accepted and the meeting concluded. A few days later Jane's lawyer delivered, via registered mail the following letter, affirming Jean's good character and honourable intentions…

"This letter serves as a formal Notice to all addressed parties regarding my letter of protest to the letter of reprimand and case of corrective action unlawfully made against me that I received regarding a formal yet unsubstantiated claim against me on DATE of this year.

This Notice serves to inform you all that after face-to-face discussions with representatives from the Human Resources Department and the offending manager Gary, I was pleased to see the that the management team in question had come to recognise my inalienable rights and had realised that further pursuit of their unsubstantiated claims through clearly illegal, let alone immoral methods was neither in their best interest nor honourable. I was further pleased to hear that they considered any of their unlawful claims to no longer be of any issue and that they wished to continue operating in business with me, putting this unfortunate and ill-intended experience behind us, where it belongs. I am pleased to confirm to all parties addressed that I, acting in honour, was in agreement and wished the same.

This Notice further informs you that I have forgiven my wrongful accusers, my abusers of my inalienable rights and that I mean them no harm and that I wish for a continued peaceful and prosperous relationship as one of the company's highest performing employees, intending to be so for years and years to come.

This notice further informs you that in the interest of all parties' legal responsibilities with upholding my rights as a Human Being, as a Canadian Citizen and as an employee of the corporation, it is advised that the corporation and its agents strictly adhere to the Human Rights Code of Ontario, The Canadian Charter of Rights and Freedoms as well as the Ontario Labour Code and that that strict adherence be in-tact at all times, never to deviate. With all clarity, be advised that if further repeated deviations from this strict adherence to lawful process on behalf of the corporation towards myself in any future regard, I reserve all of my rights afforded to me in the above mentioned Laws, Statutes and Acts and will hold all offending parties fully accountable to the maximum extent of the law.

For the public record, this specific matter has now come to a mutually agreed upon close and I personally look forward to experiencing a quick return to my normal, harmonious and harassment free working and personal life as well as a quick return to my sense of well being.

Sincerely, without ill-will, vexation or malice.

Jane"

Jane continues to work in her store with her employees and has continued to do so harassment-free. Jane's confidence grew tremendously with this experience, even though it came at an initial high emotional cost.

Allegation: Creating / Sustaining a Hostile Work Environment

Employee's Basis for Allegation: Jerry, although not an obvious visible minority, was a first generation born Canadian of both Middle Eastern and European heritage and it was only his second day on the job in an I.T. department as an Advanced Computer Support Specialist assigned to support the Senior Executives of a major Canadian banking firm. Jerry's manager demonstrated public displays of racism and bigotry towards Muslims and Arabs early on in his employment and held Jerry's background against him.

Background: The morning of his second day at the office, Jerry was hard at work getting familiar with the firm's technology platform when he was approached by his hiring manager, Donald, who asked him to join him in the boardroom as there was news of an aircraft flying into one of the World Trade Center's towers. Jerry's second day on the job ended up being the dreadful September 11th that the world would never forget. As Jerry entered the boardroom with Donald, he saw many of his new colleagues standing in front of a television watching the news and expressing their fears and concerns. Donald called for everyone's attention and said that efforts were underway to release employees for the day allowing them to return home to their families and loved ones. Donald further stated that the firm was going into a disaster recovery mode and that the Executive Team would be transferring to their designated recovery facility until further notice. Donald expressed regret over what was occurring in New York and called for prayers for the people who lost their lives. Donald then stated to the group that he didn't understand why we haven't "nuked" the Muslims and the Arabs off the face of the planet yet and that if we had done so already, we wouldn't be going through what we are today. He wished everyone a safe journey home and asked Jerry to stay behind. After everyone left, Donald approached Jerry and asked if he was able to stay to help the Executive Team transition to their operational protected location known as "The Bunker", advising Jerry that he didn't have to if he didn't want to. Before Jerry could say yes, Donald continued with his insults towards Muslims and Arabs, referring to the tragedies unfolding on the television before them. Jerry did eventually get a chance to answer and agreed to help out as much as he could. Donald thanked him and assigned tasks for him to perform.

Jerry finished his second day with rather mixed emotions. While he liked his new job and liked the people he works with, he was also seriously troubled at the racism and bigotry his hiring manager had for Muslims and Arabs in general. Jerry felt that if he didn't say anything, it would let Donald know that he was accepting of his behaviour. But Jerry also worried that since he was a new employee and also on probation, his hiring manager Donald might terminate his employment.

Jerry deliberated and finally decided that the firm would not be a worthy place for him to work at if Donald was going to continue with his hostile demeanor, so he chose to speak with Donald about his concerns the very next day. Jerry asked Donald if he could spare a few moments to speak with him privately and Donald said yes. While in a closed door meeting, Jerry politely mentioned his concerns about Donald's offensive comments in the workplace. Jerry told Donald that, while he did not agree with Donald's statements, he could accept that he has these feelings, however, it did not excuse Donald's sharing of his hatred, racism and bigotry publicly in the workplace.

Donald acknowledged that his behaviour may have been inappropriate and appreciated Jerry's bravery in bringing such concerns to his attention. Donald told Jerry that he never intended to make anyone feel uncomfortable and was going to make an extra effort not to share his personal opinions in the work environment. Jerry expressed his appreciation for Donald's understanding and thanked him for his time. Feeling better about the situation, Jerry returned to his job and enjoyed successfully accomplishing his responsibilities during his probation period. However, throughout those first three months Jerry had seen and heard on numerous occasions Donald speaking with hostility against Muslims and Arabs to his peers in public company locations such as the designated lunch room, the water cooler area and the hallways between the cubicles. Each time Donald would openly and loudly convey his general disdain for Muslims and Arabs, the instability of the Middle East, our need to limit immigration of "these types" and his support of President Bush's campaign to invade Afghanistan. Donald always went further and added that "they" should be wiped of the face of the earth and be done with already. Whenever Donald was aware that Jerry was within earshot, he would lower his voice and change the topic to something generic such as the weather. As soon as Donald thought that Jerry had left the area, he would carry on with his negative and discriminating rants. After some time, things became so bad that colleagues of Jerry spoke to him and mentioned Donald claiming that Jerry was "one of those dirty Arabs in disguise" and that "we have to keep an eye on him because we just can't trust him". They all revealed how uncomfortable they felt about the stress in the environment whenever Donald went off on another one of his tirades, but feared retaliation from him if they conveyed their feelings as he was their manager too. Many expressed concern that Jerry might come to the conclusion that when Donald voiced his opinions that their silence would be misinterpreted by Jerry as agreement. Jerry thanked his colleagues for sharing their thoughts. He reassured them that he would be patient and try to accept Donald for who he was and hope that he may change his biased opinions once he saw Jerry's strong work ethic and teamwork over time.

At the end of his probation period, Jerry was asked to fill out a probation review form, asking him to describe what his accomplishments so far and what he would work on to aspire further if chosen to continue with the firm. Since Jerry never received any criticism, formally or informally, of his work, he was confident that he would pass his probation with flying colours. Jerry completed the form and handed it in to his manager, Donald. Shortly thereafter, Jerry was called into Donald's office and was accused of doing less than satisfactory work and that numerous complaints had come in from the Executive Team about his inability to meet their technical needs. Jerry was shocked and asked why none of this was brought to his attention during his time with the firm so far. Donald said that he wasn't obligated to answer any of his questions and suggested that Jerry was going to lose his job. According to the company's policy, Donald must also fill out a probation review form and discuss it with the employee and compare differences. Jerry's and Donald's forms could not be more far apart. Jerry's was detail oriented and specific where Donald's was generic, accusatory and void of any examples. Jerry politely protested referencing his example-filled form of achievements where Donald's had none and Donald began to raise his voice in return accusing Jerry of insolence. The commotion caught the attention of Yufi, the Vice President of the I.T. department, who came out of his office and walked into Donald's office. Yufi was concerned about the yelling and asked what was going on. Jerry began to answer but was interrupted by further shouting from Donald, telling Yufi that Jerry was demonstrating a lack of respect he had never had to endure before and that he was in the midst of firing Jerry. Yufi asked both Donald and Jerry to enter his office to discuss the matter further.

Action: In Yufi's office, Jerry provided a detailed review of Donald's behavior on his second day, their subsequent discussion the next day, Donald's commitment to refrain from expressing his personal opinions at work and the repeated outbursts of bigotry towards Muslims and Arabs to colleagues in the work environment. Donald admitted to his comments on 9/11 and attributed them to his emotional frustrations at such a horrific incident but tried his very best to deny his repeated demonstrations of hatred since then. Yufi was concerned that Donald was a couple of years away from retiring and that he may have "old school" ideas about people outside his own "culture". Concerned about the sensitive nature of the matter, Yufi suspected that Donald was walking on very thin ice with regards to how he was handling himself and representing the company in this situation. He called for calm from both parties and invited Jerry to return to his work duties and expressed his happiness with Jerry's performance. Yufi investigate further by discreetly speaking to Donald's peers. Some had affirmed that he had been speaking negatively about Muslims and Arabs and that they were in open areas where other employees could hear. Yufi consulted with his HR division as per company policy and it was ultimately decided that Donald would benefit from attending cultural sensitivity training classes as well as other manager/employee relationship development courses with the hopes that they help him with his challenges. These training sessions would serve as a warning to Donald that his actions would not be tolerated anymore and continuing with this behaviour would result in Donald's long-term employment with the company being terminated. He was soon enrolled in the classes and the educational institution reported that Donald completed the courses successfully.

Resolution: Donald, however, continued to publicly demonstrate his disdains, even though it was less frequent and with a smaller group of people. Jerry went on to complete his first year with the company having won the favour of his Executive Team and his colleagues for being an industrious and studious employee who took his job seriously and performed it to the maximum of his abilities. But Donald decided to write another poor performance review for Jerry that year. The situation was the same as before as Jerry's form was full of examples that backed up his claims of success and Donald's form on Jerry was full of accusatory one-liners that were unsubstantiated.

Jerry launched an official complaint to the Human Resources department, sighting Donald's discrimination and racism towards him, referencing his experiences starting from his second day on the job, and everything in between. After Human Resources investigated the issue and had interviewed several Executive Team members including Yufi, as well as Jerry's peers, it was found that Jerry's claims were substantiated. Further, Jerry's peers affirmed their own concerns and expressed complaints about Donald's unacceptable behaviour through his constant display of hatred and racism. It was decided that Donald was a liability to the work environment in that the emotional well being of the employees was at risk and the reputation of the company was at stake overall. Thusly, Donald's employment with the bank was terminated immediately.

While Jerry had every right to be concerned about filing a complaint against Donald with HR while on probation, it might have been advantageous to review the company policies about employee's rights to a respectful environment as well as the complaint process. If Yufi had not been so intent on finding out the truth of the matter, this case may have gone a different way and Donald may have gotten away with dismissing Jerry.

Glossary

Adoption Leave
A period of job-protected leave granted to adoptive parents to care for a newly adopted child.

Arbitration
A binding process used to resolve a particular dispute to an impartial third person. The parties involved agree, in advance, to abide by the arbitrator's award issued after a hearing at which both parties have an opportunity to be heard.

Bereavement Leave
Unpaid, job-protected leave upon death of a member of an employee's immediate family.

Common Law
Refers to outcome of cases ruled in a court of law.

Compassionate Care Leave
Leave that provides an employee with time off to provide care or support to a family member who has a serious medical condition with a significant risk of death within 26 weeks.

Conduct
Personal behaviour or way of acting.

Conflict of Interest
Occurs when an individual or organization is involved in multiple interests, one of which could *possibly* corrupt the motivation for an act in the other. For example, advising on a panel to regulate activities of the oil industry in the public's best interest while sitting on the Board of Directors of a large oil company. The interest of ensuring the oil company retains its profits through less government controls is in direct conflict with the needs of stricter controls for the benefit of the public. Therefore, objectivity as a panel member cannot be guaranteed due to the conflict of interest.

Constructive Dismissal
Occurs when employees resign because their employer's behaviour has become so heinous or made life so difficult that they may consider themselves to have been fired.

Discrimination
Workplace discrimination means putting an employee at a disadvantage based on prohibited ground (Race, national or ethnic origin, colour, religion, age, sex, sexual orientation, marital status, family status, disability or criminal conviction for which a pardon has been granted). Discrimination results in barriers to workplace equity because it blocks access to equal opportunities.

Dismissal	The termination of the employment relationship for cause at the direction of the employer.
Family Medical Leave	Unpaid, job-protected leave to provide care or support to certain family members who have a serious medical condition with a significant risk of death occurring within 26 weeks.
Family Responsibility Leave	Unpaid, job-protected leave that enables an employee to meet responsibilities related to care, health or education of child or care or health issues of immediate family member.
Grievance	A wrong or hardship suffered, which is the grounds of a complaint.
Group Termination	The simultaneous dismissal of a specified number of employees over a short period of time. This type of dismissal usually requires government approval beforehand.
Harassment	Engaging in a course of vexatious comment or conduct against a worker in a workplace that is known or ought reasonably to be known to be unwelcome. Workplace harassment may include bullying, intimidating or offensive jokes or innuendos, displaying or circulating offensive pictures or materials, or offensive or intimidating phone calls.
Inducement	An act, promise, threat or item that helps to persuade someone to do something.
Insolence	Condescendingly rude or disrespectful behavior or speech.
Insubordination	Misconduct where the employee refuses to recognize and submit to the authority of the employer.
Jurisdiction	The right and power to interpret and apply the law in regards to a specific territory or authority.
Jury Duty	Job-protected leave to allow employee to serve on trial jury.
Just Cause	A legally, sufficient reason to terminate an employment contract immediately and for which, no notice or severance pay is due to the employee.
Layoff	A temporary interruption of the employment relationship at the direction of the employer because of lack of work.
Malicious	Motivated by wrongful, vicious, or mischievous purposes.

Marriage Leave	Paid one day leave for wedding/civil union of employee or member of employee's immediate family. (Québec only)
Mass Termination	See "Group Termination"
Maternity Leave	Job-protected leave designed to give expectant mothers the possibility of withdrawing from work in the later stages of their pregnancy and to allow them some time to recuperate after childbirth.
Medical Leave	See "Family Medical Leave" and "Personal Emergency Leave"
Misconduct	Work related conduct that is in substantial disregard of an employer's interests. Such conduct may be willful or intentional, but it may also be unintentional conduct that results from extreme carelessness, indifference, or lack of effort.
Mobbing	An extreme form of bullying where the victim is attacked by a group of co-workers on an almost daily basis for periods that can extend many months. This activity forces the victim to feel helpless and insecure.
Organ Donor Leave	Unpaid, job-protected leave of up to 13 weeks, for the purpose of undergoing surgery to donate all or part of certain organs to a person.
Overtime	For most employees, whether they work full-time, part-time, are students, temporary help agency assignment employees, or casual workers, overtime begins after they have worked 44 hours in a work week. After that time, they must receive overtime pay.
Parental Leave	Both new parents have the right to take parental leave of up to 35 or 37 weeks of unpaid job-protected time off work.
Period Of Employment	The period of time from the last hiring of an employee by an employer to the termination of his/her employment, and includes any period of layoff or suspension of less than 12 consecutive months.
Personal Emergency Leave	Unpaid, job-protected leave due to illness, injury and certain other emergencies and urgent matters.

PIPEDA	Personal Information Protection and Electronic Documents Act which protects individuals from the abuse or misuse of personal information collected electronically including emails, computer files and video and telephone surveillance.
Plaintiff	A person, who starts, brings a case to court or who sues or who asks the Court for a trial against a person or organization.
Probation	A status given to new or poor performing employees of a company or business. This status allows a supervisor or other company manager to closely evaluate the progress and skills of the newly hired worker, determine appropriate assignments and monitor other aspects of the employee – such as how they interact with co-workers, supervisors or customers.
Probationary Period	Period allows an employer to terminate an employee on probationary status who is determined not to be doing well at their job or otherwise deemed not suitable for a particular position. Some jurisdictions have an *at will* policy, which allows a company manager to terminate an employee at any point during the probationary period.
Reprisal	Retaliatory conduct by an employer who cause or threaten to cause any harm to an individual on the basis that they have participated in any proceeding such as filing a complaint or refusing to act unethically to benefit the employer.
Reservist Leave	Job-protected leave for civilians serving as military reservist in the Canadian Forces.
Revoke	To withdraw or cancel.
Severance	In some provinces/territories, it is synonymous with termination. In Ontario, certain employees are entitled to severance pay which compensates for loss of seniority and job-related benefits and recognizes an employee's years of service.
Sick Leave	Leave for employees who need time off for their own illness.
Statutory Holiday	Also referred to as general or public holidays in many statutes, are days of special significance that have been established by governments to commemorate or celebrate certain events, usually of a religious or historical nature.
Statutory period	Legally mandated notice period.

Suspension	A temporary interruption of the employment relationship other than a layoff at the direction of the employer.
Temporary Layoff	An employee is on temporary layoff when an employer cuts back or stops the employee's work without ending his or her employment (e.g., laying someone off at times when there is not enough work to do). An employer may put an employee on a temporary layoff without specifying a date on which the employee will be recalled to work.
Termination	The unilateral severance of the employment relationship at the direction of the employer.
Termination Notice	Written notification provided by an employer stating the date on which an employee's or employees' contract of employment will end.
Termination Pay	An employee who does not receive the written notice required by law must be given termination pay in lieu of notice. Termination pay is a lump sum payment equal to the regular *wages* for a regular work week plus benefits and vacation pay that an employee would otherwise have been entitled to during the written notice period.
Wages	All forms of remuneration. This definition includes salary, commissions, vacation pay, severance pay and bonuses. It also includes employer contributions to pension funds or plans, long-term disability plans and all forms of health insurance plans.
Wrongful Dismissal	Where an employer wishes to terminate employment, and no grounds exist for doing so, an employer is required to give reasonable notice of termination to an employee. Where reasonable notice is not given, an employer is required to provide termination pay (see above). Where an employer fails to provide such compensation, or seeks to provide inadequate compensation, an employee's legal rights may be enforced by proceeding with a claim for compensation for wrongful dismissal.

Index

V

W

www.ingramcontent.com/pod-product-compliance
Lightning Source LLC
Chambersburg PA
CBHW082130210326

41599CB00031B/5933